www.killerpresentations.com

This book is about four dimensional PowerPoint presentations. A full definition of what I mean by 4D is contained within these pages but suffice to say that for me the only definition of a Good PowerPoint slide is this:

Good PowerPoint slides do not make sense until the presenter explains them, or builds them!

In order for *Good slides* to therefore make sense they need the additional two dimensions of *Time* and *Narrative*; you need to see them build over time and hear the presenter explain them. How do you do this in a two dimensional book?

The answer of course is that you can't. The solution is to have a book that also has a website. There are 122 PowerPoint slides in this book and almost every one has been recorded and uploaded to 35 web addresses printed throughout this book.

Access requires a valid e-mail address and a password that can be found in the glossary of this book (killerpresentations.com) so you need to have a copy with you. The site also contains a discussion area, links page, tips and some free downloads.

Nicholas B Oulton

D0673473

Dedication

Confidante, mentor, supporter, coach, sounding board, realist, pragmatist, friend, mother, partner, lover, soul mate, wife: Debbie.

rning Cent
C Saltas

Killer Presentations

REVISED AND UPDATED · 2ND · SECOND EDITION ·

Power the imagination to visualise your Point – with PowerPoint™

Nicholas B. Oulton

howtobooks

LEARNING CENTRE
...LTASH
C... 658.452 OUL
ACC. No. SA012237
DATE 23/4/09 CHECKED R

Published by How To Books Ltd
Spring Hill House, Spring Hill Road
Begbroke, Oxford OX5 1RX
Tel: (01865) 375794. Fax: (01865) 379162.
info@howtobooks.co.uk
www.howtobooks.co.uk

All rights reserved. No part of this work may be reproduced or stored in an information retrieval system (other than for purposes of review) without the express permission of the publisher in writing.

The right of Nicholas B Oulton to be identified as the author of this work has been asserted by him in accordance with the Copyright, Designs and Patents Act 1988

© 2007 Nicholas B Oulton

First edition 2005
Second edition 2007
Reprinted 2008

British Library Cataloguing in Publication Data
A catalogue record for this book is available from the British Library

ISBN 978 1 84528 184 7

Photos © M62 Visualcommunications Ltd.
Typeset by Pantek Arts Ltd, Maidstone, Kent
Printed and bound in Great Britain by Cromwell Press Ltd, Trowbridge, Wiltshire

NOTE: The material contained in this book is set out in good faith for general guidance and no liability can be accepted for loss or expense incurred as a result of relying in particular circumstances on statements made in this book. The laws and regulations are complex and liable to change, and readers should check the current positions with the relevant authorities before making personal arrangements.

Contents

About the authors

Nicholas B Oulton

Nicholas is a Chartered Marketer and a professional presenter. He has over thirteen years' sales and marketing experience and has devoted the last ten years to helping people improve their presentations.

Nicholas founded m62 visualcommunications, a company set up to help clients perform better as they deliver a presentation. m62 now has offices in Liverpool, the US and Singapore. m62 has won numerous awards and Nicholas was nominated for *Insider Magazine*'s 42 under 42; he was also nominated for UK North West Entrepreneur of the year.

Over the years Nicholas has developed a method for delivering successful visual presentations that combines technology with sound presentation techniques, and which maximises the amount of information the audience retains from a presentation. This approach, backed by one of the UK's leading design teams, has culminated in m62 having an international reputation with global clients such as Jaguar, Symantec, Ford, Bayer, Panasonic, Hitachi Data Systems Limited, EDS, Storage Tek, Proctor & Gamble, Colgate, Price Waterhouse Coopers, Quintiles and even Microsoft.

Nicholas's American clients refer to him as 'the professor of presentology'. He spends nearly half of his working life in the US teaching, presenting and helping clients make the most of their presentation opportunities.

m62's *Killer Sales Presentations* seminars have been widely acclaimed as being practical, indeed an eye-opening experience and are always well received. A recent organiser had this to say about their event:

> *'Over 50 people attended the presentation by Nicholas Oulton and all feedback was positive. The only negative comments were "It should have been longer", or "Sorry I missed out" from those who had been unable to attend and had heard later how good it was.*

'All the other comments not only convinced me that it had been a very successful and well-received event, but that we must have a second helping of Nick's friendly, entertaining and extremely informative presentation. This was what people want to listen to after a day's work ... something that stimulates, educates and can be put into practice the next day!

'As someone who has extensive experience of the organisation of both corporate and leisure events, I would recommend this presentation to anyone involved or interested in PowerPoint.'

David Broschomb, Chairperson
Business Marketing Group, CIM

Nicholas can be contacted at nick@killerpresentations.com
m62 can be contacted via their website at www.m62.net

Patrick Forsyth

Patrick Forsyth who assisted Nicholas with the writing of this book is a marketing consultant and trainer with more than twenty years' experience of working with clients in various industries and around the world. He runs *Touchstone Training & Consultancy*. He also writes extensively on business matters, has more than fifty books successfully published, and also writes articles and corporate materials. His *The Management Speaker's Handbook*, also published by How To Books, offers practical guidance on the personal skills and disciplines of presentation.

Acknowledgements

Starting a business is a difficult task, far more difficult than it looks or than I thought it would be. Making it work, however, requires more than hard work and tenacity; it requires the good will of an enormous number of people. I have been lucky with investors, staff and clients, all of whom believed in the ideas in this book and put their faith in me to build a team that could turn these ideas into breathtaking presentations. Specifically, I'd like to thank my clients below who have allowed us to use their presentation material throughout this book:

AIG
Bayer
BDB
Blue Sheep
Bran & Luebbe
Brownlow Group Practice
Burns eCommerce Solutions Limited
Diaper
EDS
egg.com
Europanel
GSK
Hilton WorldWide Services
Hitachi Data Systems Limited
Imperial Tobacco
Innovex
Jaguar
Lancaster University
McNicholas Construction Services
Metalspinners
Microsoft
Panasonic
Peter Norvig – Gettysburg PowerPoint Presentation
RTC North

Bevan for similarly aiding the illiterate and Angela Kaston for managing the detail required to pull this together.

Alison Sleightholm and Clare Shields have created most of the design in this book with assistance from the rest of the m62 graphics team.

Nicholas B Oulton
Bracken Bank 2007

Testimonials

'These guys know more about PowerPoint presentations than anybody else on the face of the planet.'

VP Global Marketing

symantec.

'The best PowerPoint training I've seen. Makes you see the world in a different light.'

Peter Delahunty
Sales Director

corus

'The thought leaders in PowerPoint.'

John Timperley
Marketing Director

PRICEWATERHOUSECOOPERS

'As someone who has extensive experience of the organisation of both corporate and leisure events, I would recommend this to anyone involved or interested in PowerPoint.'

David Broschomb
Chairperson Business Marketing Group,

The Chartered Institute of Marketing

'I was impressed by how quickly you turned mine, and my colleagues', fairly mundane slide shows into exciting and motivating presentations. I also appreciate the coaching that you gave to one of the team who was quite nervous. You did a great job. Thank you.'

Chris Tobin
MD EMEA

Bayer

'We have had a number of significant wins over the last week or so. One of the largest single pieces of business for over 6 years! So the new sales presentation is really having an impact.'

Mark Beatie
Vice President EMEA

'This (training) exceeded all my expectations in terms of real life examples. I have been on many presentation courses before, but none were as useful as this in terms of genuine practical advice on winning business.'

Roger Thomas
Marketing Manager

'Our new Corporate Overview slides went over very well with our sales force. Thank you for providing what we needed, which was to polish an existing presentation to a level of high-impact graphics and animations. Your team was able to keep to our concepts and existing messages while providing us with a much better looking way to tell our story'

Sela Missirian
Director of International Marketing

'The training our global sales team received from m62 has transformed the way we communicate our value to clients. It's the most important thing we've done this year in terms of making our sales people more effective in the field.'

David Lilley
President

Innovex is a service unit of Quintiles Transnational Corp

'Our staff are more confident, professional and competent presenters and the feedback we have had has been brilliant. It really has helped develop the partnership as new agencies are always impressed.'

Gemma Dixon
Head of Training

Preface

The message in this book is likely to be a revelation for anyone who makes presentations. The possibilities described may surprise, but they are real and – very important – they are tried and tested. They can turn many a pedestrian event into something special and, above all, can maximise effectiveness in a way that directly builds business. For many applications this is the future of presentations. Make of it what you will – it may literally change your life, certainly it can change your presentations and what they achieve.

When I knew that the first edition had sold out in just over 12 months I decided to ask the newsletter readers what, if anything, needed to be added. The resounding response was for some information on the research that has guided the development of most of the ideas in this book and in particular the theory supporting ***Passive Mnemonic Processes***™ and so in this new edition I have included an overview of some of the more important ideas that have influenced the theory and practice of Killer Presentations.

Foreword

As I write this, I'm in my early fifties. When I went to school we used a blackboard and chalk. When I started work we had an overhead projector and foils. Now the laptop and data projector, fired up with Microsoft PowerPoint™, provides anyone and everyone with splendid tools for presentation at their fingertips. So why are so many truly awful presentations made every day?

In my experience, the majority of people at work today still make a pretty poor job of presenting. They proudly show you a seemingly endless parade of blue background haze with small text zipping onto the screen, usually displaying exactly the same words as are then read out to you. Insulting or what? Despite years of investment in training, most marketers and sales people still persist in talking for ages about themselves, their company, their issues, their product – and so little about you and your needs. What is to be done?

You could do a lot worse than read Nicholas Oulton, one of the best presenters I have ever seen. Most people find Nicholas an appealing character and, being a Liverpudlian, he has a touch of that magic scouse humour, (for example, see the definition of m62 in the Glossary) which all helps. But Nick has far more than just natural gifts. He has learnt from his training, he has thought really hard about presentations, he has researched his work thoroughly and he now practises his craft with exceptional skill. Nick has grown a successful international business out of creating presentations that you would enjoy sitting through – and be more likely to buy at the end.

But this book is certainly not just for sales people. You could be a social worker seeking resource for your client, or a volunteer going after lottery funds for your church tower restoration. And you might just be the chairperson of an international plc seeking to sway views in the City and rescue your jittery share price.

Whatever you do, if you make presentations where you seek to gain something from those to whom you present, read this book. Take in some of the lessons, and I promise you will give a better presentation next time.

Jonathan Hart
Regional Director, East of England
The Chartered Institute of Marketing
Moor Hall
Cookham
Maidenhead
SL6 9QH
United Kingdom

The human brain is a wonderful thing, it starts working the moment you are born and never stops until you stand up to speak in public.

Sir George Jessel

Introduction, a new approach

Spontaneous speeches are seldom worth the paper they are written on.

Leslie Henson

Just another presentation book!

Last year there were countless books published on the subject of presentations. All of them with one purpose, that of helping people stand up and deliver information to a group, or sometimes an individual, with confidence and clarity. Most of these books (I make a habit of buying and reading them) are largely similar in nature. They talk about a set of skills that we at m62 (don't worry: you'll learn about m62 soon!) call 'soft skills' – that is to say skills associated with personality and confidence: how to speak, how to stand, where to look, what to say, how to say it, and which visual aids to use and where.

So why do you need another book? All of the above are very important but they seem to me to miss the point. For the last 10 years I have been suggesting that there exists a set of 'hard skills' that can impact on your presentations, a set of skills that can be transferred easily, a set of rules based on knowledge and a set of techniques that can be learnt. These hard skills will transform your presentations without coaching or hand-holding, and with this change of perception will come a change of behaviour that facilitates better presentations.

This is not just another presentation book. It points to a different way of thinking about presentations and more importantly it points to a different way of using PowerPoint™. It does not replace the other books on your shelf, nor does it invalidate any of the sound advice contained in them, other than the role of the visual aid. It will, however, help you make more use of your soft skills by improving the impact and the audience's recall of your presentations by radically altering what you show them using PowerPoint.

The slides here are an example of a before-and-after for one of our clients, Bayer. The top one is a fairly standard PowerPoint slide, the bottom our interpretation of the same information. We think the second slide is better, this book is about why.

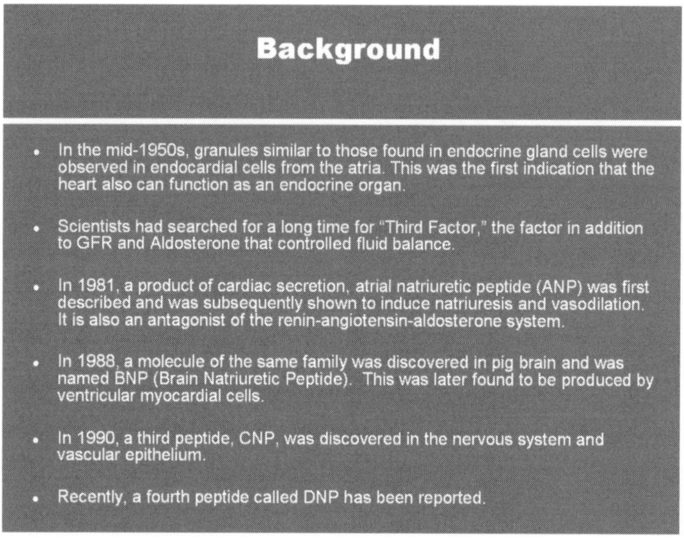

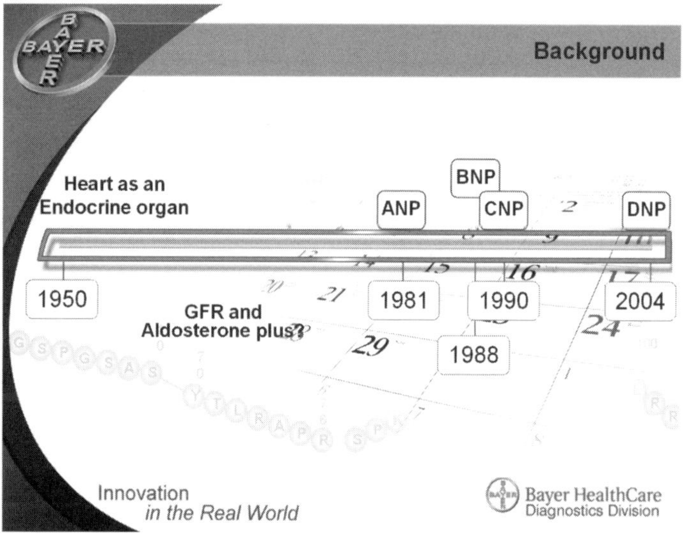

So this is a book about how to use PowerPoint – not a technical 'how to insert photo' kind of book, but a 'how to use PowerPoint to create and deliver truly effective presentations' kind of book. There don't seem to be any of these on my shelf!

Why do we present?

The first thing we at m62 do when we sit with a presenter in a consultancy session is to determine the purpose of the presentation, in fact we ask the following questions:

- What is the purpose of the presentation?
- To whom is it addressed?
- When is it?
- How long do you have?
- What do you want them to do at the end?

The answer to the last of these is probably the most important. In our experience this tells us what type of presentation we are dealing with, and for us there are only four types: *Persuasion* (on a rational level), *Motivation* (which is to persuade on an emotional level), *Education*, or *Entertainment*.

With the exception of entertainment, which we will ignore for the purposes of this book as it is clearly a soft skill, the factor that the other three have in common is that in order to attain their goals they need to impart information (motivation less than the other two). To do this they need to first gain and hold the audience's attention and then present information in the right manner, at the right time and in the right order. Simple really!

Except it isn't, is it? In this book we will examine all of the questions above and hopefully change your mind as to their importance. But before we launch into the core material, let us first examine the normal way of things.

Why do we use PowerPoint?

It is tempting to put the answer to this as 'Why not?' since it seems that this is sometimes the level of thought that goes into the decision to use it or not. We believe that there are considerable benefits to using PowerPoint but that most of its users fail to gain these benefits; indeed, as you will see in the discussion in the chapter on PowerPoint, we believe that most presentations are currently made far worse by the inappropriate use of PowerPoint. The popular benefits of using PowerPoint are that it is easy, everybody else does it (so we won't look out of place), and the audience knows what to expect.

Well, falling off a cliff is easy but that's not an excuse for doing it. 'Everybody else does it' is just as bad, and it may actually be correct that the audience expects to be abused, bored and generally disappointed, so why bother? Here's why.

PowerPoint will allow you to:

- gain and hold the audience's attention
- engage the audience in a communication process
- help the audience to understand complex ideas and relationships
- place ideas into short-term memory, which is clearly a prerequisite for placing ideas into long-term memory.

It is not easy, nor is it what the majority of other users are doing, but it is definitely worth the effort.

In short this book will help you make your presentations:

- more *impressive*
- more *effective*
- more *memorable*
- more *engaging*.

Pause for a minute and consider the last presentation you sat through. Was it any good? If so, what was good about it? Now consider the last presentation you can remember that blew you away; what was good about that?

Definition of 'a good presentation'

This is seemingly a difficult question to answer, partly because there are not that many really good presentations and partly because it is difficult to pin down the reasons for the good ones. Good presentations tend to be interesting, relevant, possibly entertaining, but almost by definition engaging. Now consider the opposite scenario: what was the last truly awful presentation you had to sit through? What was bad about it? Boring, dull, lifeless, monotonic – we can fill in the rest. We have all experienced bad presentations, partly because there are so many of them, but mostly because they are difficult to endure – sometimes the experience can border on the painful.

The worst presentation ever?

The worst presentation I have ever seen was at a logistics conference several years go. I was coaching a client through a 35 minute presentation on 'Technology For Warehousing' and he had the second slot on the second day of a three day conference. Because we were second prior to the mid-morning break we had to sit through the first presentation: 60 minutes on 'Just In Time Delivery In The Automotive Sector'. It should have been interesting enough, but the presenter, an authoritative man in his early 50s, started by handing out a copy of his slides (68 pages) and script (22 pages) and as he read his script his assistant pressed CLICK each time he moved to another bullet point.

What soon became apparent was that his script and slides where identical. He was using PowerPoint to put the script on screen, line by line. Within ten minutes (and only on slide four) the audience realised what the next 60 minutes had in store for them and decided *en masse* to go to sleep. The only thing engaging about any of his presentation was that his assistant managed to get ahead of him by two slides whilst he, head down, blindly read on – no doubt completely unaware of his snoring victims in front of him.

A change of perspective?

The point of this is that we all know intuitively what makes a bad presentation as we have all been abused by presenters over the years. We probably also know empirically what a good presentation is, from the audience's point of view.

Yet when we come to prepare our own presentation our thoughts are usually not with the audience but focused on questions such as 'What shall I present?'

This is the first reference to the 'killer ideas' in this book. We at m62 write, design and produce PowerPoint presentations in order to help the audience to assimilate the content of the presentation (what else is a presentation for?). We do not design slides that help the presenter stay on track; we do not produce lists for the presenter to talk about; we produce images that engage the audience.

Killer Idea Audience focused not presenter cued

A list of bullet points is designed to assist the presenter, indicating what he is going to talk about and in what order. They serve to prompt him to remember his lines. The performing arts phrase for this is to 'cue the presenter'.

However, as will become apparent, we believe that whilst producing cue-cards is a useful first step, they add little or no value to the audience and the presentation should be about the audience, not the presenter. Change the way you think about lists of bullet points and you will change the way you think about both presenting and PowerPoint, and be better for it. Look at the next before-and-after example, this time from Hitachi Data Systems Limited. Read the bullet points on the first slide: the key information is that this survey was completed across the whole of Europe with 800 clients and concluded that Hitachi ought to 'Go for Leadership'. Hence, the revised slide has a European map, the survey graphic and the conclusion, the rest is *patter* (words said by the presenter whilst the slide is on view). The end result is not only more attractive but actually increases the audience's engagement and interest levels. The first slide is written for the presenter ('What shall I say?'), the second for the audience ('What do they need to see?').

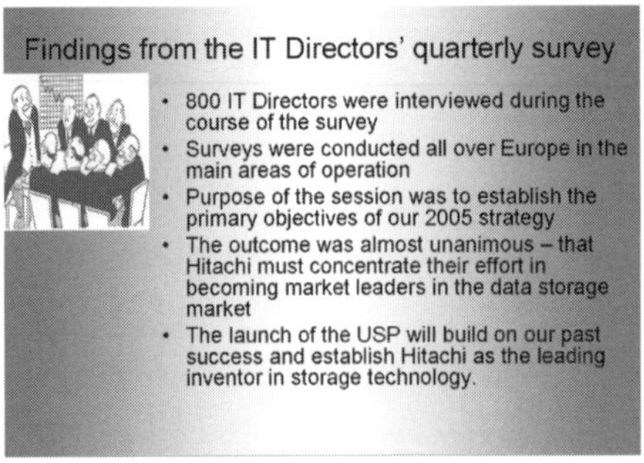

What do we do that's different?

When PowerPoint arrived on the scene it should have ushered in a new age. Many people in the business world were proclaiming a new order, a new method of communication, a method so powerful and so sophisticated it would change the way the world presented forever. It did. But the effect was not, as we hoped, for the better. Instead of the features of PowerPoint being used to produce simple attractive diagrams, well-animated and well-articulated, what we got was the bullet point, and we got it again and again and again. In fact, the only obvious difference between the old OHP acetate and the PowerPoint presentation was that the number of slides multiplied. There were suddenly many more of them; oh, and they were now in colour and able to move into view when the presenter was ready. What was spoken in presentations became what was read off lengthy text slides, or said as one slide was replaced by another.

The promise of better communication, simpler presentations, less time assimilating information and more time debating actions has been lost in a surfeit of slides, much of it prettied up by irrelevant and often annoying clip art, or even worse, the '*I have a digital camera and I know how to use it*' school of adding irrelevant pictures.

Those of us involved in promoting the 'PowerPoint revolution' got one, but not the one we hoped for. Instead of improving the world's business presentations, the approach PowerPoint has led so many people into has made them worse. It has condemned millions of people to spend more time in their boardrooms (or should that be *bored* rooms?) watching the irrelevant, soporific, swoosh of bullets flying on screen from the left.

Too often people seem to leave common sense at the door as soon as they walk in to give a presentation. Preparation now means using PowerPoint to prepare the slides; it means organising the bullet points into a logical order, and presenting simply becomes an entertaining and self-congratulatory reading of the bullet points. When the presentation material (i.e. the slides) are dull and boring, then the success of the presentation depends largely on the soft skills of the presenter; if he/she is witty, passionate and enthusiastic then the audience will respond, engaging with the presenter and not the material. With our style of presentations the material itself becomes interesting and engaging and the presenter's ability to entertain becomes less important. I am not suggesting that the soft skills are irrelevant, just that it is possible for people to give persuasive *or* informative presentations that are good and engaging, without being the company's best performer.

Alongside this massive investment in soft skills there have emerged 'how to present' courses and PowerPoint training, much of which may be useful, but which seem to us to somehow miss the key point; certainly they have failed to halt the pied-piper effect of PowerPoint use that is leading people away from effectiveness.

There *is* a body of knowledge that can be applied to a presentation; some useful theory that can improve your presentation and avoid this pitfall without too much effort – it just requires you to think about your audience and learn some simple techniques for using PowerPoint to its best effect.

This book is my atonement – I spent years convincing people to buy data projection equipment on behalf of companies such as Proxima and Infocus, hammering home benefits that never in fact materialised. Having a decent laptop and a good data projector is the basic requirement of a good presentation – people *do* remember three to four times more information if it is presented using multi-media. But multi-media is not 150 bullet points per hour, nor is it a substitute for practice and preparation.

Contained in this book are the basic techniques that we have developed to make your presentations effective. But moving away from old habits and deploying them effectively may need a change in mind set – to call it a paradigm shift is not, in our view, overstating it. Armed with a projector, a laptop and some ideas from this book, maybe you can begin to break free of PowerPoint convention, beat the cult of the bullet point and really begin to impress your audiences.

The techniques reviewed here should be accessible to the average presenter and should improve their presentations immediately. The truly gifted presenters may discover in this book much that they do intuitively and may find it useful only as a reminder. We believe *every* reader will get something from this text and that together we can begin a new revolution and use PowerPoint to:

- improve communication
- assist greater and easier assimilation of information
- shorten presentations
- stimulate debate
- engage audiences without boring them.

Having heard me knocking bullet points you will notice that they are already in use here. But a book primarily *is* text. And in a book tens of thousands of words long, every graphic device that makes reading easier – paragraphs, bold type, boxed sections *and* bullet points – is worth using. This is not a failure to practise what we preach, rather a deployment of a routine text device to make reading quicker and easier and assist emphasis.

Not a design company!

At first glance at the samples in this book you may be forgiven for thinking that m62 is a design company and that the difference between the before-and-after examples scattered throughout these pages is principally that they have been produced by a designer.

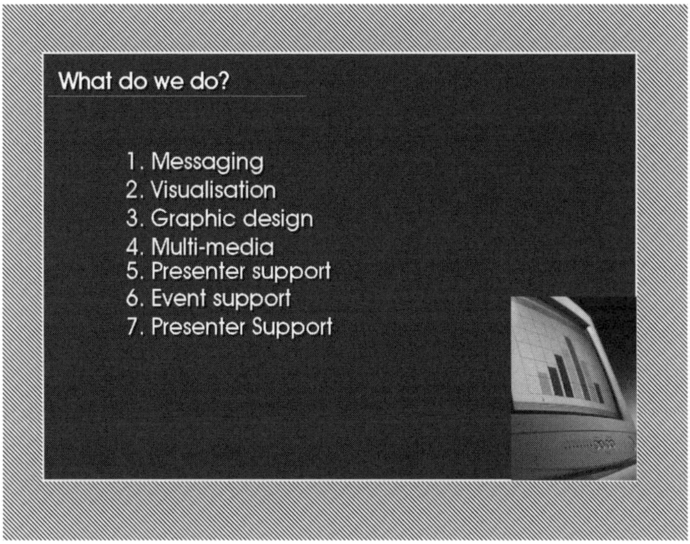

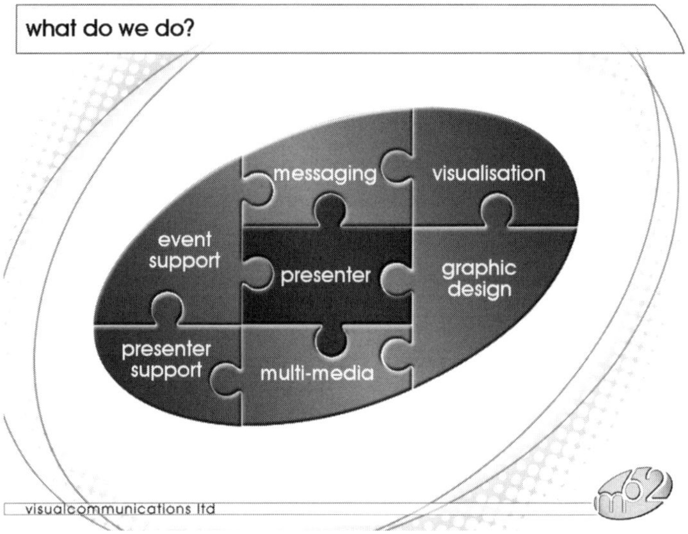

Granted the after is a more attractive piece of design, however much more than just a designer's skill has been applied to the creation of this second slide. We have looked at the first slide and worked out that the patter (verbiage that complements the slide) should sound something like this:

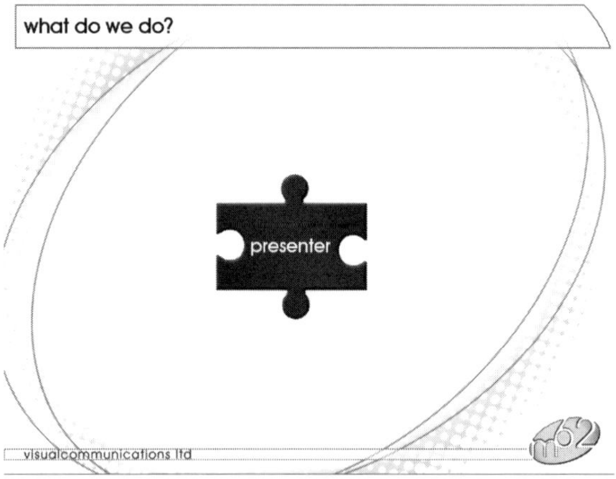

> *'The heart of our business is the presenter, and our mission statement is to help these individuals perform better at point of delivery of a presentation. In order to do this we cocoon them in a series of services that aid better presentation. Not everybody has or needs all of these services but the complete service begins with …'*

The presenter would then press CLICK* to make Messaging appear.

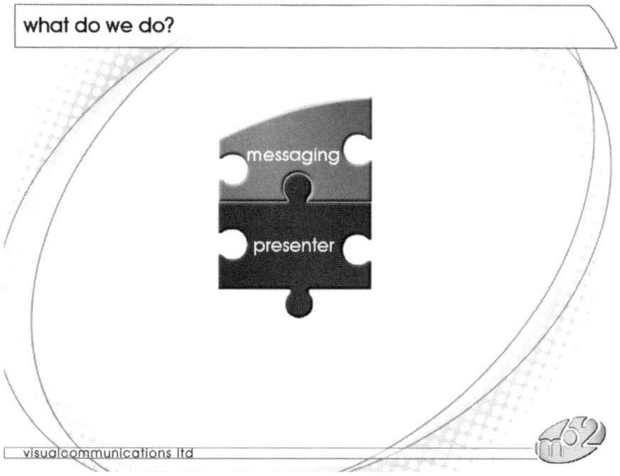

'Helping the presenter work out what to say and in what order.'

CLICK Visualisation appears.

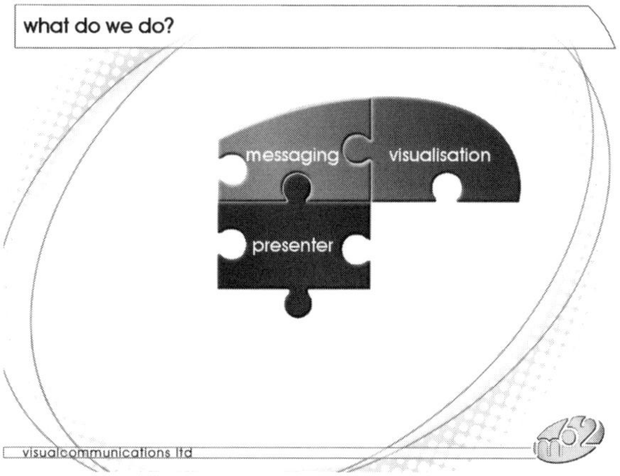

'Then, as we know bullet points don't work, we have the ability to turn the message into a series of pictures and diagrams that stimulate and engage the audience.'

* CLICK will be used throughout the book to suggest when the mouse would be clicked during a presentation.

CLICK Graphic Design appears.

> *'Then we have a team of designers who work 24/7 doing nothing else but making PowerPoint slides look beautiful for clients all over the world.'*

CLICK Multi-media appears.

> *'Then if the presentation needs it, we can add multi-media to it: if you can imagine it, then we can make it happen on screen inside a PowerPoint presentation.'*

CLICK Presenter Support appears.

> *'We provide seminars, training courses and coaching services, in fact almost every day somebody somewhere is being coached by an m62 trainer through their presentation, using technology that allows us to sit in Liverpool and listen and watch as a presenter rehearses in another part of the world.'*

CLICK
Event Support appears.

> *'And finally, if necessary, we will organise the event around the presentation so that the presenter can concentrate on the most important job (that of presenting) without having to worry about the equipment or whether the audience can hear and see the presentation.'*

With this knowledge we are able to then design a slide that complements the message thus:

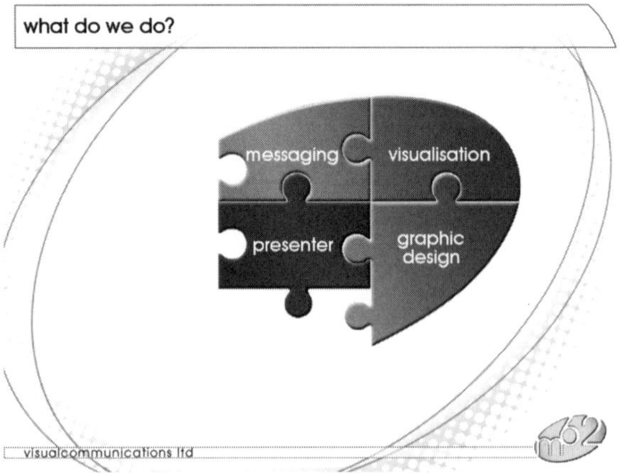

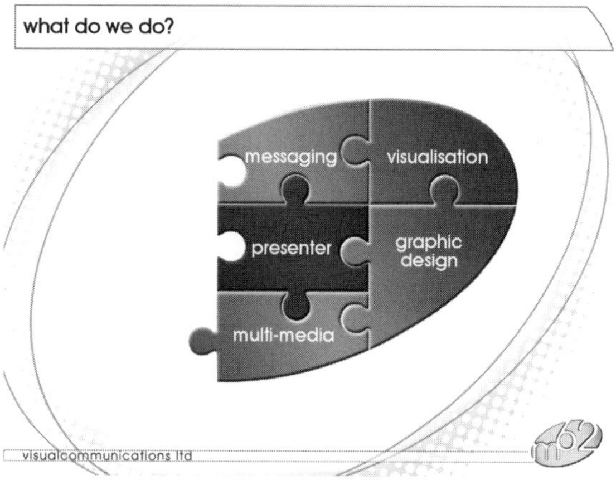
what do we do?
messaging
visualisation
presenter
graphic design
multi-media
visualcommunications ltd

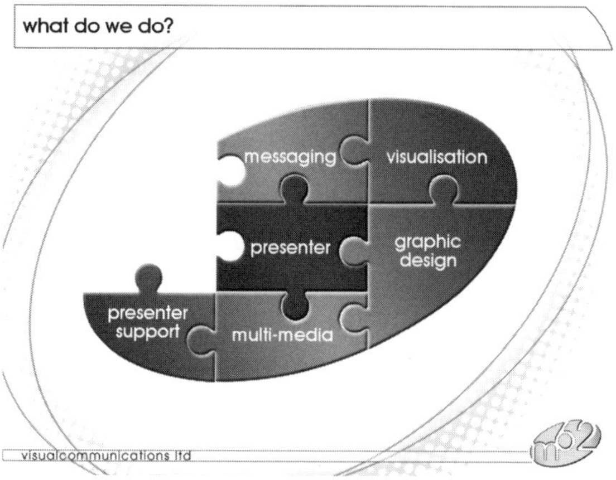
what do we do?
messaging
visualisation
presenter
graphic design
presenter support
multi-media
visualcommunications ltd

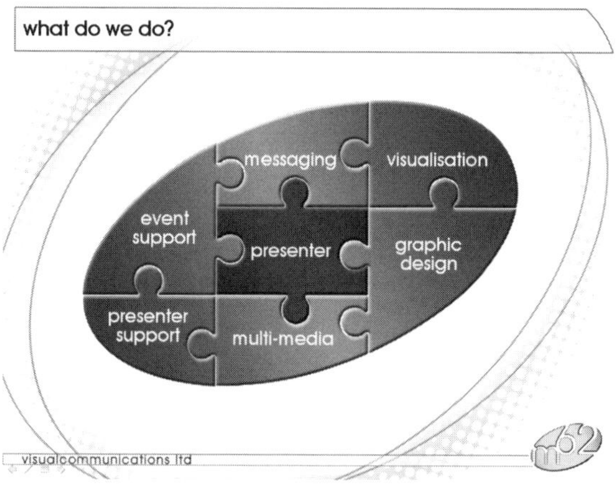
what do we do?
messaging
visualisation
event support
presenter
graphic design
presenter support
multi-media
visualcommunications ltd

You will see that the presenter piece is in the middle or 'heart' of the diagram and the services cocoon this piece. Clearly the slide builds to match the *patter*.

To see me present these slides and therefore see how the patter and visuals work together please follow this link:www.killerpresentations.com/services.html.

Turning boring dull slides into engaging presentations takes more than just design. It takes a deep understanding of communication and presentation techniques and a willingness to work at short notice against horrendous deadlines.

What's in this book?

Producing a book that is predominantly text, about a method of presentation that is predominantly about moving pictures, has been a challenge. But still there is the issue of being able to show you the examples we need to. To this end the book has an accompanying web site. You will need to register as a user, but then you will be able access a series of web links that will show you the actual slides and, in many cases, streaming video footage that shows me presenting them.

This first edition of the book has to be in black and white unfortunately, but there is a colour plate section that repeats many of the slides shown in the text. I have, where possible, chosen slides that work well in black and white to illustrate the points made.

The next issue is how to lay out the material. Most of it interlinks: how you present a slide depends on how it is designed, and how it is designed depends on how you are to present it. I hope that the interlinked nature of the material will become apparent, but since a book is not interactive I have structured it in a linear manner as best I can.

The book has essentially five sections:

1. PowerPoint

2. Messaging

3. Visualisation

4. Design
5. Delivery.

They follow a logical order and should ideally be read in sequence (although I have never managed to do this with a business book and I expect you have already looked at the colour pages – I would have).

Killer Ideas

There are a number of killer ideas in the book.

They are the most important axioms of the m62 method of presenting. I have tried to explain them all throughout the text and if you only have ten minutes then reading just these ideas will give you a flavour of what the rest of the book is really about.

For clarity here are some comments about each of the five sections.

PowerPoint

Essentially in order to make the most of these techniques a change in mind set is needed. Most PowerPoint presentations are rubbish: reams of irrelevant text, boring slides and presenters who think that reading is something we all forget how to do the moment we sit down in a presentation room. This section is about describing another way of using PowerPoint that makes the rest of the book make sense. The principal killer idea is about this change of attitude towards PowerPoint – we call it 'Visual presentations not presentations with visual aids'. I have tried to not make it sound like a rant – apologies if I have failed!

Messaging

This section is not strictly about PowerPoint although I make the assumption that you are going to use PowerPoint to present with. I give examples of where and how we have used it. But it seems difficult to separate the content from the media. A great looking presentation is not what we strive for: we strive for the audience to assimilate information in order to further a business goal. Hence, one of the killer ideas is 'Effective communication not just impressive presentation'.

Visualisation

The definition of a good PowerPoint slide is that it *should not make sense until the presenter explains it to the audience.* Our presentations are visual in nature and the core skill we have is the ability to take other people's bullet points and turn them into interesting and engaging visual slides. This section is an attempt to share the techniques we use. The principal killer idea is 'Non-self-explanatory slides'.

Design

This is the heart of the book. Here I try to demonstrate the visual techniques and devices we use every day with people's presentations. I list them with examples and explanations. Clearly it will make more sense if you understand what we are trying to do (hence the first two sections) but it might just stand alone as well. The principal killer idea here is probably '4D not 2D presenting', but most of the killer ideas are in this section.

Delivery

Since we are doing something very different in our presentations it should come as no surprise that the role of the presenter has to change. In this section we discuss what you need to do differently and why. We also look in detail at how to present specific types of slide. The principal killer idea of this section is 'Audience focus not presenter cued'.

A final note for this introduction – for the last seven years my company m62 has been putting these techniques into practice – none of them is untested. We have written and designed over 3,000 PowerPoint presentations for clients all over the world, in most of the languages you can think of. These techniques work everywhere, and they work well.

My objective for this book is simple: I want to change the way you think about PowerPoint and therefore help you make better presentations from now on. No small ambition. I hope this book helps you.

Finally at the end of each section there is a summary. It is with a great sense of irony that I have included these as bullet points to summarise each section. *I hope the humour is not lost.*

Section One
PowerPoint

PowerPoint is evil – or not!

To a man with a hammer every problem is a nail.

Confucius

Death by PowerPoint

The 'normal' approach to presentations using PowerPoint (30 slides, blue background, yellow text, all the same layout, a heading and five bullet points) is so prevalent, and so universally ill-received, that it has recently become the subject of considerable academic and journalistic comment, and it is the slides that come in for the greatest criticism.

For instance, in America a well-known and respected academic, Edward R. Tufte of Yale, who is an acknowledged corporate communications expert, has written a strong condemnation of PowerPoint in *The Cognitive Style of PowerPoint* (which you can read in full by accessing www.edwardtufte.com). One fascinating example he uses concerns the Columbia space shuttle disaster. In a slide presentation – which Tufte calls 'an exercise in misdirection' – a crucial piece of information about the foam section which detached and crippled the craft, is described as 640 times larger than ones which reassuring pre-flight advice described, was buried in small type several layers down in a busy PowerPoint list. Though the danger this might pose was actually flagged, the warning was not noticed. The main heading on the slide indicated a positive outcome to tests, saying: 'Review of Test Data Indicates Conservatism for Tile

Penetration'. One might criticise the language too, but the point remains – the key information was passed over unnoticed, seemingly mainly because of the way it was presented.

Other authors have taken issue too; another example is in the book *The Presentation Sensation* by Martin Conradi and Richard Hall.

Additionally, to reinforce any lingering feelings you may have that traditional PowerPoint style and practice are fine, try looking at www.norvig.com/Gettysburg where Peter Norvig has posted a wonderful spoof of Abraham Lincoln's Gettysburg address:

> *'Four score and seven years ago our fathers brought forth on this continent a new nation, conceived in liberty and dedicated to the proposition that all men are created equal.'*

Such stirring language and thoughts are reduced to banality by a visual presentation that is not visual, and which uses bullet points such as 'Met on battlefield (great)'. As an example of how to reduce a powerful and memorable message to insignificance; this is a classic.

In Britain, a feature by John Naughton in a serious newspaper, *The Guardian*, addressed the same issue, quoted Tufte's American article and added its own despairing spin: 'Power corrupts. PowerPoint obfuscates. Next time you have to give a presentation, leave it at home'. A similar article appeared in the *Financial Times* in January 2005.

The reason why such comment is made is obvious: the prevailing style of PowerPoint driven presentations, while they are something audiences expect and so often tolerate, do not really satisfy audiences as they should. A good, stylish presenter, with presence and panache, may be able to make up for this, but only in part. The criticism comes because this kind of PowerPoint use is worldwide and large numbers of people notice that it fails to do a complete job, though that might be better worded by saying that presenters allow it to do a poor job.

The solution

So are these pundits right? Is PowerPoint intrinsically evil? Not so. Edward Tufte *et al* certainly have a sound argument based on what the vast majority of the world's 450 million PowerPoint users are doing with it. But this is the issue; it is *how it is used* that causes the problem and the audience abuse. The PowerPoint system itself is not to blame. Transform its use and you transform its effect.

Consider a 13th century Samurai sword, crafted by someone who dedicated their life to perfection, creating a blade so sharp it can cut falling silk, so strong it can slice through trees. In the hands of the Samurai the sword represents justice, protection and a way of life based on simplicity and harmony. To many people it is a thing of beauty. Yet not so long ago in the UK such a sword was used to kill innocent passers-by, by a man clearly unhinged. Does that make the sword evil? Does it diminish its beauty or its usefulness? Clearly it does not. PowerPoint is the same: just because many of its 450 million users use it badly, that does not make it a bad piece of software. It simply exposes some inadequate communication skills.

The solution is apparent: we need not change the tool*, merely change the way we use it. A change in thinking is required: that paradigm shift we have referred to. The way many people need to think about PowerPoint must change. If we reassess the manner in which we use it, and perhaps accept that it has its uses and its limitations and that it is not the perfect medium for all forms of communication, it will work better for us.

How well do you really know PowerPoint?

What are the two most useful features within PowerPoint?

At seminars when I ask this there is no single most common answer. People mention all sorts of things: being able to change the order of slides, being able to use a variety of typefaces, etc. Those most in for ridicule will say 'the ability to add clip art' as if this is somehow the panacea to all presentation ills! What is very rarely mentioned is either of our top two.

* Although there is one feature of PowerPoint that to my mind ought to be removed and that is the presentation wizard – less hocus-pocus and more mumbo jumbo to my mind.

The use of the 'B' key

What happens in show mode (i.e. during a presentation) when the presenter presses the 'B' key? Do you know? I ask this during seminars that I have now given to probably 10,000 people. Only a handful have known, and yet I think it is probably the most important feature of PowerPoint. Why?

Because a presentation is delivered by a living, breathing person, the contribution they make to the totality of a presentation is crucial. Sometimes the full attention of the group must be on them, on what they are saying and how they are saying it. Steps need to be taken to make this so. Press the 'B' key and the screen goes blank, so that attention necessarily must then focus on the presenter. Too often, audiences are left staring at an image on a screen that is, for the moment, irrelevant to what is being said. The facility to blank out the screen is invaluable. Press the 'B' key again and the blanked image lights up again. So simple, yet relatively few people seem to know or use it. You might also like to try the 'W' key which turns the screen white.

The ability to locate a particular slide

I am essentially a salesperson (coin-operated!) and have spent many years 'carrying a bag' as they say in the US; here is a scenario that has happened to me countless times. I am in the middle of a pitch to the Marketing Director when the CEO walks in and says 'So what is this all about?' CEOs have, in my experience, many common attributes, the most significant being their attention span and their ability to influence a sale by giving their approval. If you have ever been a salesperson then you have been in this situation: you have two minutes to convince the CEO, two minutes that will probably decide the sale.

So, somewhere in your presentation you have a killer slide (see later); the slide that summarises the value proposition; the one slide you need to show the CEO, after which they will be interested, or not! How do you get there?

If you think that the process is 'Esc', followed by *Slide Sorter*, scroll down, double click the slide and then press *Slide Show*; then you don't really understand PowerPoint.

You need to be familiar with your slides, but if you want to jump to, say, Slide 24, perhaps to answer a question, hit the numbers '2' and '4' and then the 'Return' key, and up comes Slide 24. Again this is an invaluable, and often little used, feature. Also try the 'Home' key for going to the first slide or the 'End' for the last slide (try pressing F1 whilst in show mode and PowerPoint will bring up a list of in-show commands).

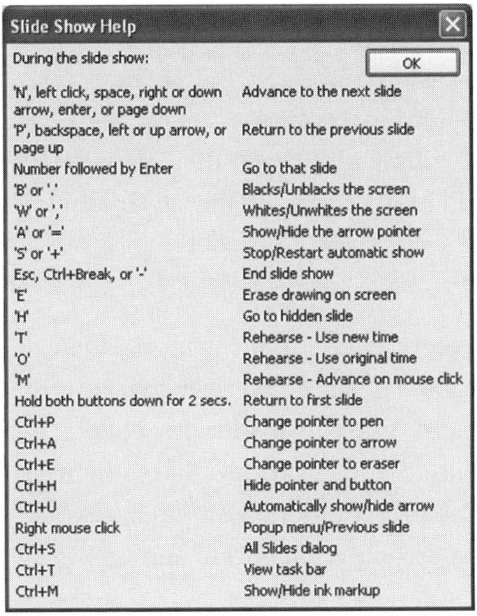

PowerPoint is surely something that must be regarded as an essential working tool. As such, we must be familiar with it. This is especially so for sales people and their sales pitches. Most sales people are drivers (that is a comment about owning cars not a personality type, although…!). There will be few, if any, buttons on the dashboard of their cars for which they do not know the function. Maybe PowerPoint should be regarded in the same way.

Having described PowerPoint as a tool, perhaps the following analogy brings the point to life. Consider PowerPoint as comparable to a pencil. Most people can write and draw using a pencil. But only after some consideration and practice, and perhaps training, can they execute something more artistic. Many can 'write with it' as it were, but it contains the potential to be used as an artist would use it. You just have to know how to do so.

PowerPoint is surely the same. Indeed when we interview for graphics staff for our team, part of the process involves giving them a piece of paper and a pencil and asking them to sketch 'customer service'. Those that can produce something good enough to hang on the boardroom wall stay for the rest of the interview – those that don't, do not.

The full extent of the possibilities PowerPoint harbours is considerable. One of the limitations of presenting these ideas in book form is that it is difficult to do justice to the visual nature of some of what we are trying to describe. However, it would be unrealistic to expect you to have read to this point without having at least flipped through the colour plates, which form part of the book – so you will have an idea of how slides can look.

Tried and tested

Before getting into more detail about what we believe PowerPoint can do when used in the right way, let us be clear that no simple cosmetic change is being advocated here. The reasons for any change must be tangible. And here they are certainly that. Judged in a harsh light of measurable results, and focusing on sales presentations and pitches where such measurability is in no doubt, the approach we advocate and employ works.

Simplistically, one might look at the success rate for sales pitches as being linked to the number of potential suppliers competing: if three companies pitch then a simple rule of thumb suggests that, given that they put over their case in broadly comparable ways, there is a one in three chance of success, of getting the business. An organisation operating professionally and feeling they have an edge, might judge their success against a betterment of these basic odds. Perhaps on such a basis anything over a 30% success rate might be judged acceptable.

Since 1997 we have been involved in creating over 3,000 PowerPoint presentations for clients. The vast majority of these were sales presentations. These typically fall into two different categories that we call *Generic* and *Specific*.

Generic sales presentations are those that are used by a sales-force every day:

- Who are we?
- What do we do?
- Why do clients deal with us?

They are broadly the same and it is possible to design a presentation that allows the salesperson to *spin* (give subtle different meanings to) the presentations to suit most client-facing opportunities. We have clearly demonstrated that a consistent, well thought-out value proposition, well-articulated in a visual PowerPoint presentation can increase sales. There is an element of self-selection in the sample set, as people often don't ask for our help unless they are losing. So assuming you close 1 in 3 of your deals, which is we feel average, then you should expect to see an increase to around 1 in 2 by sorting out your generic sales presentation.

Specific sales presentations are those that see the light of day once and then are forgotten – or at least should be, as there is a saying 'sales presentations never die, they just get recycled' – regardless of impact or success. These presentations are when the contract value is so large as to warrant special attention or the client too valuable to risk losing. In these situations no self-respecting salesperson would run the risk of not making the client feel important by writing a presentation about them, what they need and how their problems will be solved. In fact, we have done so many of these that we have developed a process for producing them.

If we believe, after taking a brief, that the difference between winning and losing a bid will depend in part on the quality of the communication, then we are usually confident enough to adjust our fee accordingly and share the risk with the client. As such we are careful to track the effectiveness of our approach. Each year since inception we have succeeded in helping clients win over 85% of their key specific bids, winning a total of over £3 billion worth of business.

How is this possible? There are a number of reasons and setting them out is what this book is all about.

We have shown the following example hundreds of times at seminars and then we show a progressive improvement in layout and design from one to the next. What these slides show (albeit simply presented on the page in black and white) is an evolutionary sequence.

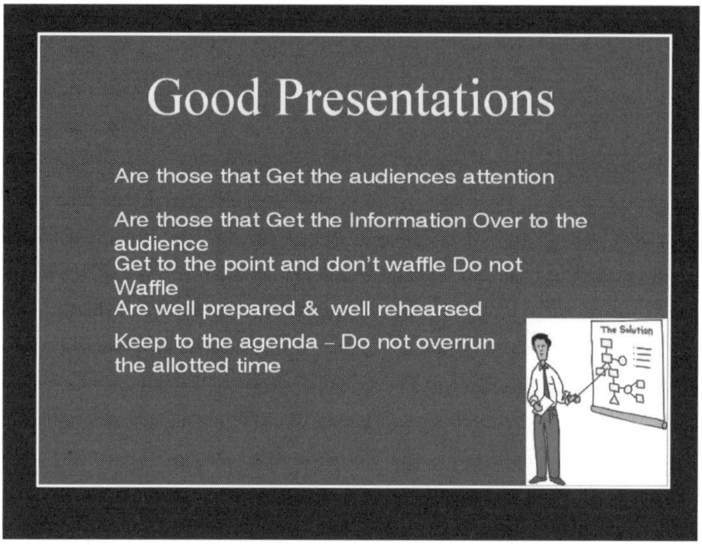

1. A very traditional slide presenting a list of points in full. Put up as one unit, it is clear what it means and it can be read more quickly than a presenter can read it aloud, leaving the audience bored and with people's minds wandering until the speaker catches up and moves on.

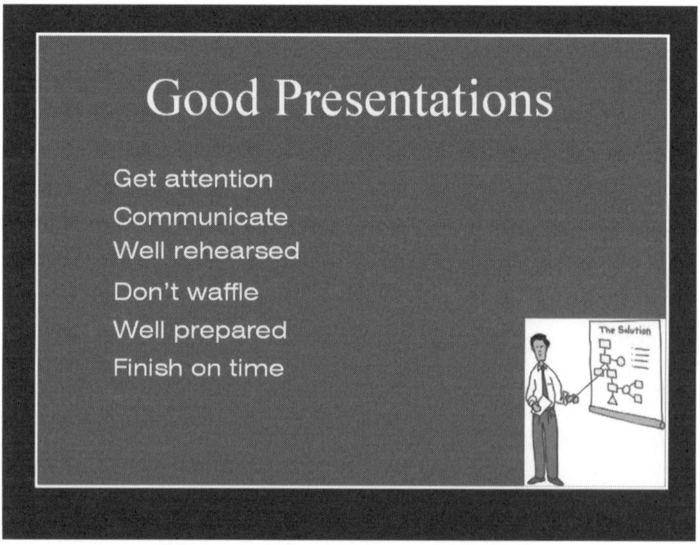

2. The second slide reduces the text and looks better because of it, the audience have less to read, and so may listen to the presenter. But as they still know what is going to be talked about, they may tune out anyway until the next slide is delivered. It is still a list.

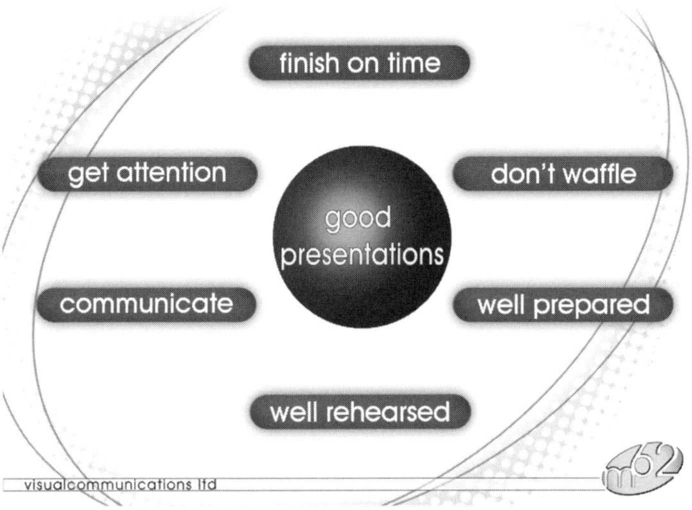

3. The third slide is laid out not as a list but as a Mind Map™ type layout, with the central idea in the centre of the screen and the bullet points laid out around it. To improve the slide further, it is built up with five CLICKs, preventing the audience members from reading ahead and so forcing them to listen to the presenter. Most people agree that this third version is a significant improvement on the first; however I still don't like it too much. It is still self-explanatory. What is the purpose of the presenter if the audience can discern the information on their own by simply reflecting on the completed slide? There is a better way.

4. I want you to look at the fourth slide. I introduce this to the audience as articulating the same information as the last three slides but in a visual manner, then I CLICK and two balls appear labelled *Presenter* and *Audience*. I pause, look at the screen and then look at the audience. They all follow my gaze to the screen and then look at me expectantly, sometimes with a confused look on their faces. The incomplete diagram does not of itself articulate my point, they know that *something is missing* and they want to know what I have to say over this diagram that makes the point. Stop for a minute and examine the last sentence '*they want to*

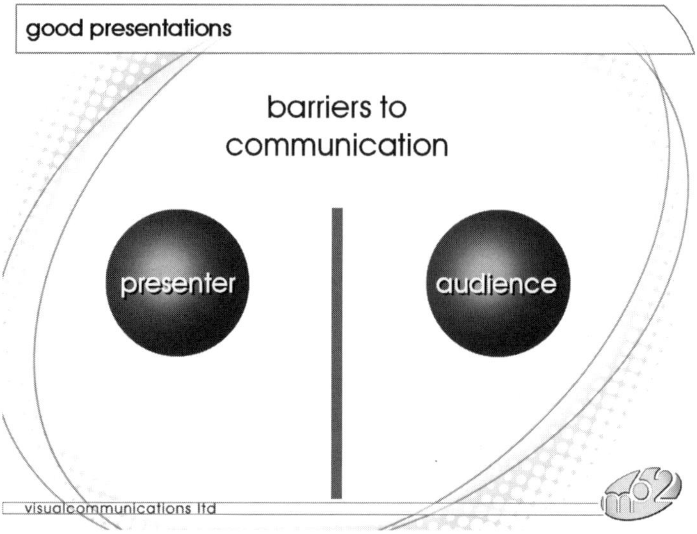

know what I have to say'. When was the last time you were in a presentation and *actually wanted to listen to the presenter?* More importantly, how much more effective would your presentations be if your audience listened to every single word you said? The audience are at this point utterly engaged in communication with me, I have their rapt attention and usually you can hear a pin drop. I point this out to them and then say 'there are three essential ingredients to an effective presentation', I look at the screen (still two balls) – I have done it again in a different

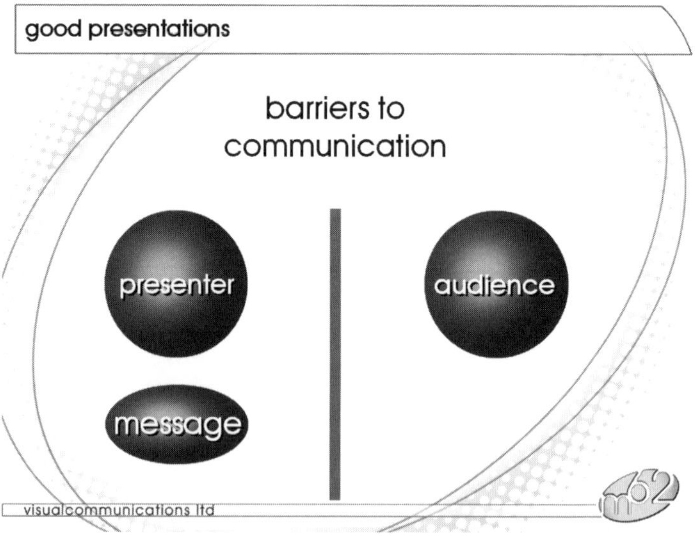

way. They have just been told there are three things, but they can only see two. This creates something we call *visual cognitive dissonance* (apologies to the psychologists reading this for bastardising a proper term). The beauty of dissonance is that it compels a resolution; in this case the resolution is to watch and listen, which, let's face it, has got to be the Holy Grail of presenting. CLICK

5. Then I finish the diagram off, I explain that the line in the middle represents barriers to communication and that the third element has to be a message (SMART, see later). The definition of a good presentation is this and only this: 'To what extent do we manage to get the message…' CLICK (message begins to move to the right) '… across to the audience'. Nothing else matters – they don't have to like it, agree with it or enjoy the experience; they just have to understand the message.

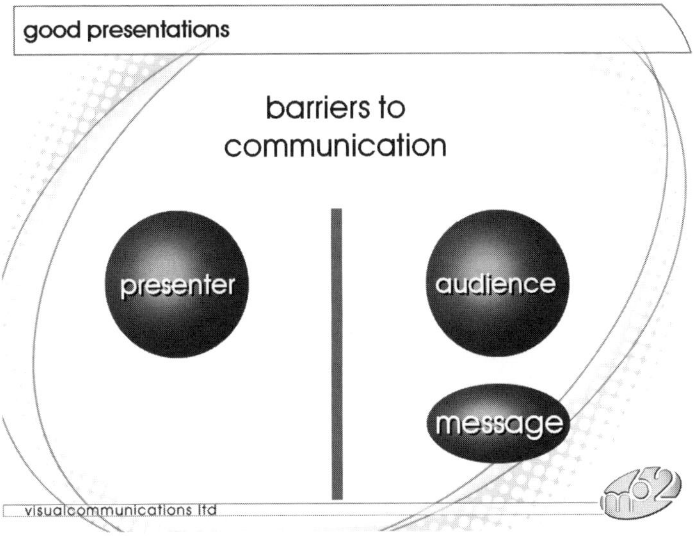

Again this is best seen presented and can be viewed on www.killerpresentations.com/cuecards.html

This demonstrates two more of our 'killer ideas'.

Killer Idea Slides should be non self-explanatory

By designing slides that do not present an instant message but initially intrigue and then help the audience to visualise the argument, you encourage the audience to pay attention and, by increasing their engagement with you, make it more likely that they will retain more of the message for longer. In this way what the presenter says – *patter* – becomes an integral part of the overall flow of information; a seamless part of the whole.

Killer Idea Visualisation

A picture really does paint a thousand words; certainly it does a better job of communication than words alone. Until recently I thought that psychologists said people process images four times faster than text, however I recently found a reference to visual processing being 400 times faster* than hearing spoken words – images are 'language independent' and can add an element of emotion as well as conveying the core content of a message.

Distraction, the presenter's enemy

The audience can only remember that which it heard, or saw; if your listeners weren't paying attention, they will have zero retention of the information. Later we will look at the audience's attention span for this reason. Clearly then we must allow the audience to pay attention to the appropriate piece of communication.

I will mention this several times in this book as it pertains to each section. There are four sources of distraction:

- Content
- Presenter
- Design
- Animation.

Let's look at them in turn.

* *Emotional Branding* by Daryl Travis (Prima Tech), Chapter 6 'Right brain, left brain, no brain at all'.

Content

The biggest problem with presentations that we encounter is that they have too much information in them, much of it interesting but irrelevant and this is then delivered too fast for the audience to cogitate much if any of it. The rule should be only to include information that is 100% strictly relevant to the arguments being made. Anything less than this encourages the inclusion of information that 'may be useful' or worse 'may be interesting'. These pieces of information have a habit of distracting your listeners and, worst of all, prompting them to stop paying attention to the presentation as their mind wanders down a path inspired by an irrelevant observation.

Presenter

Presenters distract audiences in two ways: either by saying something or by doing something inconsistent or irrelevant (or just plain annoying). For example I once watched a businessman attempt to make a serious point whilst wearing a skirt (don't ask!) – very distracting.

Design

If the audience walks away from the presentation discussing the design of the slides and not the message, then we have failed. The design needs to be good enough to allow the message through but not in any way divert attention. Irrelevant pictures in the background are one distraction, as are relevant pictures that can't quite be seen, prompting the audience to try to decipher the imagery.

Animation

This is the most frequently misused distraction technique. We use animation to draw the audience's attention to the place in the slide we want them to look at, but it is easy to draw their attention to the wrong place or to anaesthetise them by over-using irrelevant animations. Please see the section on animation to see our objective quality rules regarding animation; these are designed to avoid unintentional audience distraction.

Each of these areas of potential distraction has its own section in the book. Much of the content is simply-applied common sense. In order to communicate effectively the audience have to be paying attention to what we are showing them and listening to what we are saying – all at the same time. The less we distract them, the more they pay attention, the more effective the presentation. What we do is not complicated, just different from the norm.

Which version?

I started m62 in July 1997 and Microsoft had just released Office™ 97 but most of my clients were still using Office™ 95 and therefore PowerPoint 95. So the first couple of hundred presentations at m62 were developed in 95. Office 97 was a vast improvement and quickly became the norm, however it failed to produce smooth text and as a result we often produced text outside of PowerPoint and inserted it as a picture file. This looked much better but made editing difficult.

PowerPoint 2000 added a much better text engine and we stopped producing text in Photoshop™. But the big change was PowerPoint 2002™. The single biggest advantage was the ability to have items leave or move on the screen. Microsoft completely redesigned the 'custom animation' and made it significantly easier to use.

We now standardise on PowerPoint 2003, in fact we encourage clients to upgrade as it is so far ahead of the older versions. We now develop in 2003 and supply the PowerPoint Viewer with each presentation (not available in 2002 which caused us some problems).

We are providing suggestions to Microsoft's development team for features that would help for the next version, and if they manage to incorporate these we will dutifully upgrade and insist clients do likewise.

One addition to PowerPoint that my design team find very useful is the PptExtreme toolkit, which can be found at: www.PptExtreme.com. This adds some time saving shortcuts that do not affect the finished file (so other users can still see all of the presentation).

Summary

1. Presentations are for the audience, not for the presenter.
2. Use non self-explanatory slides (create **visual cognitive dissonance**).
3. Remove unnecessary text.
4. Don't use complete sentences: single words or phrases will do.
5. Pictures not words where possible.
6. No complete slides, always build.
7. Don't distract the audience.
8. Upgrade to PowerPoint 2003.

Section Two
Messaging

If what you have to say is not more beautiful than silence, shut up.

Confucius (NBO translation)

I think this is a particularly apt quote. As I mentioned in the introduction, it is difficult to separate a presentation from its content, and whilst much of what is in this section relates to presentations in general, regardless of whether they use PowerPoint or not, I feel that we have to examine content in the light of certain facts.

The psychology of memory is complex and in this second edition there is an additional chapter at the end of the book that covers some of the more simple ideas from this area. At a simplified level, memory can be divided into Working Memory and Long Term Memory. LTM is the store for all our actual memories but Working Memory is the place where information is encoded for storage, and decoded for retrieval. As I will explain later Working Memory has four fundamental elements that are largely to do with sight and sound and the recreation of these inside our heads. Working Memory is basically an attention system, that is to say it governs 'how' and 'what' we pay attention to.

Vision is handled by one side of the brain (right) and language the other (left). Furthermore we learn to interpret images immediately upon birth, whereas language skills don't really start to develop until the age of two. Visual information is processed much more quickly than language-based information, presumably because vision is innate and language a learnt process that requires conscious thought.

Attention span

If the purpose of a presentation is to transmit information to the audience with the intention of either educating or persuading them, then it is important that we understand how people retain information. We know, for example, that the amount of information learnt during a presentation deteriorates exponentially, that is to say you remember more today than you will tomorrow and more tomorrow than next week, etc. But what about the amount of information actually attained during the presentation? This depends on a number of factors – not least how well it was presented – but the single biggest determining factor has to be whether the audience were actually paying attention or whether they were thinking about something else. They can surely only be expected to remember that which they actually heard, or saw.

Because it is difficult to measure information retention,* we will concentrate on attention; after all, one leads to the other. There is some research into the psychology of attention** and, as we will see, it is not guaranteed. Attention starts relatively slowly, builds quickly to a plateau and then drops away again, the final drop being somewhat sharp. The figure shows this graphically.

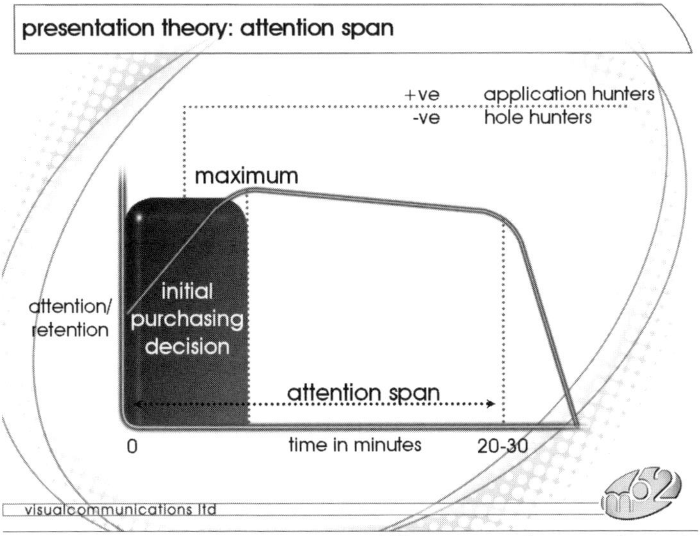

www.killerpresentations.com/attentionspan.html

* We have tried, but it involves testing the audience's comprehension after the presentation.

** See *Video in Business Applications* by Hugo De Burgh and Tim Steward and 'Attention Span and its Implications for Trainers' N Oulton, *Critical Thinker* 1993.

The time between the start of the presentation and the point at which the individual 'tunes out' is called the *attention span*.

You can measure your own by taking a stop watch and good book (a novel, not this one!), start the watch and start reading. The chances are the first time you check the watch is a good measure of your current attention span.

Even while reading this, if you watch for it you will be conscious of your mind wandering from time to time: checking the time, thinking of what you must do next, wondering if you should pause and make another cup of tea (go on: the caffeine may help too!) or a telephone call. This always happens, and even if what you are reading is something particularly interesting you will still find your concentration waning. It is worth noting that women generally have a better ability to hold their attention than men (that is why girls in single-sex schools do well working at their own pace – better than girls in a co-educational environment, who have to endure the boys getting bored and disturbing their concentration).

As the figure shows, all sorts of things contribute to whether audience attention is focused on a presentation or not.

In the figure opposite, the 'notation positive' correlation means that as the factor increases, so too does the attention span. Conversely, 'negative correlation' is the undesirable alternative. 'Balanced' means that a lack of the factor can be as detrimental as too much of it; hence a balanced approach is needed.

Of course, every individual's attention span varies depending on what they are faced with. For instance, it will tend to be less when they have to concentrate on something complex. It varies between individuals too – one person may be unable to concentrate on say, a television programme that fails to grip them, and another easily able to see it through the hour.

While all sorts of things can affect the attention given to a presentation (even a heavy lunch or having a difficult decision to make later can distract an audience), some things can clearly hinder and these include:

Factors Affecting Attention Span		
Presenter	Enthusiasm Voice Animation Passion Pace	Positive correlation Monotonic reduces attention Balanced Positive correlation Balanced
Audience	Intellect Interest level Opinion of Presenter Sex Age Language	Balanced Positive correlation Positive correlation Females typically higher than males Increases with age, flattens after teens Familiarisation increases attention
Subject Matter	Relevance Familiarity Complexity Clarity	Positive correlation Positive correlation Negative correlation Positive correlation
Venue	Effort to See Effort to Hear	Negative correlation Negative correlation

- **The subject matter:** must be made interesting and relevant. A level of detail that reflects the audience's prior knowledge and experience, clear, easy explanation and use of 'their language' are all essential.
- **Physical barriers:** clearly if people find it hard to see or hear this creates difficulties – the venue and environment must be organised to assist the process.
- **The presenter:** enthusiasm is infectious. A clear, confident voice, varied tone and pace, suitable gesturing and a demonstration of expertise and belief will all boost attention.

That said, consider some fundamental factors about this, and also some solutions.

Strategies to extend attention

First impressions last it is said. Certainly the first few minutes of a presentation are vital. A good start, one that grabs the attention, and that may usefully employ media such as sound, animation or video alongside what the presenter does, is a prerequisite for success. But other detailed factors help too.

You can maintain attention for longer if you read the audience and act to boost any flagging attention when necessary. There are two different techniques for doing this that we call 'hard breaks' and 'soft breaks'. Hard breaks include coffee or comfort breaks, a change of location or format. A hard break is some kind of definite break allowing the audience to think about other things (although depressingly these days it often means a 'let's check our Blackberry' break).

Soft breaks can be used more often and include:

- a change of pace
- a new topic
- variety in media
- a change of presenter or presentation
- asking a question
- examples, anecdotes and digressions (especially if they reinforce the main theme as examples do).

After a break, continuity needs to be picked up; sometimes this involves a summary. Once that is done, you have made a new start and attention is rekindled.

Any presentation can become dull and over-complex unless care is taken. If it is also too long or poorly-targeted this will compound the problem. Prevailing standards are not so high. This creates a powerful opportunity for those determined to create a good presentation to shine – and succeed.

To add a measurable element here, we recommend no more than two soft breaks that will extend a session to 90 minutes; then a hard break is necessary.

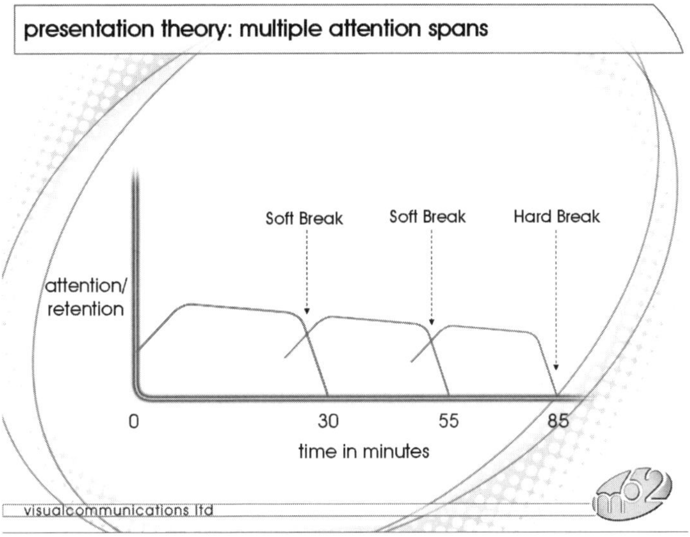

Timing

The duration of presentations is crucial. They must not go on too long. Sales pitches last ideally 20–30 minutes and certainly not very much more, though they can, of course, lead into less formal elements and discussions. For the record, longer events such as a training course (lasting perhaps for several days) can only be sustained by organising them into smaller segments – the kind of breaks involved here was touched on earlier.

Get their attention

Look again at the graph; you will notice that the audience typically does not pay much attention during the first few minutes of a presentation. There are principally two strategies for dealing with this. Most presentation books suggest that you employ some sort of gimmick at the front of a presentation in order to grab the audience's attention – multi-media works well, sound is compelling, or some theatre. However, I prefer to adopt another strategy, particularly with sales presentations. We accept that they will not remember the content for the first few minutes; using that time to create impressions, usually with credible facts and figures, that lead to a sense of trust in the organisation, without needing to be actually recalled. For example we might spend three minutes talking about the company, its locations, number of employees, market size, etc. – all interesting information that adds to credibility, but all facts and figures that can be instantly forgotten once the audience has decided that the company is credible.

Initial Purchasing Decision

At the start of a presentation the audience members are usually not paying complete attention, however they are making a *non-cognitive decision*, usually based on the presenter, about whether this is going to be a productive use of their time. This constitutes what we call the 'Initial Purchase Decision' (or IPD), but you may be familiar with this theory as '*First Impressions Count*' or '12 paces, 12 inches, 12 words'.

Two routes are open to people at this point, they adopt one of two states of mind that condition how they spend the rest of the presentation:

- **Application hunting** is the name we give to the positive one. In this case, people conclude that the answer is 'Yes, this sounds worthwhile' and they decide that they will concentrate as matters proceed. Specifically, they enter into an internal dialogue that asks questions of the developing presentation along the lines of: 'I wonder if ... I wonder if this would help with this or fit with that'. They engage in actively searching out applications for the ideas being presented. Provided their view proves accurate, this state of mind may continue throughout the presentation – nevertheless, it is best regarded as inherently fragile.
- **Hole hunting** is the alternative. Their initial assessment comes up negative and if they do actually listen and enter into an internal dialogue, then it is one of trying to find fault with what is being said. They look for holes in the argument.

Of course, these are two extremes and there are possibilities that exist between them, but often such a presentation does polarise views. The response must be to recognise the process – wholly reasonable from the listeners' point of view – and aim to get a positive decision made. This influence must happen within some three to five minutes or the moment will pass; that is when the IPD is made. Unfortunately too, once the initial purchase decision has been made in a negative way, it is often very difficult for the presenter to reverse it.

Summary

1. 20–30 minute presentations adjusted to match (audience, content, venue, time of day).
2. No more than three × 30 minutes between hard breaks.
3. First four minutes will probably not be remembered in detail only in impression.
4. Write content of first four minutes to influence the IPD.
5. Application hunters are an easier audience, particularly for sales.

- Measurable: To ensure action takes place afterwards (here you might link to any appropriate measure: from agreements or actions that group members take, or commit to, to the volume of applause received at the end!).
- Action Orientated: For the objective to be based around something for the participant to do, take action or something within your control.
- Realistic: It is desirable to be realistic about expected outcomes – hence in this case, a short book of short sections, (if it took you too long to read, the effort might prove greater than any benefit from doing so).
- Timed: To be achieved within a defined time frame (about three hours if you have a good supply of coffee.)

Formalising objectives prompts other questions, and answering them focuses the objective. *How much* do you want *who* to buy and *when?* What actually needs to happen? For instance, there is a difference between a presentation designed to persuade a known decision maker to say 'Yes' there and then, and one designed to prompt a recommendation, say from key members of the audience to a decision maker not present. If this analysis produces a complex picture, so be it. The job is to ensure that the presentation addresses exactly what really needs to be done in all respects. Objectives are thus not simply important in their own right, they should assist the process of going about assembling and delivering the presentation and ensuring that it will work. In a word, objectives are directional.

Not so long ago I started a consultancy session with a salesperson pitching to keep a contract worth £6M ($12M) over the next two years. I started by asking about the purpose of the presentation: I was told that it was to keep the contract. The salesperson had a look on his face that clearly said that he thought this a stupid question. I then asked him, if this was the objective, who the person who signed the purchase order was, and whether that person was going to be in the room during the presentation. It transpired that the salesperson knew who the decision maker was but he didn't know if he was going to be there. To which I then asked, if the decision maker was not there, how could the objective be to win the business? Clearly the audience was not capable of fulfilling this. Over the next two hours we developed a strategy that culminated in him phoning the decision maker and asking him to come to the presentation, and when the decision maker agreed we asked him what he wanted to see. The answer guided the presentation content and ultimately won the client the contract.

So, always be clear about your objectives. It is a good discipline to write them down. It is not a chore – to be effective, you should have done the thinking that enables you to encapsulate them briefly. List what you want to achieve, what the audience want, and how they will benefit from being party to the presentation.

So, ask yourself whether you are clear in this respect before you even begin to prepare. If you know *why* the presentation must be made, and *what* you intend to *achieve* then you are well on the way to success. Time spent sorting this, and making sure you have a clear vision of what the objectives are, is time well spent. It may only take a few moments, but it is still worth doing. Or it may need more thought and take more time. So be it. It is still worth doing, and in any case it may well save time at later stages of preparation.

All right, so you are clear about your purpose, you have specific objectives – what else is important at this stage? The answer here is dependent upon which type of presentation you are to make.

Four types of presentational intention

In my experience there are essentially four main kinds of presentation, and the difference between them lies, unsurprisingly, in their intention. A presentation can aim to:

- **Persuade:** to get someone to agree with your point of view to the point where they will commit to the action you suggest as a conclusion on a rational level (buying the product or service in the case of selling, or taking a step towards doing so).
- **Educate:** or inform in a way where the main aim is to impart information; though in transferring a skill there is also a clear link to prompting action.
- **Entertain:** the purpose of the presentation is for the audience to enjoy the experience.
- **Motivate:** to persuade on an emotional level to change (or re-inforce) behaviour.

Here we are interested primarily in persuasive and educative presentations; the other two can be left to the soft skills public-speaking experts, though an element of each may cross over into any other.

Persuading and educating

Certainly, sometimes both persuading and educating may have to be addressed in the same presentation, but it must always be clear which is occurring. The objectives set the scene: if you intend to prompt someone to agree with you, or buy from you – and thus that they must accept the credibility of what you say, then you are *persuading*. If you simply want them to know something, then you are *educating or informing*.

The two different type of presentation are just that: different – not just in their objectives, but almost everything:

- pace
- duration
- content depth
- question-handling.

The example we use most to describe the difference is question-handling; there are further details and an example in the front of each of the sections, but suffice to say that as a 'teacher' I must answer students' queries. The implication here is that educational presentations must *answer questions*. But this is *not* the same in selling. In a sales pitch, questions are often best not answered directly, but responded to with another question. Again, more later.

This much alone will begin to focus a presentation in the right kind of way. The process we are touching on here is important. As we are focusing particularly on sales presentations we need to investigate more about exactly what it is in a pitch that can make it successful at persuading and link it, indeed all that has been said so far, to the nature of a winning killer presentation.

Solution selling

Frequently this provokes objections from people who sell complex or technical products or services. The argument is that in order to sell my product I have to teach the prospect about it. This is possibly the most difficult type of selling, primarily because the salesperson has to fulfil both roles:

salesman and teacher (or technician). The best rule of thumb is to distinguish these roles by using both a salesperson and a separate technician or educator. If this is not possible then use two presentations – the education piece and then a separate sales piece; *what is it?* – teach, *why buy it?* – sell.

If you must teach and sell at the same time during a presentation then we advise that you use two different backgrounds in the presentation, one for teaching slides and another for sales slides, and coach them to behave differently in each scenario. You will find your sales people more effective if teaching and selling are kept separate if at all possible.

Language of objectives

Once you have written down your SMART objective, the language used in the objective can help you identify the type of presentation and therefore the appropriate structure.

Persuasive presentation objectives use words like *buy*, *sell*, *agree*, *commit*, *give*, and *concede*: all words that require persuasion and ultimately an element of belief. Therefore persuasive presentations are about generating belief.

Teaching presentation objectives use words like *teach*, *explain*, *understand*, and *remember*: all words that require knowledge. Therefore teaching presentations are about transferring knowledge.

By analysing your objectives you can quickly determine the type of presentation, but a word of caution. Sales people always think the objective is to sell, teachers always think the objective is to teach; neither is absolute. For example if I want to sell you anti-lock brakes, I first need you to understand what they do (teach) and if I want you to learn Pythagoras' theorem I need you to see a need or application for that knowledge (sell).

Audience objectives

Having decided on your own objectives, it is now important to consider the audience's objectives. Whilst these are perhaps secondary, it goes without saying that if we give a presentation that fails to meet their expectations, we are unlikely to achieve our own objectives. This is nowhere more important than in a marketing presentation. We have a number of clients who hold seminars or roadshows to attract new business (we do ourselves), but if you advertise that the presentation is about learning (e.g. 'New tax rules and their implication for business owners' – a genuine example) then you had better deliver a teaching presentation before you pitch. We usually recommend that these become two different presentations, delivered by the expert who teaches and the salesperson who, after a successful training session, then stands up and does a short sales pitch. We have shown that this can be dramatically more effective than the usual 'buy our services' approach many organisations use.

Summary

1. Why?
2. Set objectives, research if necessary.
3. SMART objectives.
4. Look at language to decide structure.
5. Are you selling or teaching, not both if possible?

Presentational intentions: educating

Tell me and I'll forget;
show me and I may remember;
involve me and I'll understand.

Chinese Proverb

There is a saying that 'those who can, do and those who can't, teach'. It is clearly a saying uttered only by those people who either have never taught or have no idea about how to go about it. I was fortunate at school and had some incredible teachers, particularly for mathematics. As I passed my exams a year early, I had a year at school at the age of 16 when I didn't have any maths lessons to attend. I was asked to help teach some students who were having difficulty. The experience has stayed with me my whole life. The lessons I learnt about teaching mathematics to 12 year olds have helped me teach a huge number of subjects to a huge number of people; presenting, selling, diving, sailing – subjects too numerous to list. Here's the point: there is a process to teaching, and if you follow it you can teach almost anything to anybody.

The process of teaching

My experience is that the process of teaching goes something like this:

- **Credibility:** they have to think you know what you're talking about even if you don't!
- **Motivation:** they have to want to learn.
- **Language:** there has to be an understanding of the language used within the subject matter (e.g. it is difficult to teach a person to sail without using the words 'sheet in' or 'duck!' [duck as in 'lower your head' rather than 'best served with plum sauce']).
- **Basic concepts:** the simple ideas that build to complex ones.
- **Complex ideas:** the ideas underpinning the subject.
- **Understanding:** the pinnacle of success when they understand the subject and can make use of it (possibly even teach it themselves!).

Put simply, you teach by finding out what the audience know already, then breaking down the things they need to know into bite size chunks that they can understand, and then presenting it to them in a language they are familiar with. Sounds simple, but is probably the hardest thing in the world to do well.

When I am explaining this in a seminar I use the following diagram.

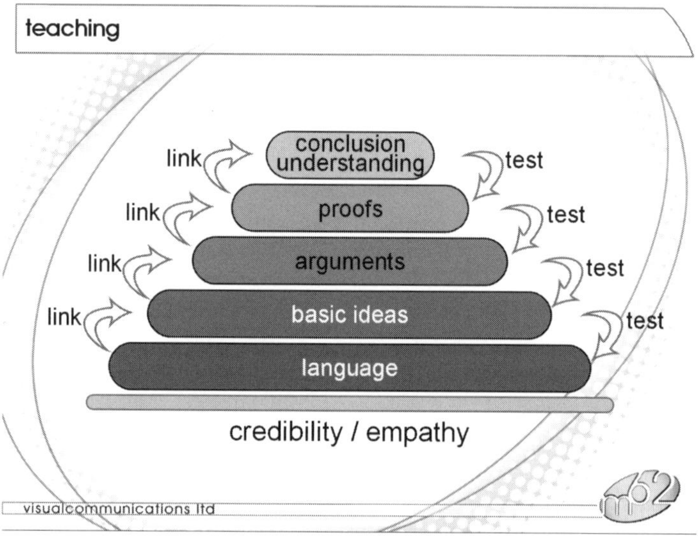

www.killerpresentations.com/teaching.html

I call this the pyramid of learning, each layer is bigger then the one above it suggesting that in order to teach you have to have good foundations. Each layer is linked (by showing the audience relevance!) and then at each stage the presenter needs to check understanding by asking questions.

Structure

So broadly we would structure a training presentation like this:

- Who are we?
- What are we going to teach?
- Why do you need this?
- Language definition
- Questions and answers

- Basic ideas
- Questions and answers
- Arguments, proofs
- Questions and answers
- Conclusions
- Questions and answers.

Teaching presentations are never the same. Audiences always have different levels of understanding and assimilate information at different speeds. The most important skill for the trainer is to keep people engaged (the right slides clearly help) and this necessitates an element of audience control to maintain the appropriate pace and path of information delivery. Questions asked by the audience will divert the path and may require you to skip through the material in a non-linear fashion.

Audience participation is critical to success in teaching environments. As the Chinese proverb at the head of this chapter says, involvement is the key to understanding. You cannot teach by preaching. Therefore teaching presentations must be flexible and the presenter must be ready to move wherever is required in the material. Whilst we don't advocate actually hyper-linking sections, we do suggest splitting the presentation into sections and saving them as separate files. This helps the presentation become interactive rather than linear.

Pace

Again, the single biggest mistake in this type of presentation, as with all presentations, is in providing too much information too quickly. Present too little information and interested audiences in an interactive environment will ask for more detail; present too much detail and audiences go to sleep regardless of the environment. The key to success is to pace the information to suit the audience; frequent questioning not only involves them in the process, but it also allows the presenter to gauge the pace: if they are lost then slow down; bored, then speed up.

Questioning

Questioning is an important part of the learning process – both questions asked by the presenter to check or gauge understanding and those asked by the student. They are important partly because of the reasons why the questions are asked and partly because of what they reveal about the inquirer.

Open and closed questions

Amongst many things that are necessary in training people to dive, one must ensure that they truly understand and appreciate Boyle's Law. This is the law that links the volume of a gas to the pressure it is under. Take an inflated balloon under the water, and the deeper it goes the more the increasing pressure of the water compresses it – it gets smaller. Conversely, as it rises towards the surface, with the pressure reducing, the balloon expands.

Why is this important? Imagine you are at a depth of ten metres and you hold your breath and swim to the surface. As the air expands in your lungs (balloons), it has nowhere to go and it can cause serious damage – ultimately bursting a lung or causing an air embolism.

The trick to diving then is not to hold your breath, ever! So that as the air in your lungs expands it can escape and do no damage. Continuous breathing is essential to diving safely but is difficult to do and counter-intuitive since it is instinctive to hold your breath underwater.

Now suppose a student having listened to the above explanation was to ask the following closed question:

> *'So are you suggesting that if I held my breath at 20 metres and started to ascend quickly I would be dead before I passed the ten metre mark?'*

Clearly the answer is 'Yes'. However what is interesting is not the answer but the question. Look at it again, but this time ask yourself 'Does this student think he understands?'

Because he has phrased a closed question you can hear that he is seeking affirmation for something he thinks he understands; by asking this question he is checking his comprehension.

Now consider the same enquiry but asked as an open question:

> *'So, what happens if I surface from 20 metres?'*

The probability is that the questioner does not fully understand, he certainly doesn't think he gets it, and more information is necessary. This is almost a cry for help.

Teachers probably do this instinctively, by listening carefully to questions and determining whether they are open or closed we can tell where the student is in his search for comprehension and therefore gauge how effective our teaching is.

Effect on attention span

Earlier I said attention span is only really about 20 minutes; this tends to be longer in teaching presentations, if the audience has the desire to learn; but it is still not an hour, nor is it all day. The harder the subject matter and the longer the course the shorter these segments need to be. No more than three attention spans without a hard break, and remember that at the end of the day (when they are tired) attention span may drop to ten minutes, and so the last section should be no more than 30 minutes in duration (as opposed to 90 minutes first thing).

The re-cap

Particularly when teaching, where the objective is to impart knowledge, it is important that after each break (hard or soft) the presenter recaps. This is primarily to ensure understanding but also to help the audience position the information, both in their minds and in the context of the course outline; people like to know what they are doing, why, and what's next.

After a soft break I usually recap the content of the previous attention span and after a hard break the contents of the previous segment. Usually

I will ask a question or two to check understanding and to draw the audience back into engagement.

Summary

1. Slow methodical and meticulous.
2. Flexible flow through the material.
3. Key to understanding is involvement.
4. Pace at the slowest member of the audience.
5. Questions are used to test understanding and encourage engagement.
6. Questions asked by the audience are major indictors of success or failure of the teaching process.
7. Re-cap habitually.
8. Unless you really enjoy teaching or have the patience of a saint, leave it to the professionals.

Presentational intentions: persuading

Management cannot be expected to recognise a good idea unless it is presented to them by a good salesman.

David M Ogilvy

There are many ways of viewing the sales process. People talk of 'consultative selling', 'solution selling', 'interactive and creative selling' (what else?) and refer to patented approaches such as SPIN™. Essentially, the overall approach that all these espouse is logical and depends on a similar view of how people buy. The sale process should certainly not be structured just on the basis of *what we want or find easy to do.*

A good definition of selling (one that reflects customer focus and an understanding of the buyer decision making process), is simply: 'Selling is helping people to buy'.

Each year billions of dollars are invested in training salespeople on sales techniques and relationship building. Everybody knows that you cannot help people to buy until you have uncovered and explored their needs. And so salespeople are trained to know how to open and close a sales call, how to ask questions, how to handle objections, when to explore options, the stage of the sales/buyer cycle when you should present solutions, and how to ask for the order.

Organisations know that to achieve their goals it is imperative to have a common sales process in order to manage opportunities more effectively and more efficiently. There are many benefits that are realised by having a common sales process, one being that a sales force has a common language. When a salesperson is selling to me, I can tell very quickly whether they are trained to a particular process. This gives me comfort in knowing that I'm dealing with an organisation that recognises the value of training and developing their salespeople.

However, of all the billions of dollars invested in training, very little, if any of that is invested in the sales *presentation* process. And they're missing a golden opportunity. The difference between winning and losing is a razor's edge – the *competitive* edge. The competitive edge, especially in a 'beauty parade' pitch, is more often than not, the presentation. PowerPoint is an incredibly powerful sales tool that can give you that edge. With the correct presentation process you can kill the competition, and not the audience! (Which is largely what happens now, you may have heard the expression Death by PowerPoint).

A persuasive sales presentation process

We tend to assume that decisions in the business world are all rational. This is unlikely as there is always an element of the emotional. The decision maker may 'like' the salesperson, have a relationship they value or just dislike something. However, our experience is that rational arguments are far more persuasive than emotional ones and only fail when they are either slim or badly articulated, thus allowing the emotional arguments to prevail.

To this end we tend to assume that the single most important factor in influencing a decision is how well the rational arguments are made. In essence how well the sales presentation is written, designed and delivered. We do not ignore the relationships that will influence the emotional decisions, nor do we ignore the impact of design and multi-media in manipulating the emotional decisions, but here we will concentrate on how we deliver the rational arguments.

A typical presentation process would look like this:

1. Empathy.
2. Credibility.
3. Benefit.
4. Justification.
5. Close.
6. Questions and answers.

Empathy: people buy from people, especially people with whom they have a connection. That is, you must demonstrate an understanding of the audience to whom you are speaking. This starts in planning – which must originate a tailored presentation, one appropriately directed at the organisation and the people to whom it is being delivered – and is augmented by the presenter's manner and how they handle the initial stages of the presentation. Whilst, realistically, many people make presentations that are, in fact, similar to numerous others they have made. What matters here is the feeling. If a presentation appears to be too 'standard' – *it's obviously what they say to all their potential clients* – then this is resented, and is likely to be seen as not taking sufficient trouble, or as a sign of insufficient understanding. This can then dilute attention and effectiveness.

Credibility: sell yourself, your company and your product in that order. There is a role here for evidence and proof (including external facts and figures); another element of this is the presenter's credentials. As a parallel example, there is a good deal on the cover, and on certain pages inside, about the pedigree of the authors of this book. The background here is a necessary part of building up credibility. Without it a book that sets out to change your view of presentations, or at least of certain kinds, and which is critical of much current practice, would seem less appealing. If you did not feel that what is being said came from a reliable source, discusses proven methodology and is based on experience, you might well view it very differently.

A number of different things may be necessary here within the course of a presentation, that progressively build a feeling that the presenter's credibility is sound. Returning to the case of this book, one extra element is the quotations featured in various ways, endorsements, which provide a form of independent comment. While some such details may therefore be important here, they must be expressed succinctly, do their job of building credibility, and positioned early on.

Beware! There is a style of presentation where the need for establishing credentials simply takes over and submerges, or postpones, other detail; or both. One example we witnessed was in a London-based financial company, who will not be named to spare their blushes. For a while every presentation they conducted began with the same 34 slides detailing the history and organisation of the company. These were used, in part, because they were familiar. They were felt to get the presentation and the presenter off to a good start. Their lack of relevance, for certainly the detail was way beyond what was necessary, and the time it took to go through them negated their having any good effect. Indeed, having made people think 'Boring', they prevented the remainder of the presentations from striking the right note. The initial purchasing decision was made, negatively, long before this part of the presentation was complete.

Benefits: the value proposition

The art of selling is about *Feature, Advantage, Benefits*. The core of any sales presentation needs to be about describing benefits. It is not our intention here to go into the classic details of the plethora of sales technique that constitute the full sales process. But for the record, benefits are those things about the product or service and its provider that do something or mean something to the customer. Features are simply factual points about the product or service and the organisation selling them. Most often benefits should lead the argument; after all, features give rise to benefits – what make them possible – and benefits link most closely to customer needs. But there is still some confusion about features and benefits (even in this day and age, we find a worrying proportion of participants on sales courses who cannot differentiate accurately between the two).

What we do need to do here is to make clear what seems to be the best way of dealing with this factor in the context of the overall approach we commend and use.

For all the complexities of the buying/selling process, potential customers ask themselves three fundamental questions when considering the merits of a product or service:

- **Do I need it?** Unless what is being sold actually meets a real need, there is little likelihood of a purchase being made.
- **Can it be delivered?** Having decided that they do want it, then they have to decide that they believe the claims being made are genuine and that the benefits being described can be delivered.

- **Can I afford it?** This is where a decision is made about value: does your value proposition – the overall package that you offer – satisfy the client's buying criteria?

In many cases, traditional sales presentations are quite good at this, a persuasive case is made and there is much talk of benefits. But, if no sale is confirmed, then where is the cause most likely to lie? In our experience, and there is no doubt about this, if there is a failure, the most likely cause is that the presenter failed to create genuine *belief:* the customer is not convinced that the product is for them, is of good value and that it can/will be delivered. This principle cannot be overstated, hence the next killer idea.

Killer Idea **Persuading requires belief**

A sales presentation must create *belief* – the way it is conducted must reflect this, it is the central bedrock of any success. In order to succeed you must describe value, but then you must articulate it in a way that ensures that the prospect really believes that you can deliver.

As this figure shows there are many paths that can be taken as the sales process proceeds, but only one that leads to success. A sales presentation must present the value proposition and this must then be supported by a compelling justification that is truly credible – *believable*. We call this step 'justification' and it is critical. Where the sales process overall is contingent on the value proposition, by the time you have arrived at the pitch presentation this should be fairly solid – if not you're going to lose, whatever the presentation is like. Assuming your value proposition is sound, the real issue for the presentation is whether they believe that you can execute.

We have found only four types of proof: *Testimonial, Technical, Process and Logical.* Unfortunately, we do not have the space here to discuss these at length nor show examples as I would like to, suffice to say that *Testimonial* (which subdivides into three: 1st, 2nd and 3rd person) is always the most credible.

During seminars, I usually ask for a show of hands for people who have ever received an e-mail or letter from a client saying thank you or well done. There are usually lots of hands. Then I ask how many of them have

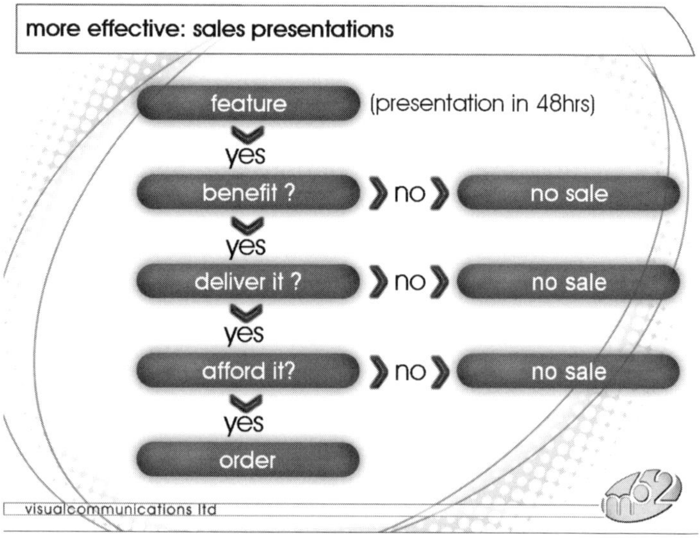

www.killerpresentations.com/salespsych.html

ever thought to put this in a PowerPoint slide and show a prospect – few, if any, hands. What a waste of an opportunity! At m62, we even put customer quotes on our business cards.

Close, questions and answers, close

That done, all that remains is to ask for the order – to close (closing is another important sales technique, but beyond our brief here to deal with in detail).

Hopefully this will raise objections (e.g. too expensive) that we can isolate, pre-close, counter and then close. If we are unlucky they will have no objections.

Effect on attention span

Let us now relate this to our original premise about the question of attention span. Where does the value proposition fit within the total presentation? If this is the most important thing, and if attention wanes if people are not rapidly engaged with what is being said, then logically it must be delivered early on. That means maybe after just three or four minutes, and certainly ahead of the audience making their initial purchase decision. It is indeed a key part of what can prompt them to make a positive one.

However complex it may be, and however much more there may be to say about it later, the value proposition must come in at this stage. It must be capable of being described succinctly. And in doing so, will utilise one slide – the one we call, unsurprisingly, the 'killer slide'. We will have more to say about the precise nature of this in due course. One point meantime, and let us put this as a check – think of a presentation you have made, or indeed one you plan to make. Does it have one key slide that plays this sort of role? As we have said, it should have, so, assuming it does, where is it placed? In a presentation using, say, 30 slides it should not be further in than around number five or six. If it is much later than that, you risk losing its effectiveness; and if it is the last slide, then we would suggest you need to seriously rethink your approach.

The figure below shows the positioning of the killer slide (labelled 'benefits') and the following list summarises the nature of the structure we are looking at, and the sequence we believe it should follow.

- **Introduction:** four to five minutes long establishing credibility, ending (if budget allows) with a piece of media to ensure attention.
- **Benefits:** a description of the overall value proposition that is on offer to the prospect (not just a general statement about it.) This is usually five headings surrounding the title 'Why us?'
- **Justification:** taking the five elements of the value proposition in turn and offering proof of their need (if necessary) and proof of your ability to execute (essential).
- **The close:** ask for the order.
- **Question and answers:** these often delay a response to any initial close and must be dealt with effectively to reinforce belief; they are an important – and usually expected – part of any sales pitch.
- **The close:** finally, this time (though there are, of course, circumstances where a decision follows later and discussions and other processes perhaps continue in the interim).

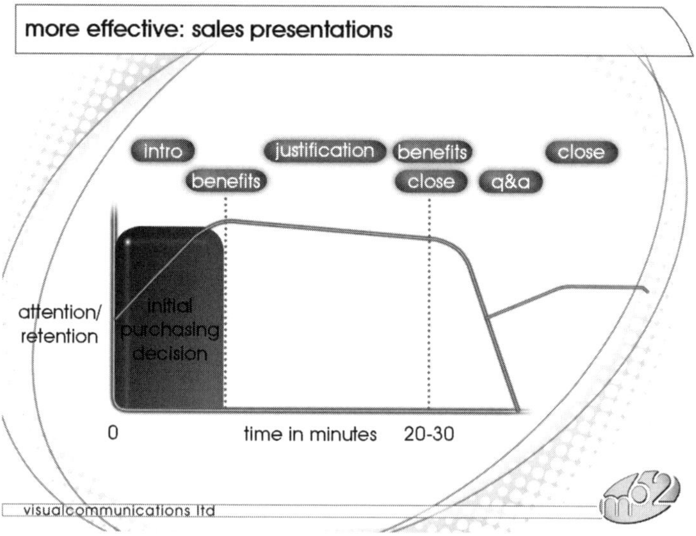

www.killerpresentations.com/salesstructure.html

The figure provides an effective route map. It indicates the path to success. It also shows what needs progressively to be done to align it to the audience's attention span. This is radically different from the 'me, me, me' style of presentation castigated earlier.

Can this structure really be so mechanistic? Each customer, and thus each presentation, is, of course, unique. But the detailed differences always fit into the overall picture and structure described. How do we know? m62 have helped clients create over 3,000 presentations. Every one used this structure, and every client experienced an increase in conversion rates. In major presentations (potential order value more than £1 million) we regularly achieve better than 85% success and are sufficiently confident to be paid, in part, on results.

Approached along these lines, presentations will never seem pedestrian or 'standard'; indeed, because they are customer focused, that would be difficult. Add good delivery and good visuals, and the chances of success are excellent.

The killer element

All the principles set out here are tried and tested, based on the many presentations we have originated for clients (and ourselves), which in turn have achieved a high success rate. One element here, and one we promised more detail about, is how to encapsulate the core message about what you offer, and construct, the killer slide. Whenever we are involved with this process we avoid past practice and try hard not to make assumptions. Rather we go back to basics and analyse the situation 'with a blank sheet of paper'. Nothing can be decided, much less put over in a presentation, until a clear idea exists as to exactly what stands the best chance of prompting a positive buying decision. Not only is this information crucial, but in most cases it must be capable of being expressed succinctly. The core message must be there, understandable and powerful, but must not take forever to present and articulate.

The process we use for identifying a value proposition is this:

1. Brain storm.
2. Delete irrelevant or inaccurate.
3. Collapse redundancies.
4. Rank according to customer need.
5. Rank according to competitive advantage.
6. Select best 5.

The purpose of this is as much to gain agreement about the common message as it is to find the best value proposition. The process takes about an hour with a client one-on-one, and can take a day in a workshop setting with all the key decision makers from an organisation (longer if you involve salespeople – all of whom generally want their say!).

We will digress for just a moment. The technique to use here is the one that takes a feature and follows it with the words, 'which means that …' For example, if a catering equipment company makes a flat grill unit for use in restaurants and hotels, they might describe a particular model as having a cooking surface of 800 square centimetres (which is clearly a feature). But this is easily transformed:

> *'This model can cook six steaks or a dozen eggs at once and will be just right to help cope with the rush you said always occurs at breakfast time (because this model has a cooking area of 800 square centimetres)'.*

This is a good example because, whilst few people can probably instantly and accurately imagine 800 square centimetres in their mind's eye, it is certain that any restaurateur will be wholly able to imagine the description of what it will do, and see how it can help.

The So What? game

Every salesperson will tell you that they understand the difference between a feature and a benefit. They will also tell you that they always discuss benefits with clients and never features. Even so in helping clients write over 1,500 sales presentations I cannot remember a situation where I have had only benefits in the answer to the question: If I was a prospect 'Why would I choose you?' (Alarmingly the most common response to this is 'We are cheaper.' A more convincing argument for a lack of sales skills there is not. Bad salespeople sell on price, good salespeople sell on value.)

There seem to me to be a number of reasons why the responses we get are often features not benefits; the first is language. By this I mean that the presenter is so familiar with the benefit behind the feature that talking about the feature automatically makes him think of the benefit. For example, we use 'more impressive' as a *benefit* statement, but if we are to be analytical this is actually a *feature* of our service – the benefit is actually 'audiences frequently confuse an impressive presentation with an impressive organisation, so having a really impressive presentation can help you win more business.' The benefit here is winning more business, the feature is an impressive presentation.

My role as the outside consultant in these discussions is not to offer advice as to what the benefits may, or may not be, but simply to ensure that the audience see clearly the benefit and that this is not hidden by fogged thinking or imprecise language. The trick to doing this is by asking a series of stupid questions, to be precise a series of questions that more often than not appear to be inane but that actually force the presenter to think through their sales logic. By asking 'So What?' after each response to the initial question above we usually get to the benefits relatively quickly, for example

'Why would I choose you?'
'Our equipment is faster than the competitors'.'
'So What?'
'Having quicker equipment means you can increase productivity.'
'So What?'
'Well it's difficult to get trained staff these days, so improving the productivity of the existing staff is the single biggest challenge to most of our prospects today.'

The benefit here is increased productivity, not speed. Of course the smart salesperson asks the prospect first if they have staff issues and whether faster equipment would help long before the presentation.

We call this exercise 'The So What? game' and it is very useful although, be warned, it can make you unpopular or – worse – appear stupid. Let's look at an example from a logistics company and examine their value proposition.

Here we take and rearrange the way the key factors are expressed:

- **Bulk liquid transport facility**. As stated, this is certainly a feature, but it is a capability on which they have a monopoly in their area of operation. So, for the customer, the ability to use a local supplier in this way effectively becomes a benefit.
- **Large fleet of vehicles**. Again just the large number is a fact – a feature – but linked to delivery possibilities, it is instrumental in ensuring that the service the client wants will be received, and that is a benefit.
- **Sophisticated I.T. systems**. Whatever software and systems they use is hardly of interest, but what they will do certainly is – the ability to plan and track consignments to a high level of accuracy is a benefit, and that is precisely what the systems are there to do.
- **Blue chip clients**. In a service business, the benefit of the right sort of client list is one of low risk – safety in numbers; or at least the right sort

of organisations making up the numbers. Checking has clearly been done by past and existing users, satisfaction seemingly experienced by others (the kind of others who would stand no nonsense) and this provides a benefit in the nature of an assurance or guarantee.
- **Competitive pricing policy.** This links to the blue chip clientele: the organisation is determined to provide value for money and many others see this as cost effective.

Next, with a list of this sort noted, it must be prioritised, (preferably based on sound facts about what customers explicitly want and like), in order to select the five key reasons to buy.

Now, as promised, let us address the question of the five points. There are three reasons why we advocate five points:

1. It is unlikely that the audience will acknowledge all five, and only three reasons to buy seem to leave audiences feeling that the proposition is light. More than six and we run into a working memory problem, and so five seems to be the optimum number.
2. Added to this is the fact that breaking a 20–30 minute presentation down into an introduction followed by five sections seems to time the presentation very well, allowing three to five minute sections for each stage.
3. Five lays out on a slide in a much more attractive way than four.

Visualisation

A final point here: when a slide is actually used and shown, it is best if the five points are presented one at a time. Thus one point is made and shown at a time, and the overall picture builds up and grows in power as it does so.

To reinforce what is an important part of the overall approach, here are some other examples.

So far, so good. What we now have is a basis for the core of the sales message and also for what we have referred to as the killer slide. But how is this sort of information presented on the slide, and just how is it used? The next section adds some thoughts about the picture that is building, and how to make the overall presentation persuasive and powerful.

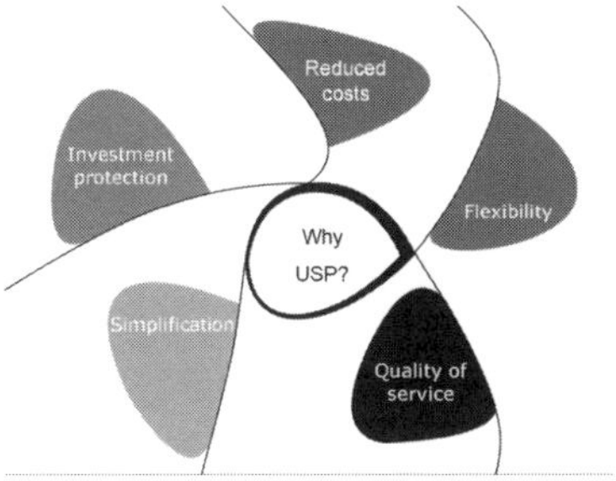

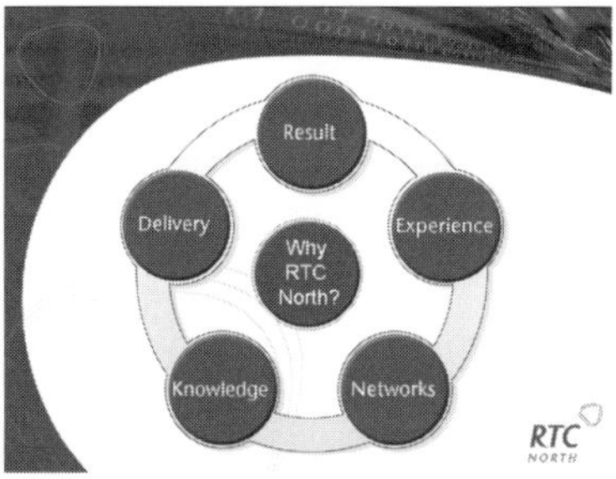

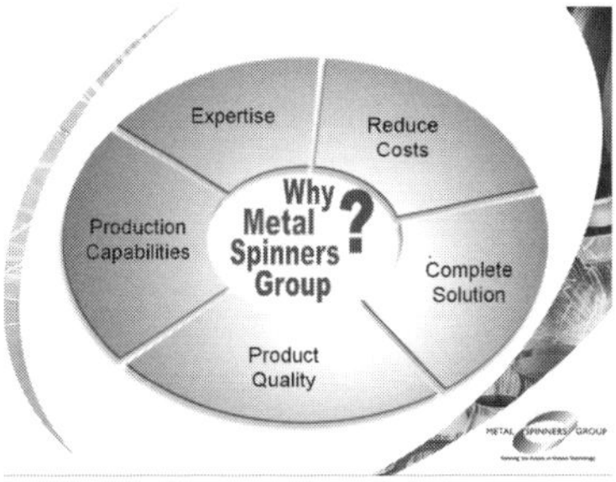

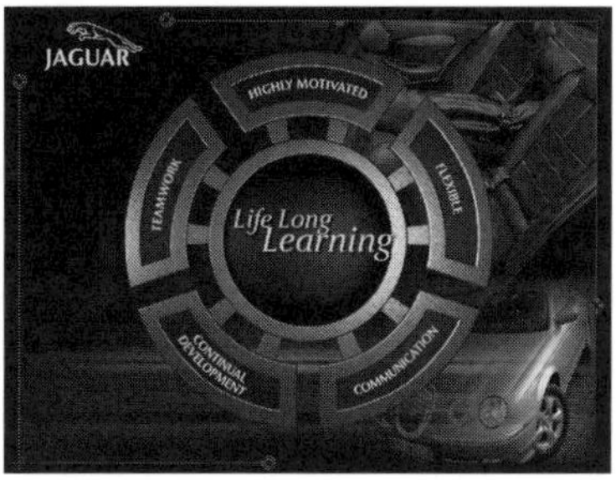

Summary

1. So What?

2. Benefits not features.

3. Presentation content is largely proof of ability to execute.

4. Use the value proposition to structure the presentation.

Section Three
Visualisation

One picture is worth ten thousand words.

Frederick R Barnard

(So why do we use a thousand words and one picture, usually an irrelevant pie-chart, in our presentations?

NBO)

Killer Idea Kill the cue-cards

Let us add to this by suggesting a short test you can try out yourself. In the first chapter of this book we showed three slides with bullet points aimed at demonstrating what factors produce a good presentation. All featured the same six points. Without turning back the pages, how many of the six points can you remember, having read them only a few moments ago? Think about it for a few seconds and write down those you can recall.

When we ask this at m62 presentations people can often remember only one or two points, despite the fact that we are talking about a time span since they saw them of not more than two or three minutes. The exception to the rule are the highly analytical people in the audience who habitually write everything down from the screen (about one in 50). The interesting question to ask these people is how much they can remember of what was said around the bullet points. The answer is usually not very much: they were not listening, they were writing! It shows that the first two of those slides were in a form that is of more use to the presenter than the audience; they provide the classic cue as to what to say. Yet an audience will apparently remember only 15–20% of their content.

Now think about the fourth slide (still resist turning back). This was the diagram that defined the nature of a good presentation and around which the patter that would accompany it at a real presentation would be hung. How well can you remember that? Can you sketch it out? At seminars almost everyone in the group can do that. Normally more than 95% of the audience have perfect recall of the graphic shown at the end. As has been said, this may help prompt the memory. It shows the difficulty we are at pains to confront.

What is more, they find that having the diagram in mind enables them to explain to someone else the concepts that were expressed to them.

I have been using this diagram to explain this point for ten years and a couple of years ago a guy on a plane recognised me and said that I had changed the way he presented. I asked him how and he drew this diagram. The question is then simple: what would you rather have, a series of bullet points that cannot be recalled minutes after you have used them, or a series of diagrams that not only can be recalled, but can also change behaviour?

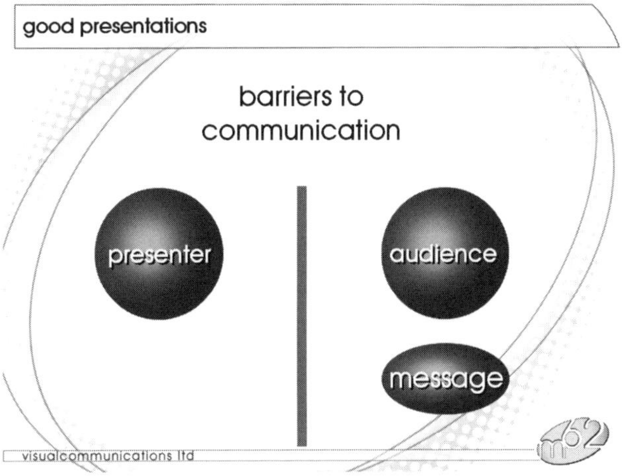

Let us look at some statistics from the psychologists again. Classic bullet point presentation means that the audience take in 80% of the message from the presenter and 20% from the visual aids. But retention is, as we have discussed, a problem. They will only remember 20–30% of the message, even just a little later and we all know this will be less still after just one day.

More statistics – people remember about:

- 10% of what they hear
- 20% of what they read
- 30–40% of what they see
- 60–70% of what they see *and* hear.

The case being made for a different vision and use of PowerPoint reflects this truth. In this way 80% comes from the plethora of information, concepts and diagrams on screen, augmented by the 20% from the presenter (assuming the patter is well prepared and presented and that the two elements fit seamlessly together). In the old way a presenter is lucky if members of an audience remember one in four of the points made whilst a true multi-media presentation may well achieve fully three quarters of the message being retained. Hence the old adage 'Tell them what you are going to tell them, then tell them it, then tell them what you've told them and then summarise by telling them again'. The first figure here is seriously scary for any presenter; the difference between the two is significant by any measure.

Think what that means in a sales situation. Most purchasing decisions are not made during a presentation, they are made later (sometimes *much* later). So while purchasing decisions are made on the content of the presentation, they are in fact made on what can be remembered of that content. Is a positive buying decision more likely to be made on around a quarter of the content of the case you made, or on three quarters of it? And in a competitive situation how do old and new style presentations stack up against each other? What we are setting out here might almost be described as something that gives you an unfair competitive edge.

In reality the information presented does come in two forms: what you see and what you hear (occasionally more, if, for example music is added). If the right patter is added to visuals that are genuinely striking and which fit well with the way people want to take information on board, then presenting is actually easier to do. It may also be more satisfying – more fun even – because it is always better to be doing something you can clearly detect is going well, rather than something accepted on sufferance.

Remember too that in judging sales presentations, the style is used by the audience to assess the seriousness of intent. If the presentation is put over in a lack lustre way, and consists largely of reading lengthy text slides, then is it reasonable for the audience and potential client to suppose that this should be seen as a professional approach, one prepared with due diligence just for the recipients and designed to do a good job for them? It is unlikely, surely. The good presentation earns the attention it gets and then benefits from that, not only in terms of having its content appreciated, but in terms of being thought well-prepared. It is a useful bonus if, amongst the comments you get, are such as: '*That was very professional ... They went to some trouble over that*'.

A presentation with clear objectives, put across by a presenter who has originated the visual and verbal aspects together, which works by presenting a strong case in a novel way and one which people see and hear so that they retain the maximum amount of the content in their minds – is a winning formula. This is the killer presentation of our title.

The right look and use

The traditional way of doing the sort of thing described above is through a list. At its simplest, and returning to the earlier logistics example, this might look something like this.

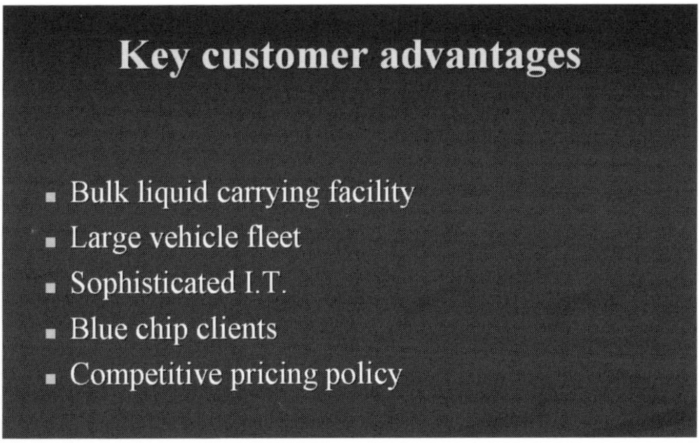

Such slides, especially in such a key role have already been commented upon – savaged if you like. There is more to say, however, to show just how powerful is the preferred approach we are describing – and, bear with us, it starts with a rant.

The kind of slide that turns audiences off most surely is the one with the list where the extensive words are read out verbatim. It might start out something like this:

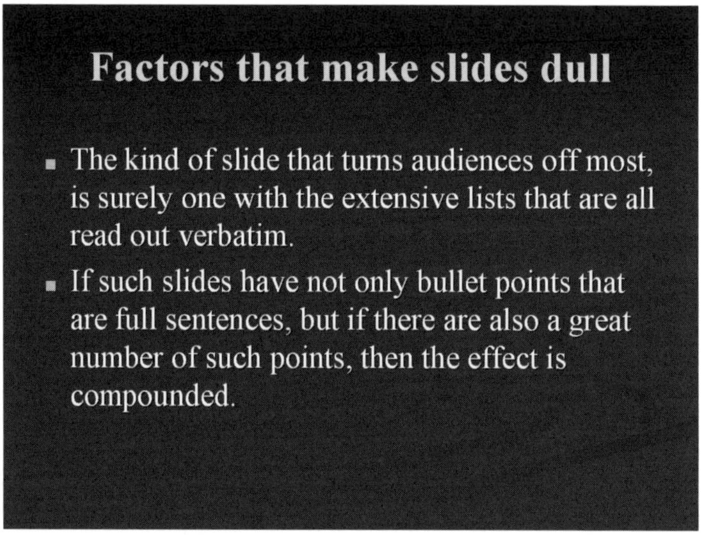

And so on. We have all seen slides with the equivalent of a short novel on them (fair enough, so this is an exaggeration – the length of a short story). Dull, inappropriate and likely to prompt a tedious presentation, one at which almost everything said is read from the screen. So what happens? Well, the slides may get used just like that, and many are, but sometimes, someone – the presenter themselves or a colleague, perhaps – admits that the overall effect looks … *a little dull.*

Crass Little Inserted Pictures Always Rubbish & Trite: C.L.I.P. A.R.T.

They decide something must change. So, working their computer literacy overtime, they add a little picture – fitting in a piece of clip art. This is how a slide that links somehow to the subject of meetings, perhaps describing a project and setting out the review process, ends up with a picture of a little group of brightly coloured cartoon characters sitting round a table gazing out from the bottom left-hand corner of the slide, and jostling the type into odd shapes.

What a change! What this is now is a dull, inappropriate slide with an inappropriate piece of clip art added in, and doing nothing to rescue the situation. It does not help. People do not say 'Wow!' and hang on every word of the text just because the picture is now there. Really, they do not. The overall effect is still bland, and in many cases – certainly for something intended to be a killer slide – the creation of it is a waste of time and effort. Yet people are curiously wedded to this style. For example, in one international organisation during a sales workshop, participants spent a day creating and making presentations, all accompanied by endless very wordy slides. Suggestions that this might be changed were initially vehemently rejected: *it's what we always do!* Yet after some hours of being on the receiving end, and being the audience for their own style of presentations, the point was made and they raised suggestions for change. Suddenly their perspective was very different.

This slide is not there primarily to act as a cue to the presenter, so ill-prepared that they must read out every word. In any case, very few people can either write the kind of material that reads well when read out, or read well in that kind of way (actors are rightly paid large sums of money to create audio books, for instance, because it demands a real skill). More evidence that very few people can naturally read well is provided by something we see practically every day: the effect that teleprompters have on our politicians. Many read their speeches (many no doubt written by someone else, which cannot be helped), but the only punctuation they use is to pause where each line ends; and, because of the physical nature of the teleprompter, the lines themselves are very short. So, what you hear sounds rather like the following looks:

Good morning ladies and,
gentlemen I am so very pleased to,
be here in your beautiful city and have the,
opportunity to speak to you about my,
congenital punctuation blindness.

Remember that an audience can read the words on a slide considerably faster than a presenter can read them out loud. Most presentations sound infinitely better if the speaker is well-prepared, and interpreting the brief notes in front of them in light of that preparation – speaking fluently from an outline, rather than reading a full text. If you reduce the words to a list of headings then what remains will certainly be much more manageable (though granted you may need to add in some notes for yourself, to act as the cue that is otherwise now missing).

Let us return to our logistics example of earlier, instead of displaying the Value Proposition as a list we used a five pointed star like this:

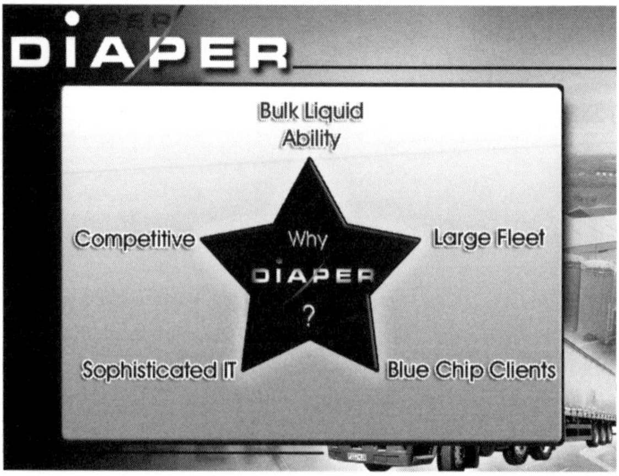

Section One
PowerPoint

Tried and Tested

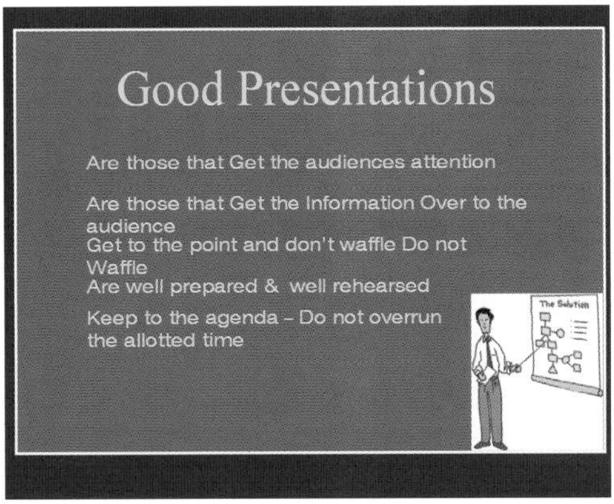

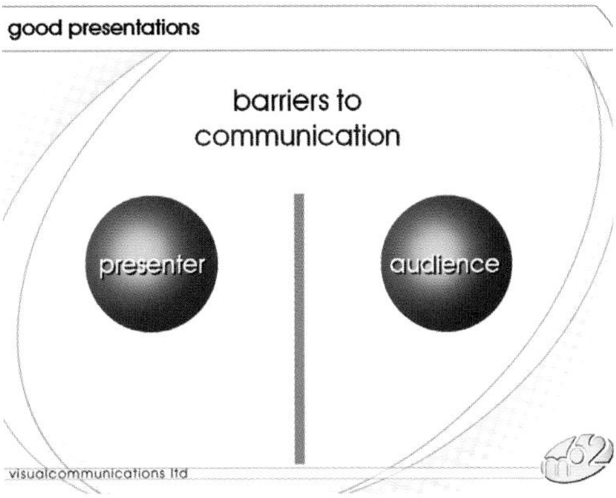

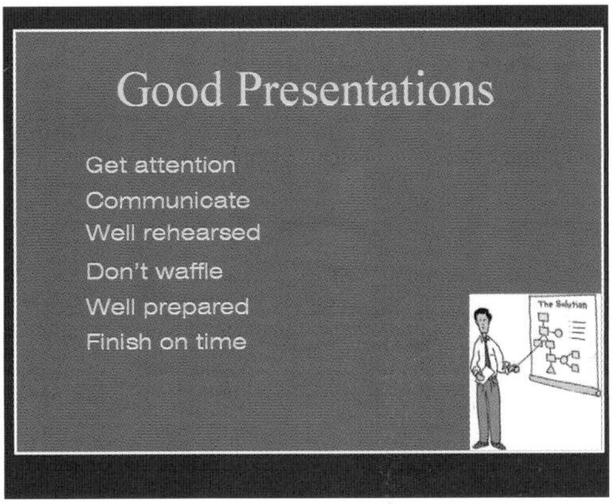

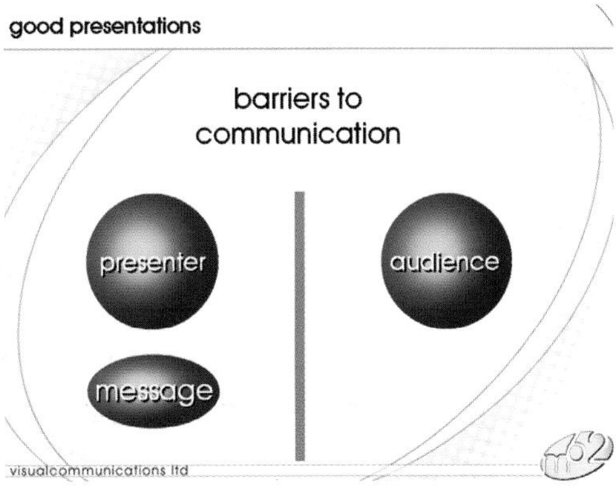

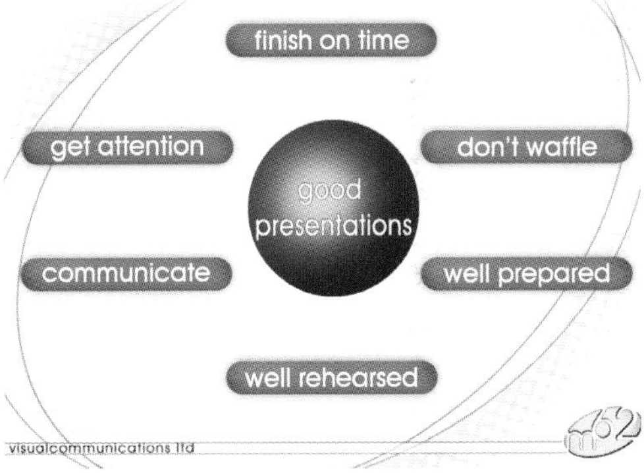

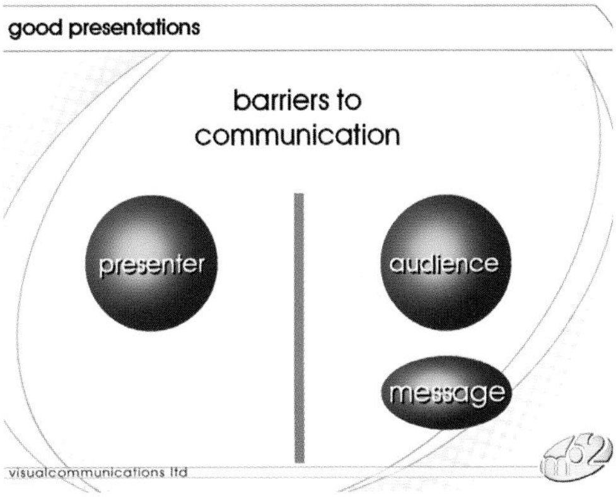

www.killerpresentations.com/cuecards.html

Section Two
Messaging

Attention span

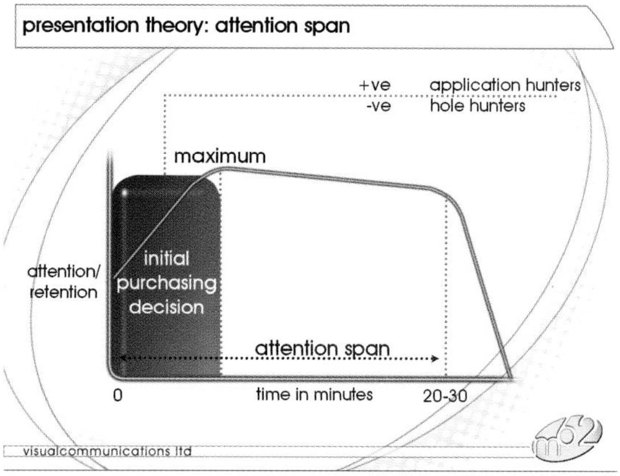

www.killerpresentations.com/attentionspan.html

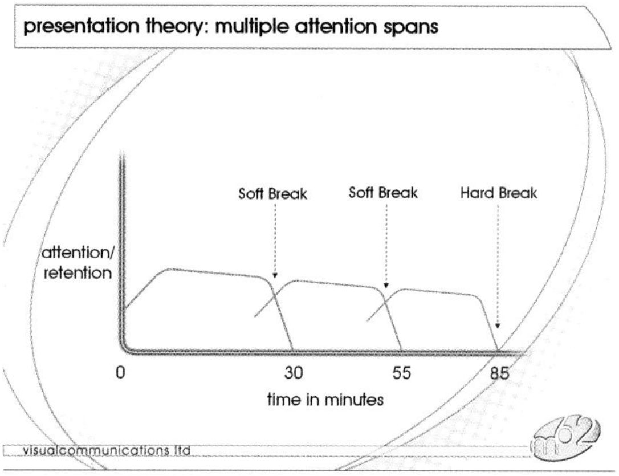

Presentation Intentions: educating

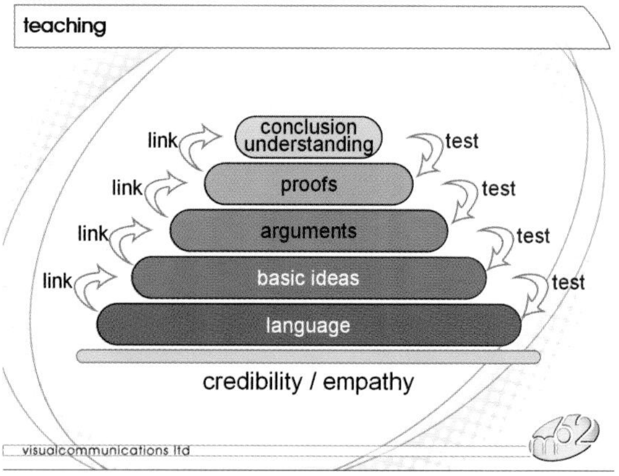

www.killerpresentations.com/teaching.html

Presentational intentions: persuading

Persuading requires belief (killer idea)

www.killerpresentations.com/salesstructure.html
www.killerpresentations.com/salespsych.html

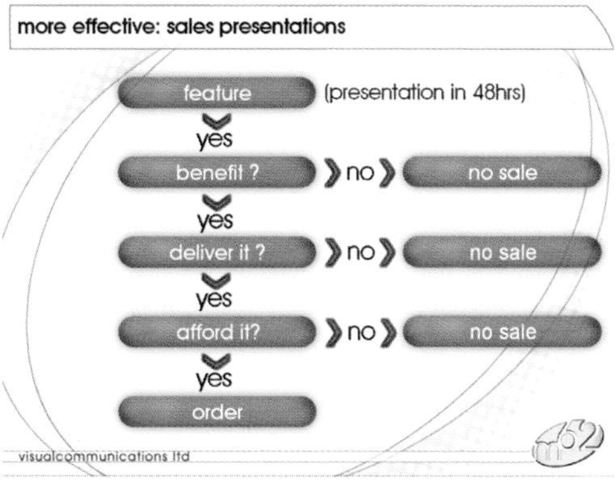

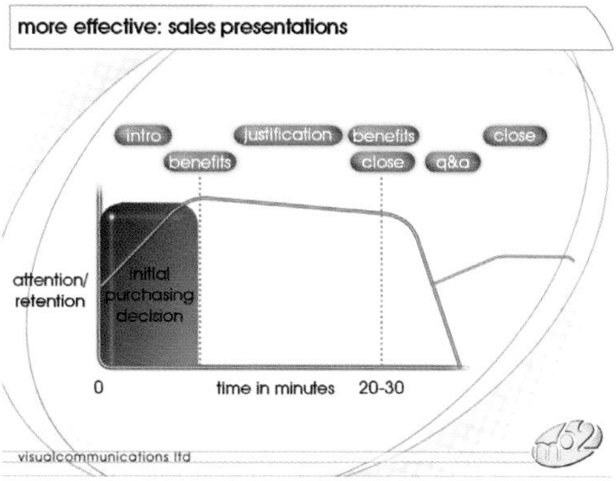

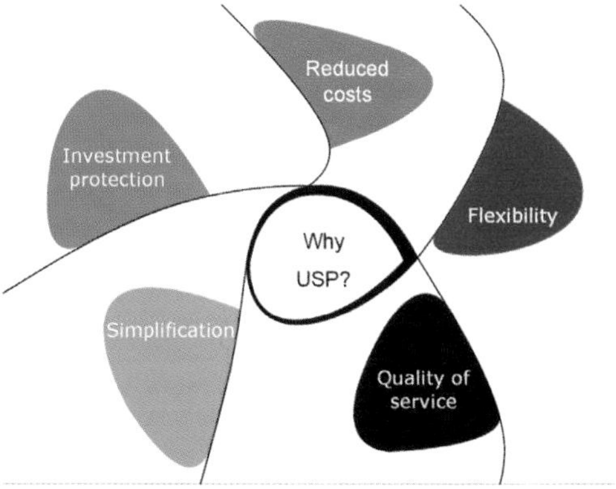

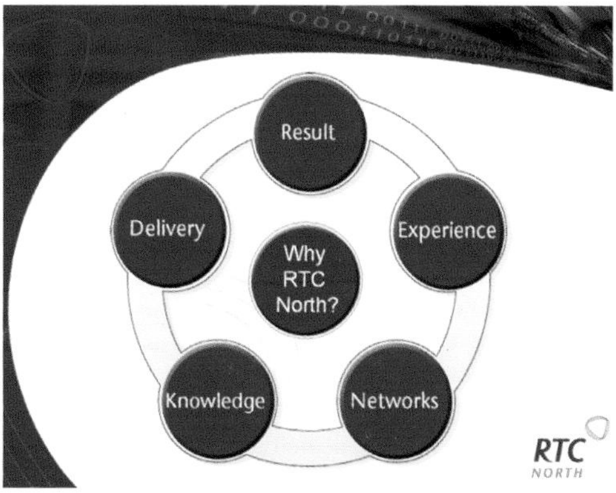

www.killerpresentations.com/usp.html
www.killerpresentations.com/metalspinners.html
www.killerpresentations.com/rtc.html
www.killerpresentations.com/jaguar.html

Section Three
Visualisation

A visualisation example

Background

- In the mid-1950s, granules similar to those found in endocrine gland cells were observed in endocardial cells from the atria. This was the first indication that the heart also can function as an endocrine organ.
- Scientists had searched for a long time for "Third Factor," the factor in addition to GFR and Aldosterone that controlled fluid balance.
- In 1981, a product of cardiac secretion, atrial natriuretic peptide (ANP) was first described and was subsequently shown to induce natriuresis and vasodilation. It is also an antagonist of the renin-angiotensin-aldosterone system.
- In 1988, a molecule of the same family was discovered in pig brain and was named BNP (Brain Natriuretic Peptide). This was later found to be produced by ventricular myocardial cells.
- In 1990, a third peptide, CNP, was discovered in the nervous system and vascular epithelium.
- Recently, a fourth peptide called DNP has been reported.

www.killerpresentations.com/timeline.html

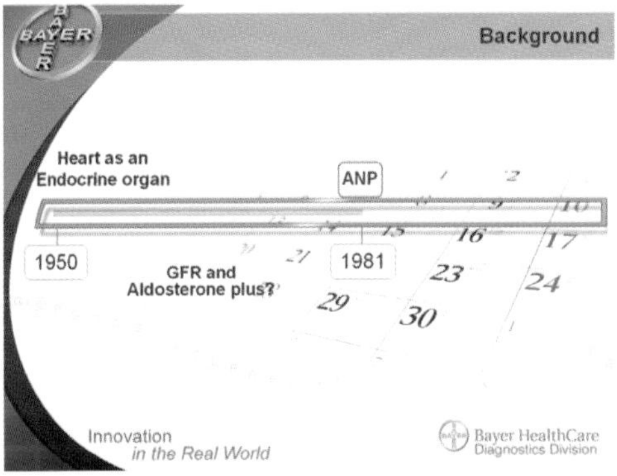

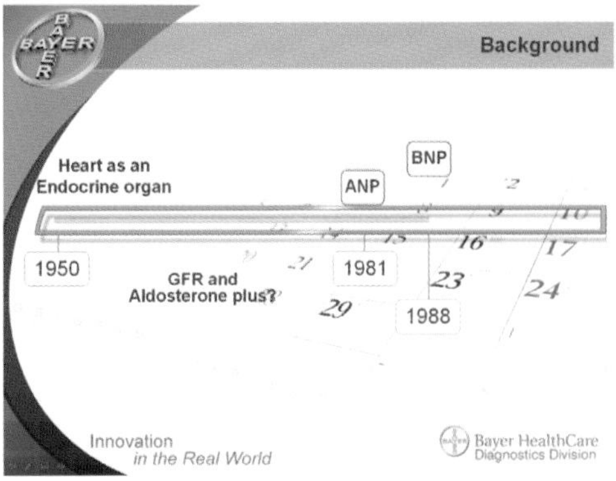

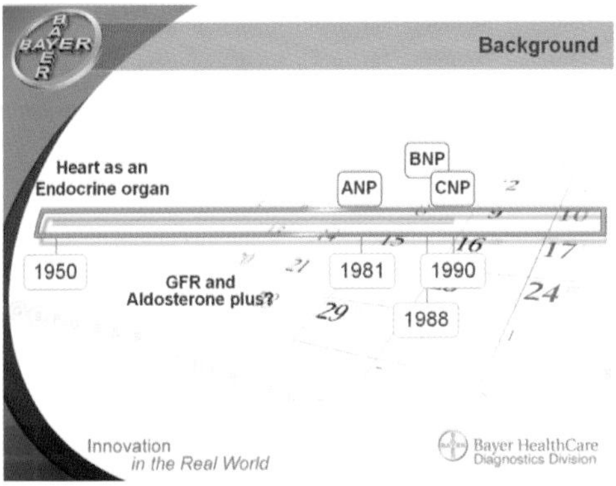

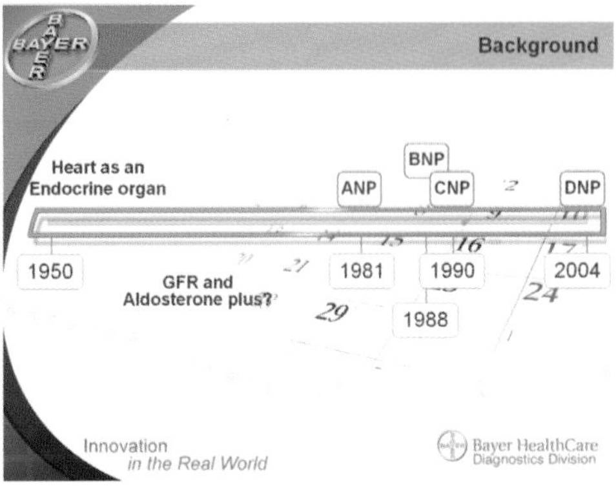

Pacing information flow (killer idea)

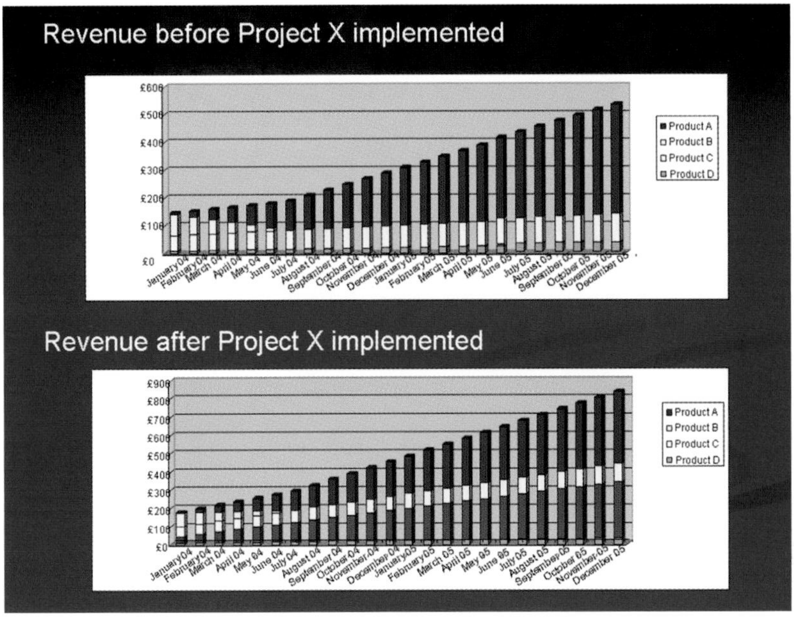

www.killerpresentations.com/informationflow.html

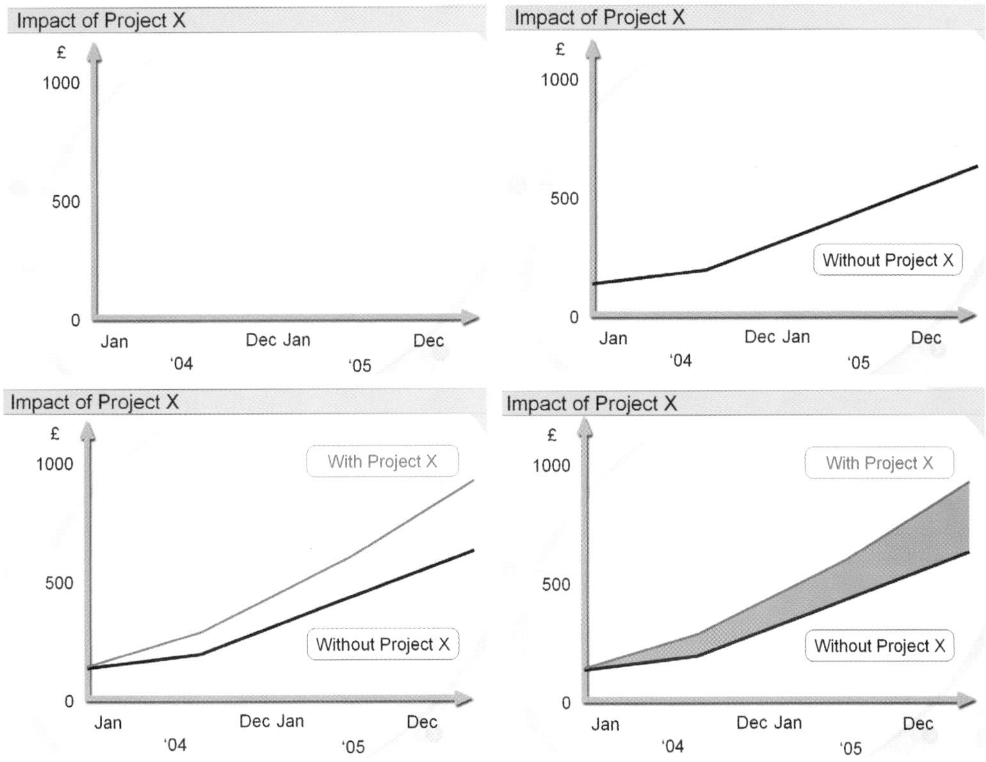

Four dimension presenting (killer idea)

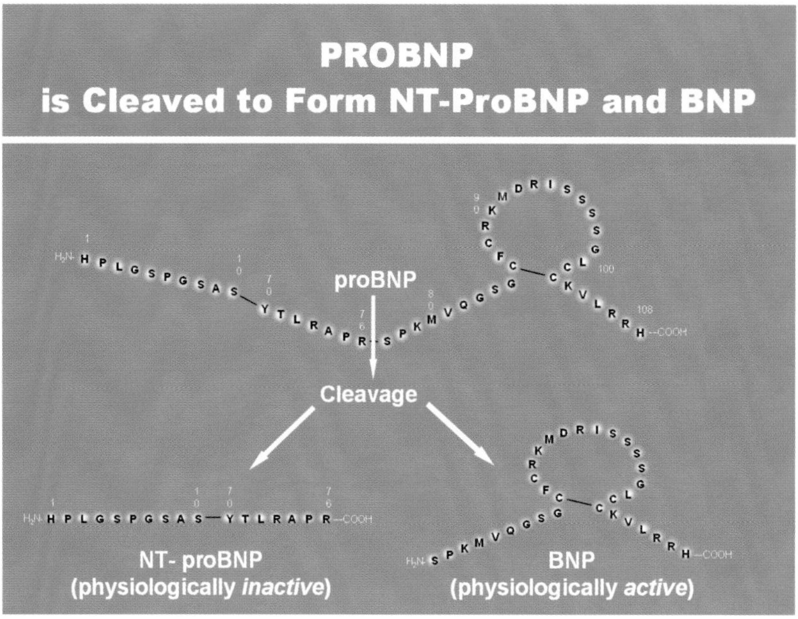

www.killerpresentations.com/4Dexample.html

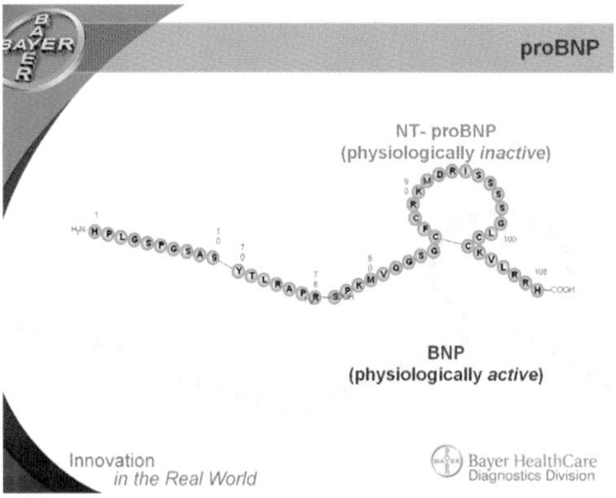

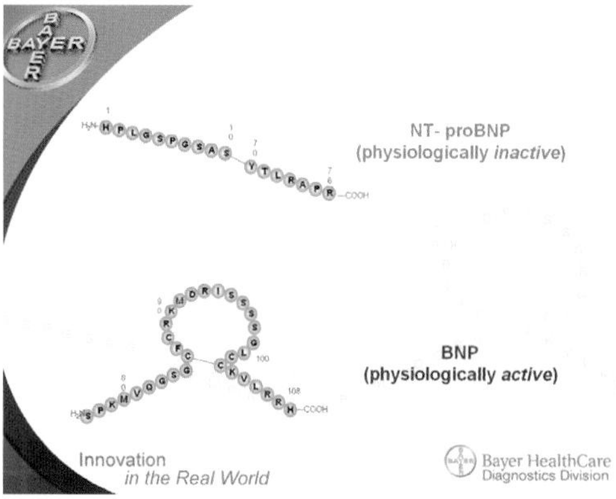

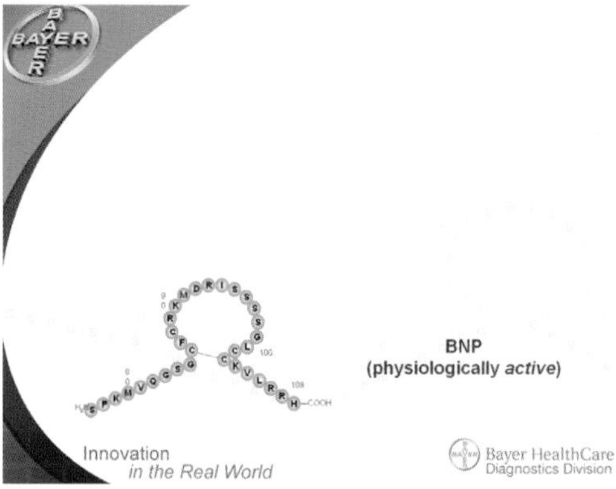

Visual devices

Build up (killer idea)

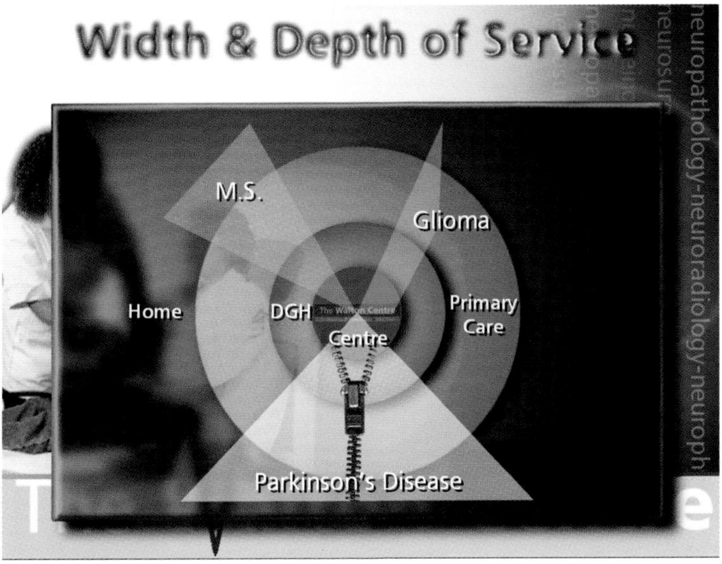

www.killerpresentations.com/Walton.html

Fade down (killer idea)

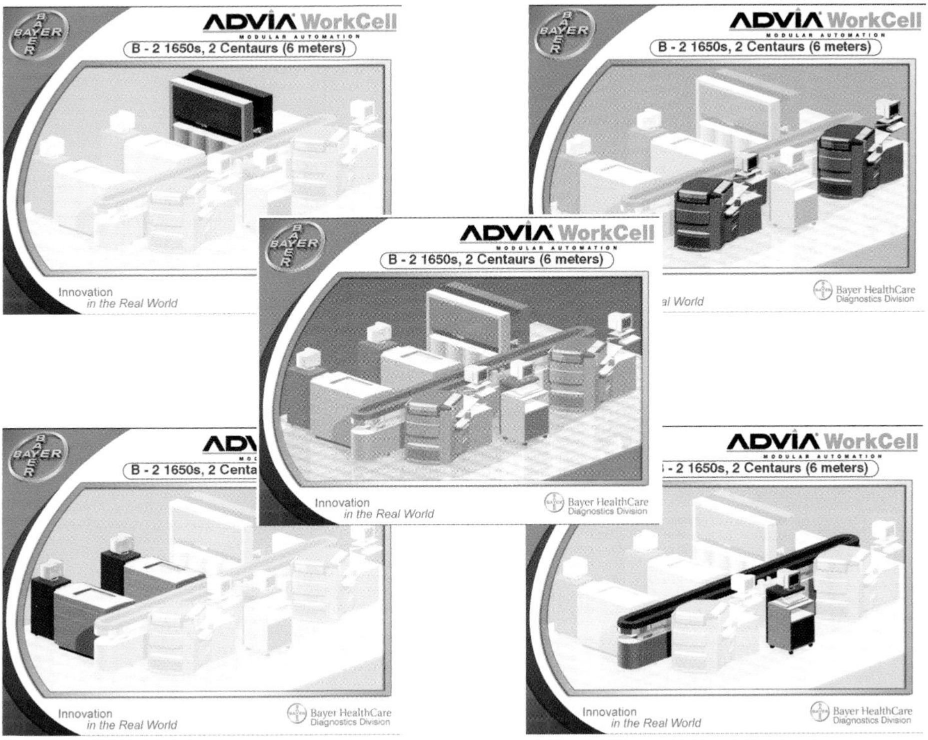

www.killerpresentations.com/fade.html

Highlight (killer idea)

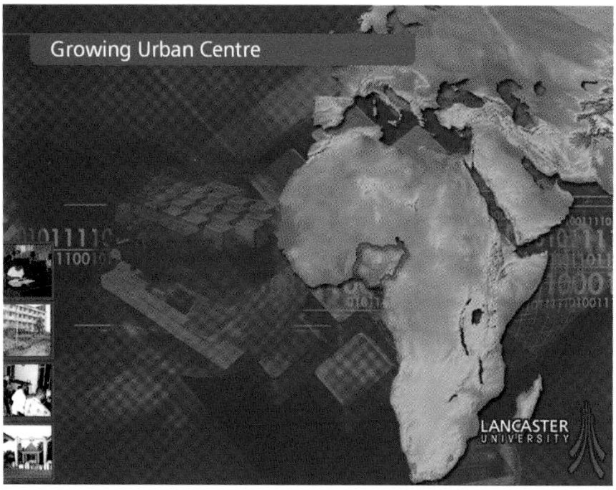

www.killerpresentations.com/highlight.html

Zoom-in (killer idea)

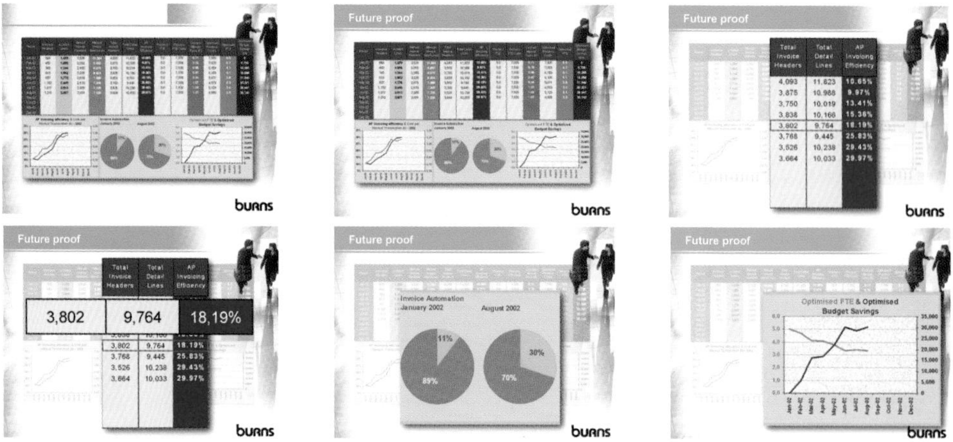

www.killerpresentations.com/zoom.html

Diagrams

Lozenge

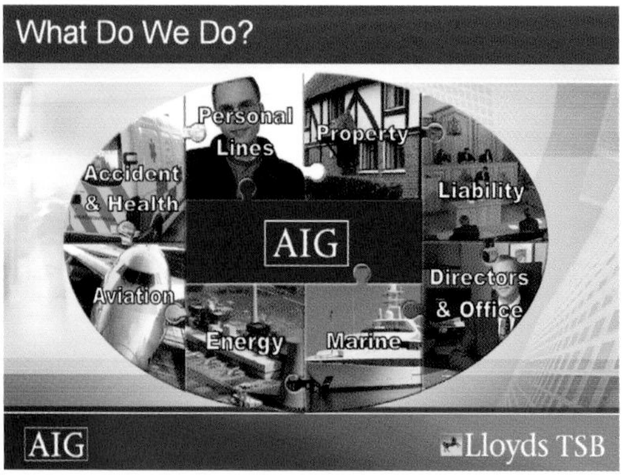

www.killerpresentations.com/lozenge.html

Schematic

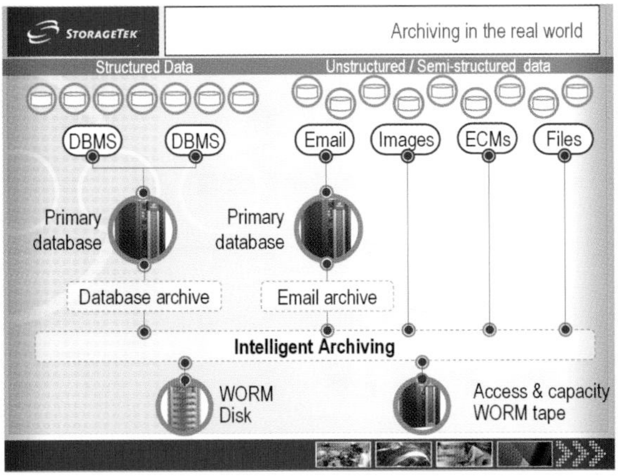

www.killerpresentations.com/schematic.html

Pyramid

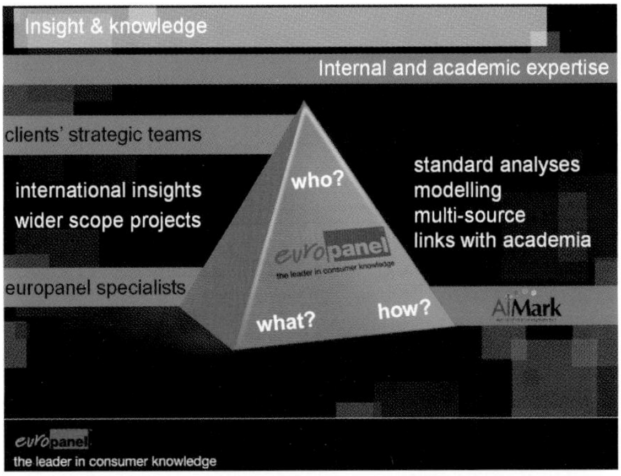

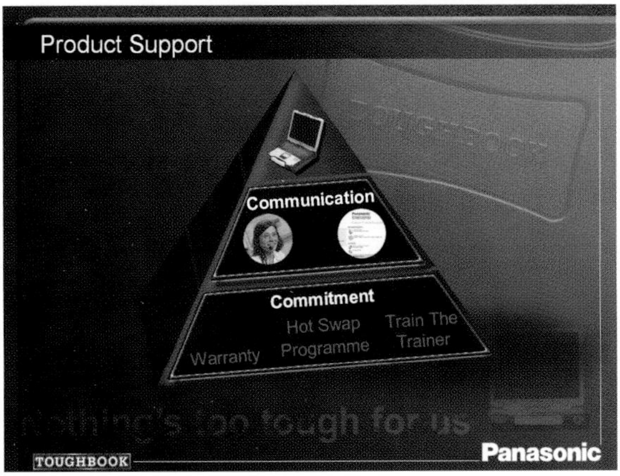

www.killerpresentations.com/pyramid.html

Venn

www.killerpresentations.com/venn.html

Matrix

2×2×2

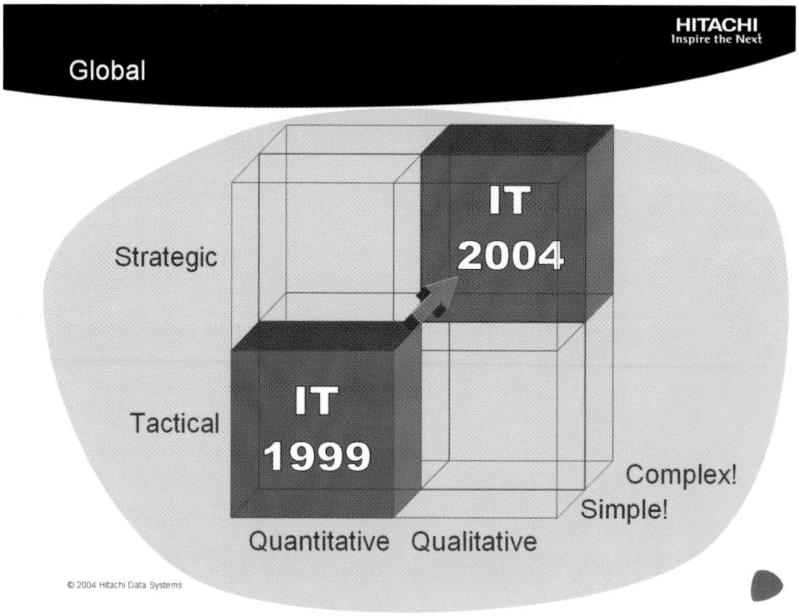

www.killerpresentations.com/2×2×2.html

2D model

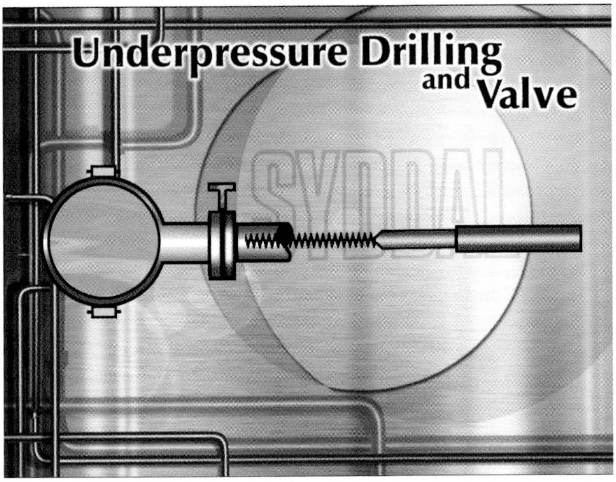

www.killerpresentations.com/2D.html

3D model

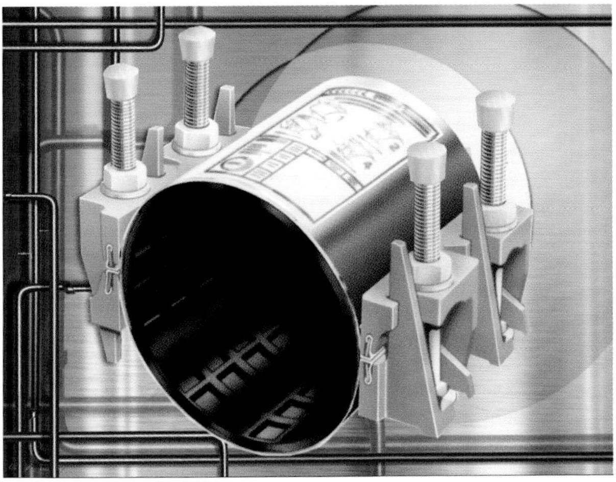

www.killerpresentations.com/3D.html

4D model

By www.killerpresentations.com/4Dmodel.html

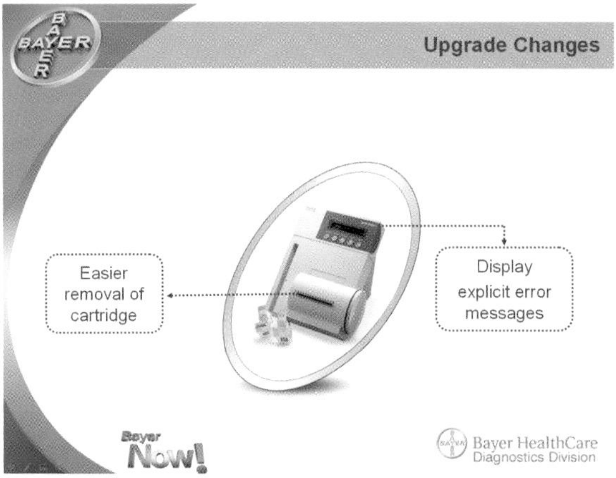

Photographs

Maps

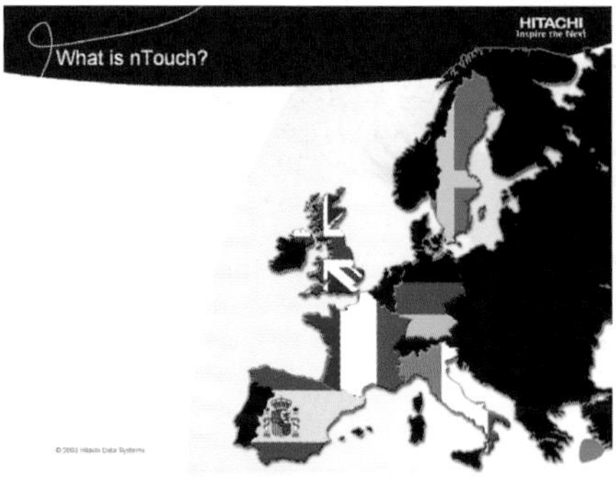

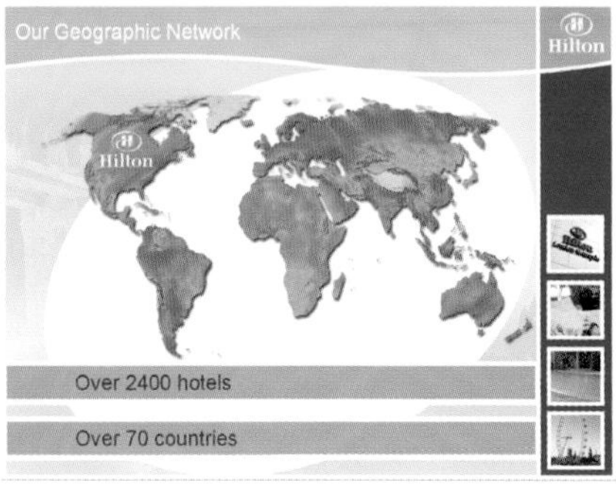

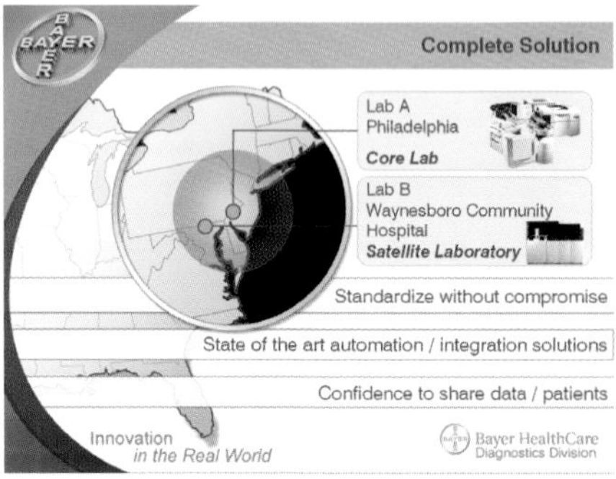

Screen grabs

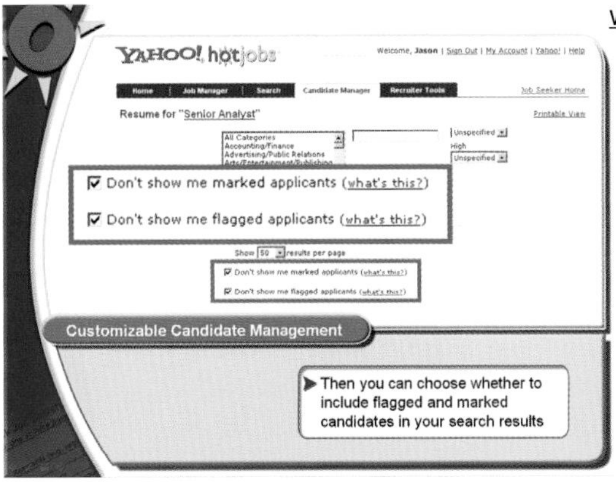

www.killerpresentations.com/screengrab.html

Visual segue (killer idea)

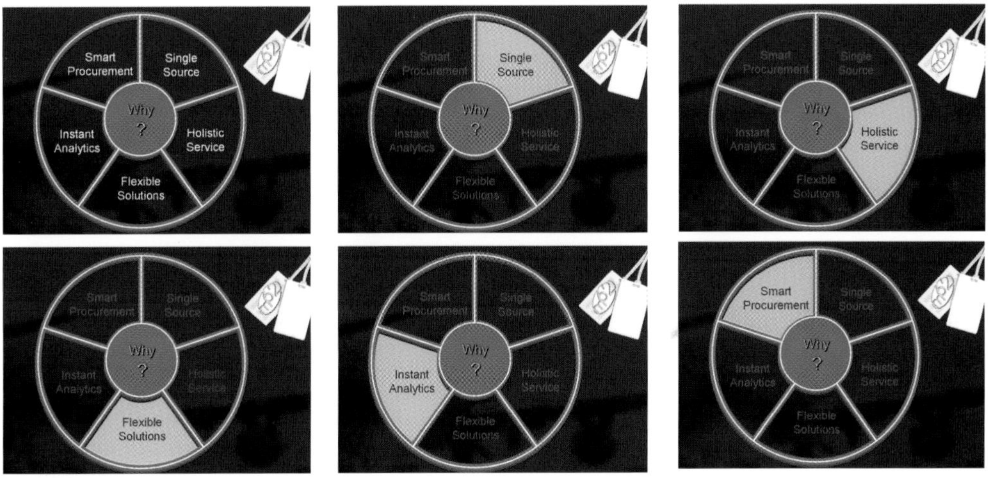

www.killerpresentations.com/seque.html

Title bars

www.killerpresentations.com/titles.html

Graphs

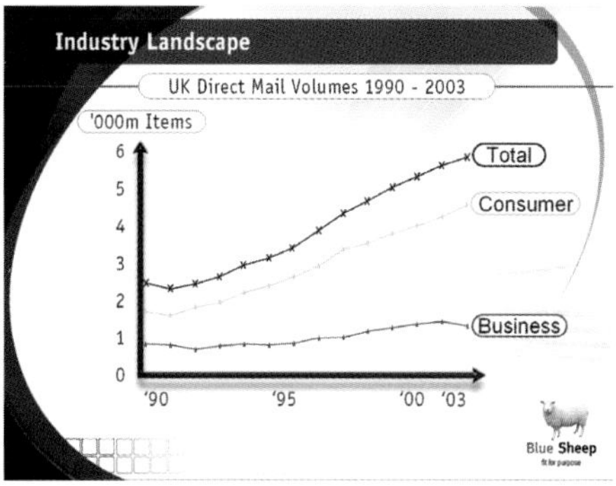

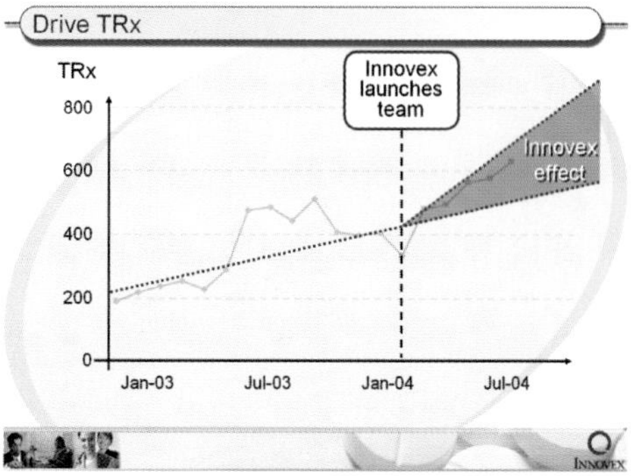

www.killerpresentations.com/linegraph.html

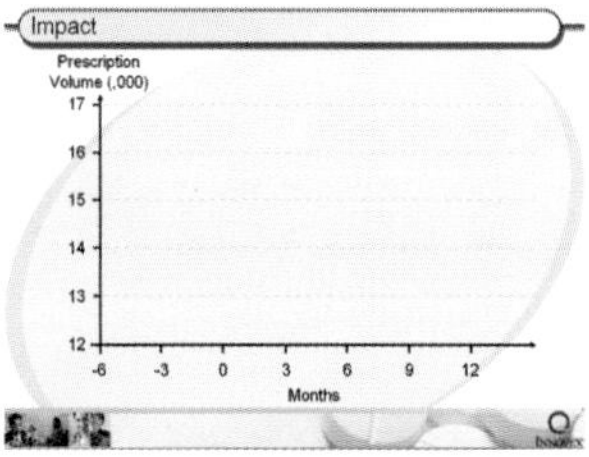

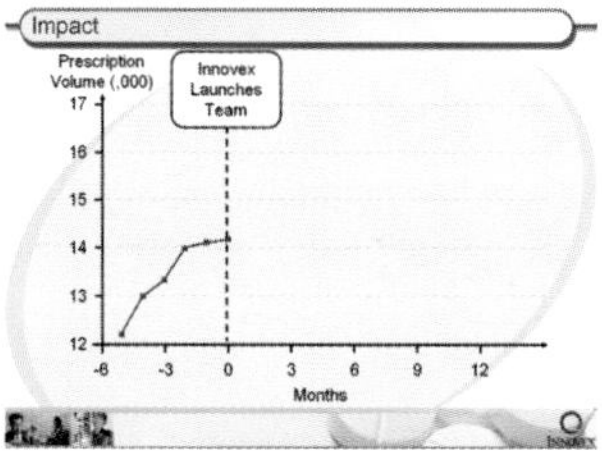

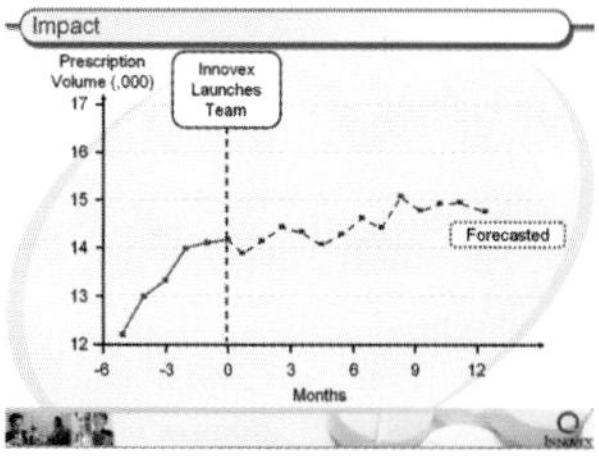

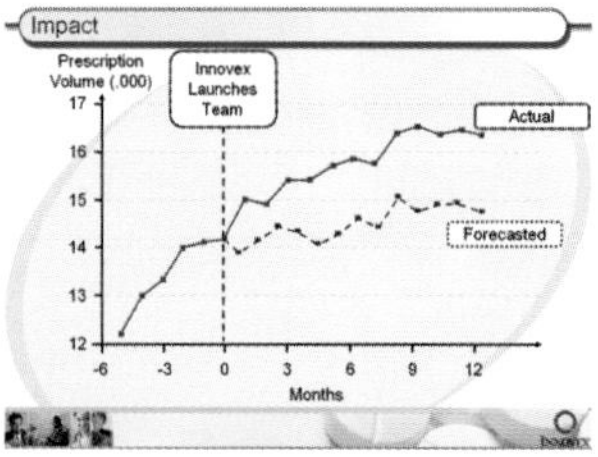

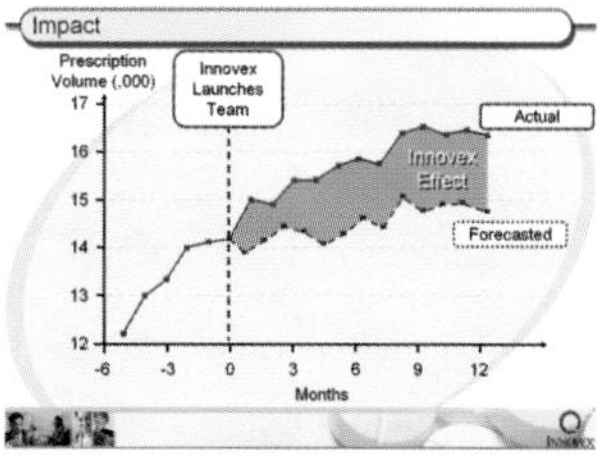

www.killerpresentations.com/graph2.html

The right graph for the right purpose
Pie charts

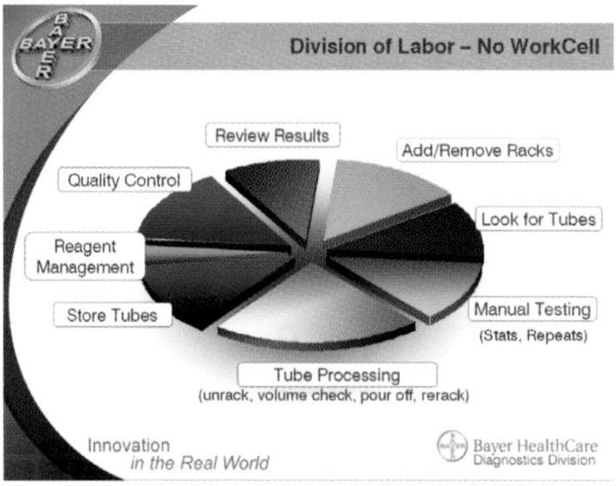

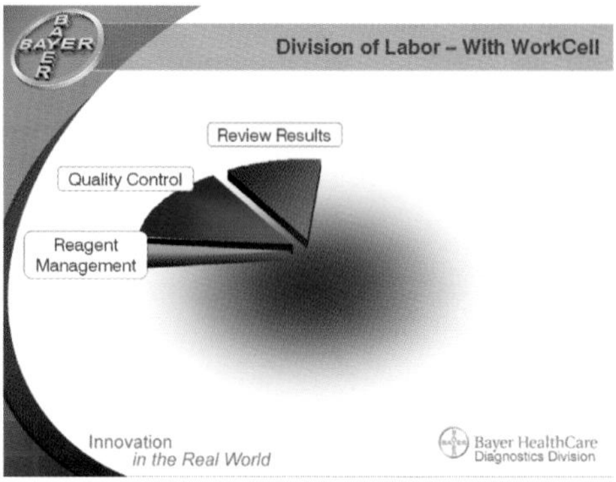

www.killerpresentations.com/pie.html

Scatter plots

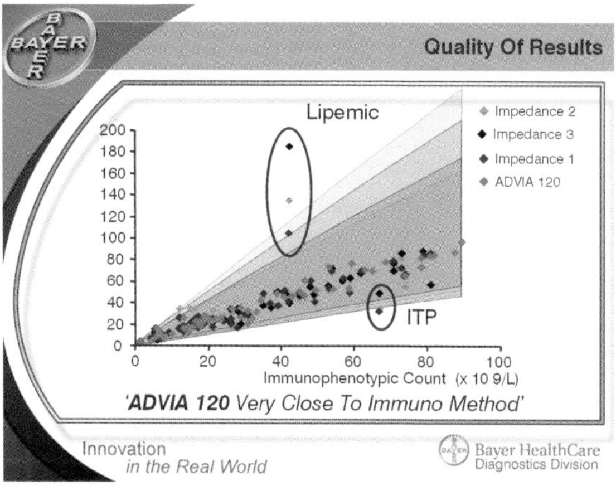

www.killerpresentations.com/scatter.html

Bar charts

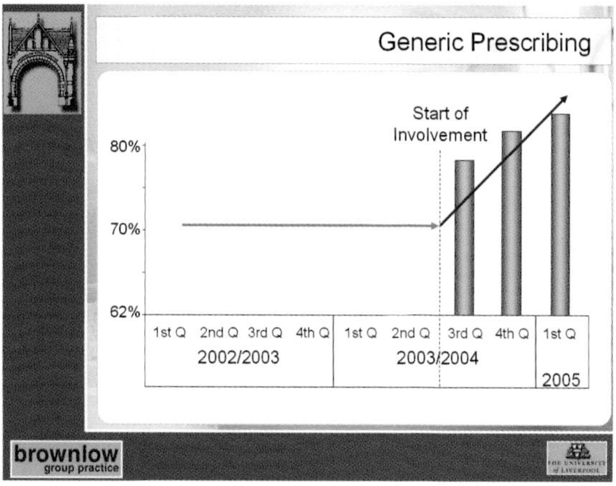

www.killerpresentations.com/bar.html

Ordered lists: flow chart

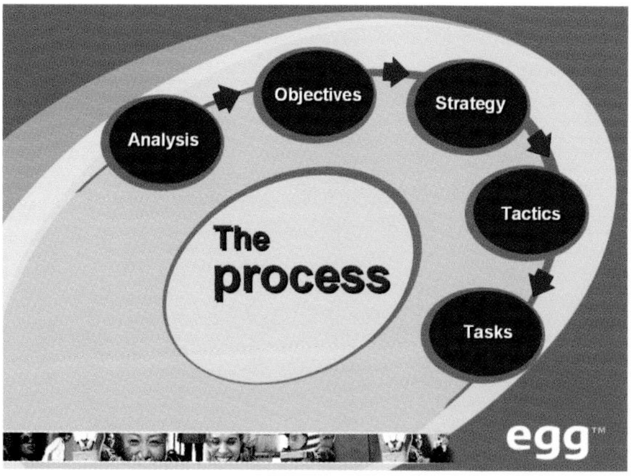

www.killerpresentations.com/flowchart.html

Section Four
Design

The communication problem: perception

Proven Track Record
Innovex Worked Bricks

www.killerpresentations.com/innovex.html

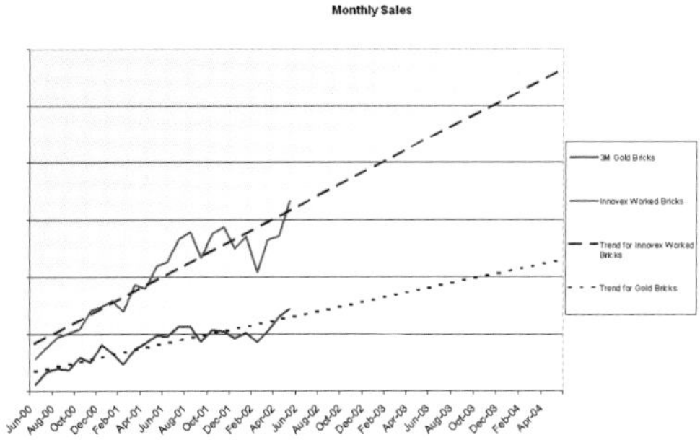

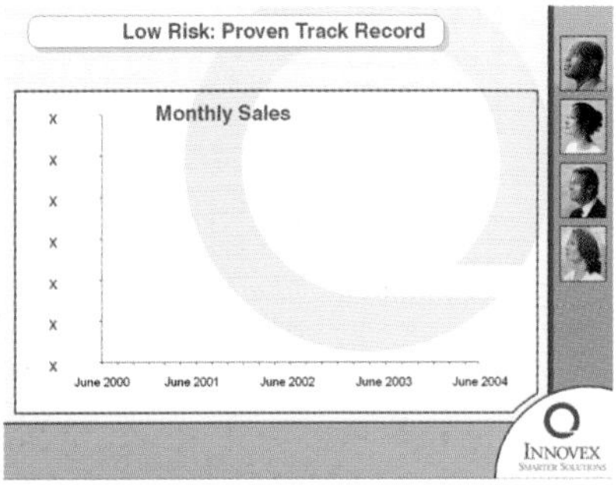

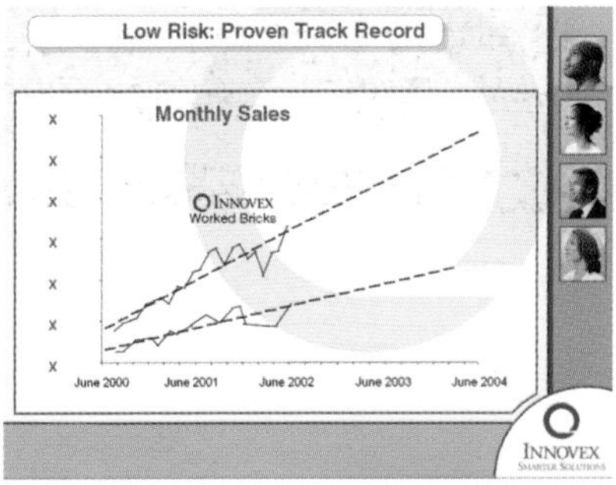

The slide builds ending with just the first heading appearing, the others require a CLICK. Not only is this more engaging for the audience but when you ask the audience to recall the five points an amazing amount of them draw the star first and then label the points, which strongly suggests that avoiding the habitual list is a worthwhile exercise.

A visualisation example

Look at the next slide – this is a typical PowerPoint slide, even down to the colours: self-explanatory, and often presented by reading.

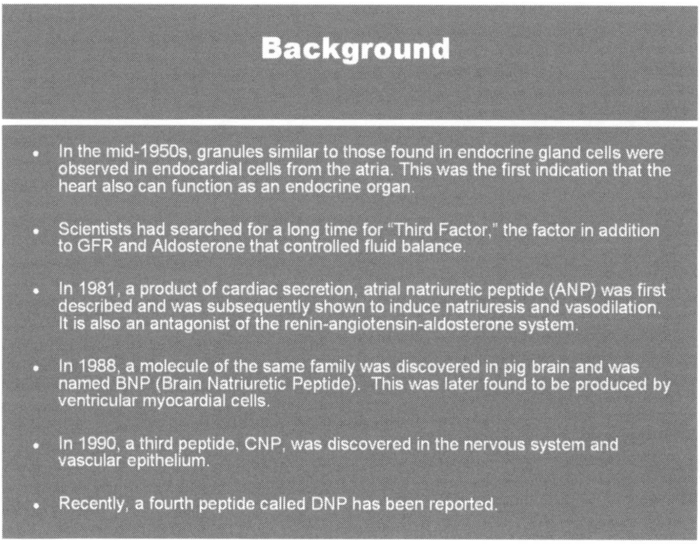

At the risk of again repeating myself, this slide will encourage the audience to disengage. Look carefully at the slide and read the text. Clearly you need to be a cardiologist to understand the content but you do not need to be a cardiologist to 'see' the picture hiding in the text, can you see it?

We find that about 1 in 50 people can 'see' the picture that supports this patter. The clue is the timeline: note that four of the bullets have a date. The slide is of course talking about the development of something over a period of 50 years and so what would be more interesting and engaging would be the sequence shown below.

What you can see here is a sequence (one slide but four CLICKs) that builds up as the presenter reads the bullet points of the previous slide. Try it. Or if you prefer, use the following link to see me present them. *www.killerpresentations.com/timeline.html*

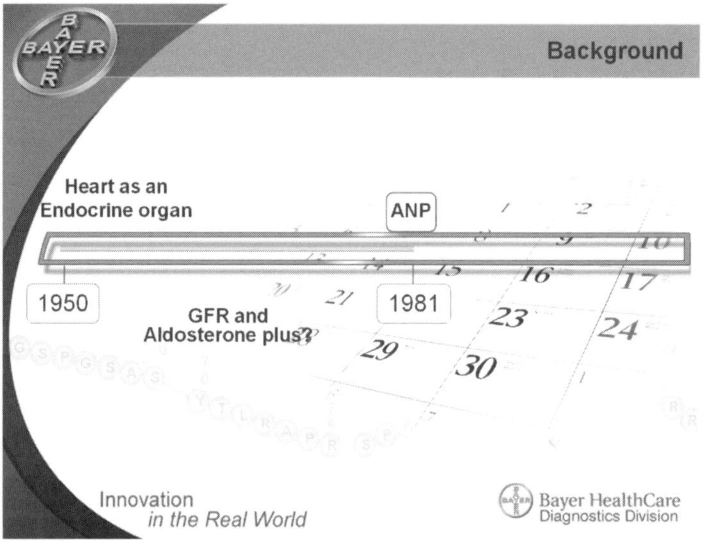

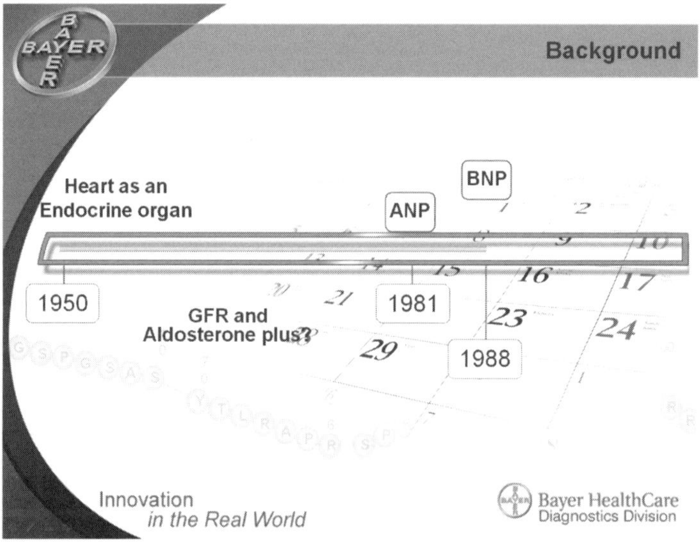

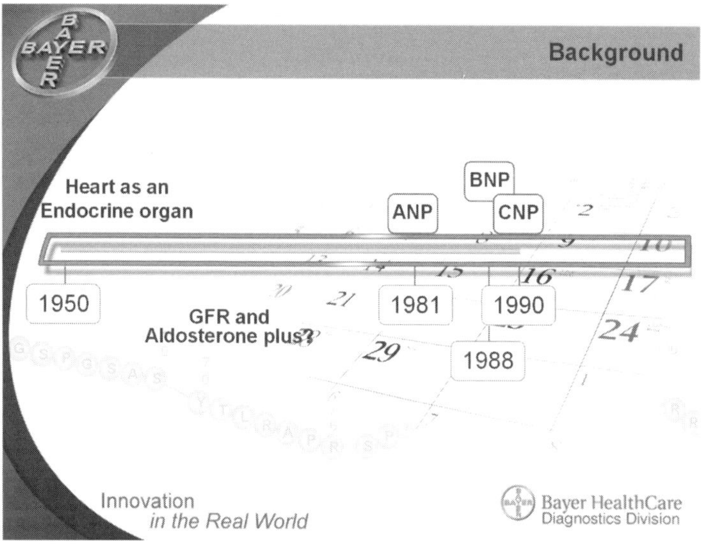

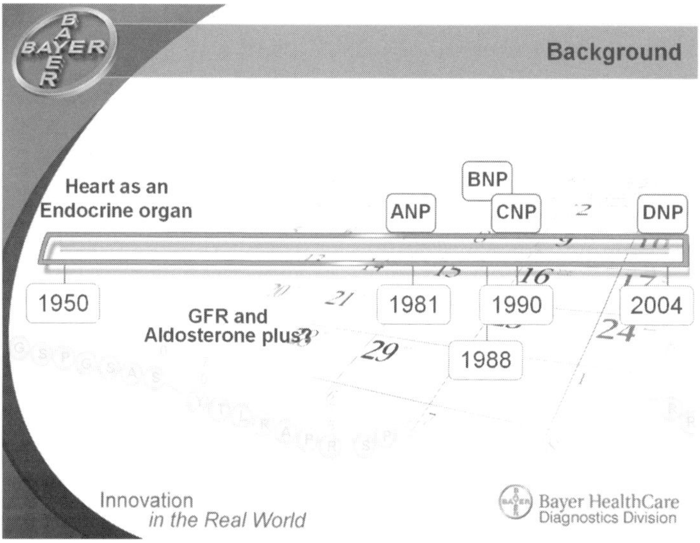

What you should see is a much more engaging piece of presentation; what is probably more interesting is that it sounds like I know what I am talking about, which of course I do not. I know nothing that is not included in the original presentation. I just have a good memory and can reproduce the patter over these slides. But it sounds better doesn't it?

Why? Because presenting, for all that personal flair may be able to contribute to it, is as much a science as an art. People remember more of what they see than what they hear: 10% of what they hear and 30–40% of what they see. This is partly why radio advertising is less effective than television advertising. What we are advocating is a seamless flow of visual information as the core of the presentation, delivered in a way that maximises the audience's attention and retention. I believe that the reasons for this increase are to do with increased engagement with both sides of the brain.

A major part of our message here is that what works best, and we will set out just why, is visualising the message. Now, for many people, the concept of using visual aids needs no advocating; they readily accept the point that many presentations are better for including the use of some slides, though how well they really work is another matter.

For some years, since early in the computer revolution, many visual aid methodologies have been in decline. Though they still have their uses, 35mm slides, overhead projector (OHP) slides and even whiteboards, flipcharts and the humble blackboard, are being used less and less. For simple applications, when even a handwritten note or rough diagram on the acetate of the OHP may still suit, such use will doubtless continue. For instance, many meetings do not involve a presentation prepared in advance, the presenter's role is as a facilitator and what is put up on screen may only be conceived as the session proceeds. In training too, where much of what is done is not as prescribed as a formal presentation, but develops on the day in line with the mood of the meeting, such methods as overhead projector slides will doubtless continue to serve a purpose for a while, albeit amongst a mix of other methods.

But for many, many people the ubiquitous PowerPoint is the method of choice for those preparing a presentation and knowing that the task must include the creation of some slides. We all work at computer screens these days, and PowerPoint is simply one of the many applications to which we must get used; indeed its very availability on the desk in front of us is one of the main reasons for its choice. Laptop computers mean that choice can be with us anywhere.

PowerPoint as an information structuring tool

The old process, seeking to save time, will always link one presentation to another whenever possible. Think of a presentation you know, have seen or made perhaps. It is likely that preparation consisted of:

- finding an earlier presentation that was in some way close – 'a good starting point'
- discarding some slides as unsuitable
- adding in new slides (including those from other presentations and even from other people)
- arranging the new set into a suitable order
- considering what will be said alongside each (with much of this being what will be read off the slides).

Why is this so typical? Leaving aside time saving, it is because we don't easily think in lists. PowerPoint helps us list things, so much so that the output often becomes a list of lists. We start with plethora of points without a suitable sense of order, and the process imposes order – we like this, order out of chaos, and regard it as a step nearer a good presentation.

My view, based on our experience, is that this is wrong. It is not a good way of preparing. It is an introspective, presenter-focused method that is likely to create a presentation that fails to do the audience justice. While a presentation must, by definition, be linear, the thinking that produces should not be. The style of preparation discussed promotes linear thinking and this, in turn, hides useful and interesting linking of ideas. It is however a starting point. It does begin to structure thoughts and we can take what it produces and, by visualising it, turn it into the right kind of form to maximise its effectiveness as a presentation.

In detail the totality of the alternative way can be set out as the following sequence which is the process which we at m62 go through in developing a presentation for our clients.

1. Set objectives.
2. Media selection.
3. Define presentation type.
4. Organise presentation structure.
5. Decide presentation content.
6. Visualise it.

7. Presentability check.
8. Design slides.
9. Animate slides.
10. Practise.
11. Deliver.
12. Evaluate.

Set objectives

SMART if possible as this helps sharpen the language which helps identify the presentation structure.

Media Selection

PowerPoint is not the panacea to all presentation ills, sometimes a site visit or a product demonstration is a better communication device.

Define presentation type

As we argued earlier, be either *persuasive* or *educational*, rarely both. Use the language of the objectives to help identify the appropriate structure.

Organise presentation structure

When we know the type we can select the appropriate structure. We usually do this prior to building content as it helps us define what should and should not be included.

Decide presentation content

This is usually a list of bullet points, in fact it is probably what most presenters do now. We don't just show it to the audience and hope it helps them.

Visualise it

If you have read this far you will know that we don't see much value in text, so the next stage is to take the text and find the diagrams or other pictures that help make the points visual. This usually ends with a storyboard, for us completed in PowerPoint including animation and builds but no design. We use this format to help articulate what is desired on the finished slide both to the client and to the design team.

Presentability check

Visuals are great but only if you can actually present them, we work out at this stage whether this visual can be presented and if so how; in short, *what would we say over this visual to make it comprehensible to the audience*?

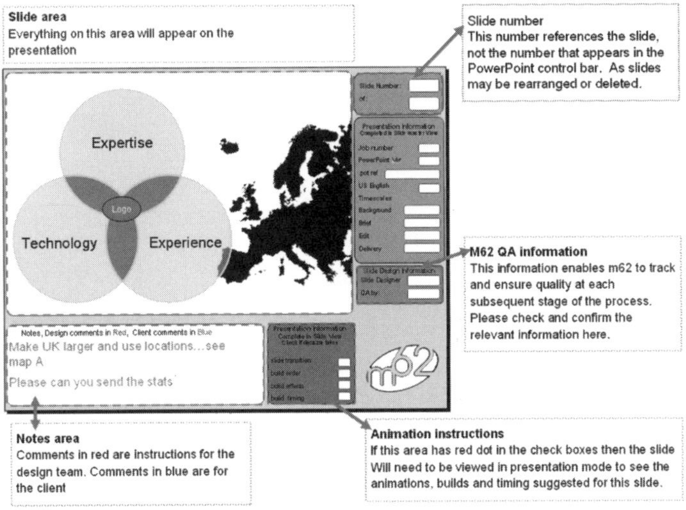

Design slides

When we are happy with the content, storyboard and potential patter, then and only then do we give the presentation to the design team, they will produce the slides exactly according to the brief, often in less than four hours!

Animate slides

When the slides are designed they are then built and animated.

Practise

This is the most important stage and the only one after the initial objective setting and content agreement, where the presenter has to be involved. Inevitably there are minor changes and tweaks, usually to the animation build sequences.

Deliver

Actual delivery can now take many forms: one-on-one, conferences, webinars or web-enabled virtual meetings.

Evaluate

Generally presenters get so wrapped up in the rehearsing and giving of the presentation (adrenaline rush) that they forget that a good debrief is essential.

Killer Idea Kill the cue-card, use images not words

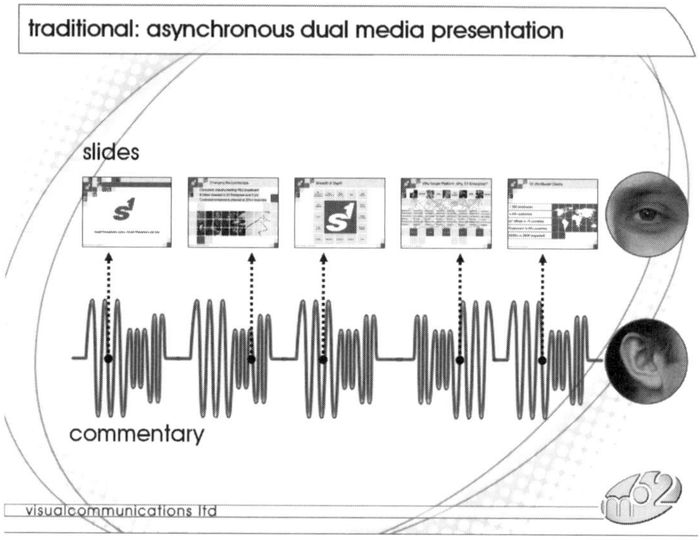

So it is clear that there needs to be a shift from designing slides that help the presenter remember what to say, to slides that help the audience understand the message. The art of achieving this translation is what we refer to as *visualisation*. Graphically the difference can be illustrated as two different tracks: the traditional and the 'multi-media'. The difference is in how the slides are designed and also how they are presented. In a dual media presentation the presenter and the slides are two separate communication pieces with the occasional reference from one to the other.

Killer Idea Multi-media not dual media

This is different: here we see a seamless interaction of two separate streams of media, merging to form a continuous flow of information using sight and sound from the presenter to the audience. This is what makes for effectiveness. A good example of this can be seen by watching BBC current affairs programmes.* The images and the narrative are blended seamlessly creating a steady flow of multi-media information. At the other end of the scale, try watching CNN, this is not nationalistic pride (most communication professionals would acknowledge the BBC as being the standard for broadcast media) but just a comment on what actually works. CNN have a continuous stream of headlines running across the bottom of the screen and generally too much information on the screen at any point in time. The result is that you get far less from it than from the BBC. If you compare listening to the radio with watching television, you will perceive something of what visuals add. This should help explain the power of m62's multi-media presentation style.

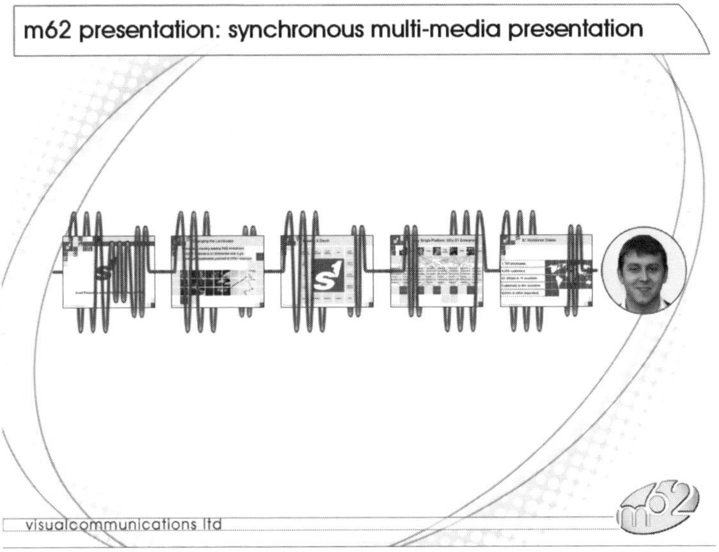

*For the purpose of this exercise look at BBC terrestrial broadcast not their interactive services or BBC24 which are aimed at a different audience.

The elements that are involved here in producing a multi-media style include:

- diagrams
- animations
- photographs
- flow charts (These are very useful and produce order where order is important. They should always be used progressively, adding each element as it is discussed and highlighting the part that is being discussed as the overall picture becomes more complex.)
- video.

More information on these key elements is contained below in the visual devices section of this book.

Killer Idea Pacing information flow

Glance at the graph below for two seconds only and then read on. How much information did you get from the quick glance? The answer is probably not a lot. Now study it for as long as it takes to work out what it is trying to say. It took longer than two seconds, but you assimilated more information. Every reader will have looked at the graph for a different

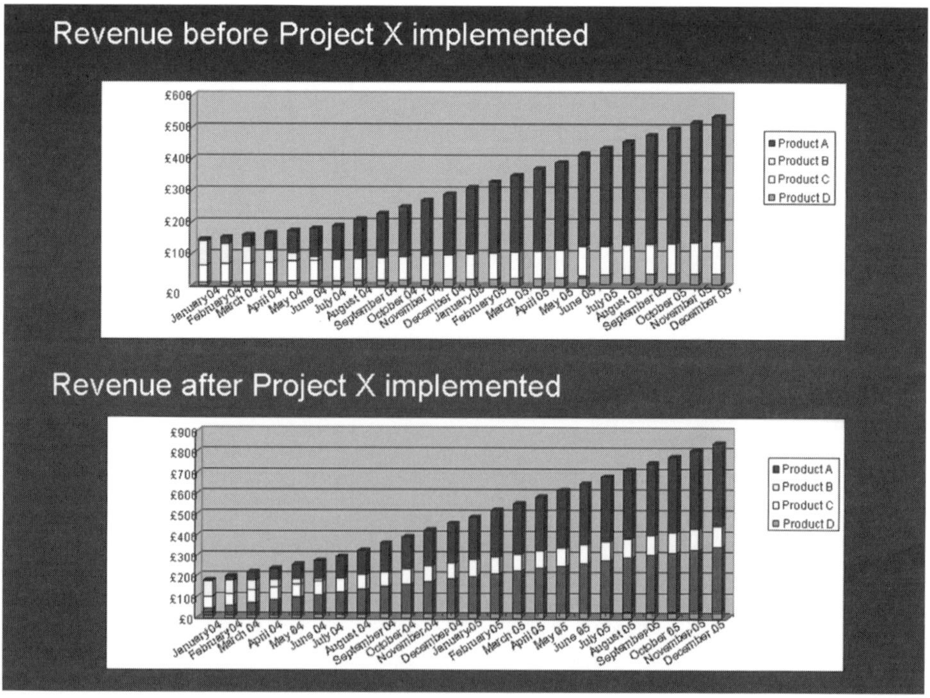

length of time and some of you will have turned the book through 90° to read it more easily.

If information is printed (we call this '2D presentation') and given to an audience, the pace of information flow is controlled by the reader – they can pause to reflect or even put it down and come back later. Ultimately the audience dictate the speed of information flow. For example consider this book, have you read from the start of this book to here uninterrupted? Probably not. Have you read every word printed in this book from the start to here? Again, probably not (don't worry we are not offended).

In a presentation it is the presenter who controls the pace not the audience; the presenter decides when to click to the next slide often regardless of the audience. There are therefore three characteristics that give our presentations impact: the first is that the amount of information is limited, the second is that the pace of the information is strictly controlled, and the third is that it is laid out in order to assist assimilation.

Now look at the next sequence, the images appear and the patter is typed next to each build:

> *'What I am about to show you is Moving Annual Totals (*explain if necessary*) for the organisation for the last 18 months. The scales here show zero to plus $1,000 million.'*

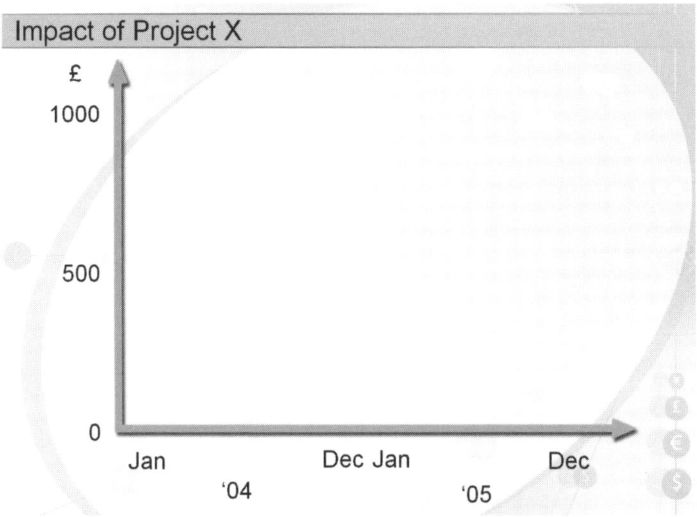

CLICK

'Look at the revenue projection before we factored in the influence of Project X.'

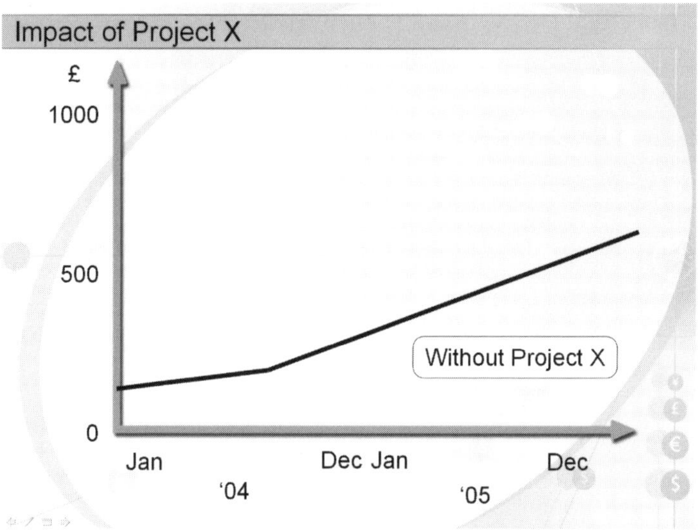

CLICK

'Now look at our actual MAT figures'

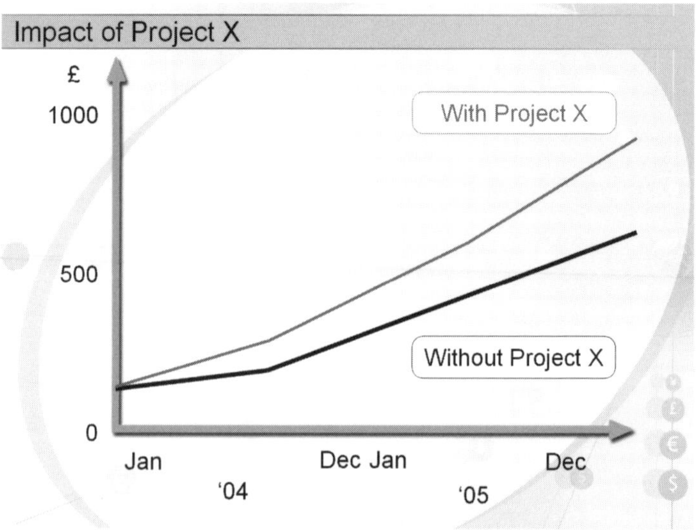

CLICK

'The impact of Project X was therefore this area here…'

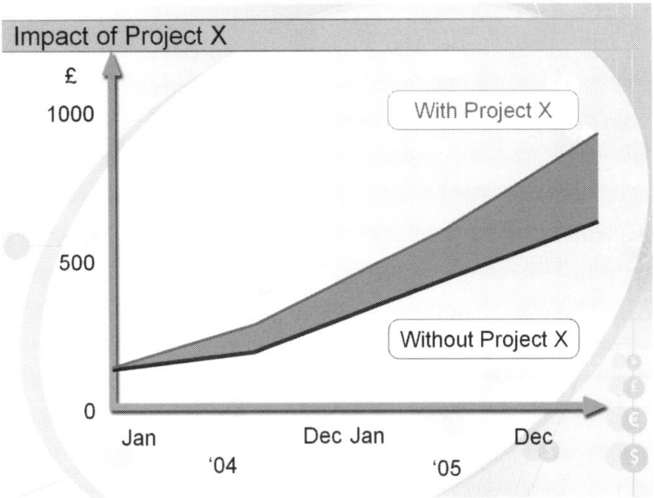

CLICK

'I therefore submit that Project X has cost the business far more than it was worth.'

The example above can be seen presented by following the link: www.killerpresentations.com/informationflow.html

What was the difference? Less information presented at the right speed to ensure assimilation. The ability to design a slide so as to ensure a smooth presentation of information is a core skill, which is why 'pacing information flow' is a Killer Idea.

This idea applies to any slide, text only, graphs like the example above, or any of the visual devices discussed later in this section. We are not treating the audience as if they were stupid; we are simply ensuring communication (the purpose of presentation).

The reason that most presenters present information like this too quickly is understandable: they have seen the information before, perhaps hundreds of times and they have had considerable time to reflect upon it and draw conclusions; the audience has not. This is probably the first time they have seen the information, so it must be presented at a pace they can cope with, not the pace the presenter chooses. By building the slides with this number of CLICKs we force the presenter to present correctly.

More examples of this are provided later, but first let us extend the idea of 2D presentation.

Killer Idea Four dimension presenting

Two dimensional presenting describes the use of a static image or text. This is most easily exemplified by reference to a slide which is both shown on a screen and printed out as a hard copy: if the two versions appear the same and no information is lost then the slide is 2D.

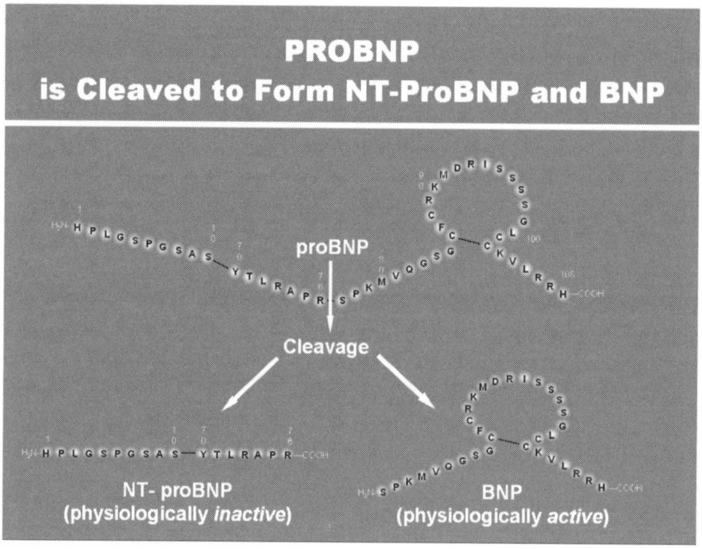

Consider the slide here; this is exactly how we would reproduce the information in a book, with arrows to indicate movement.

Step into m62's world and we have two additional dimensions to consider. The third dimension is time. We have the ability to modify the image over time, for example the graph can grow or change as the presenter builds the slide.

The fourth dimension is narrative (or patter). We have the ability to explain what the audience are seeing as the image changes.

One three-build sequence is shown here as three end-slides. Between the first and second the chain actually breaks apart and moves on the screen to the final resting position shown in slide 2. It obviously loses something in print.

As this slide is animating, the presenter explains what the audience is seeing. The motion is compelling and almost all of the audience pay attention and most will remember the points made, because they were watching closely and paying attention.

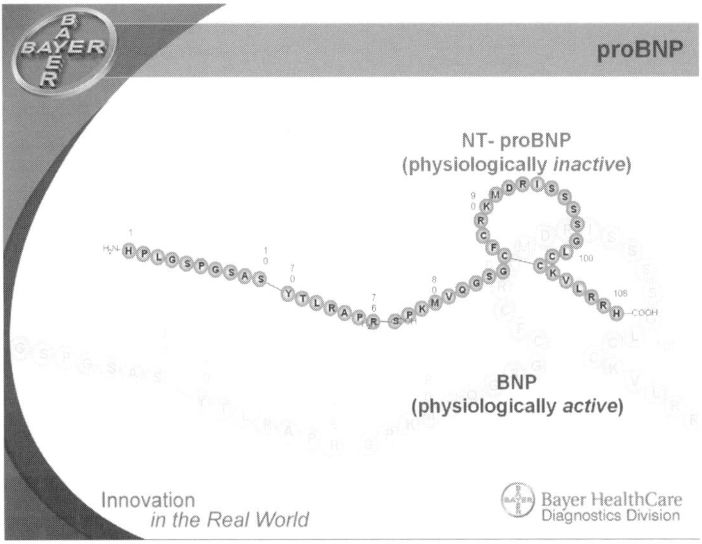

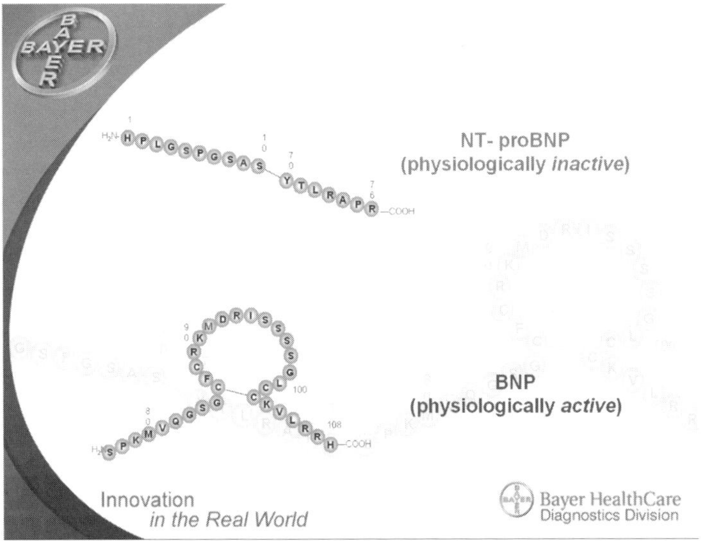

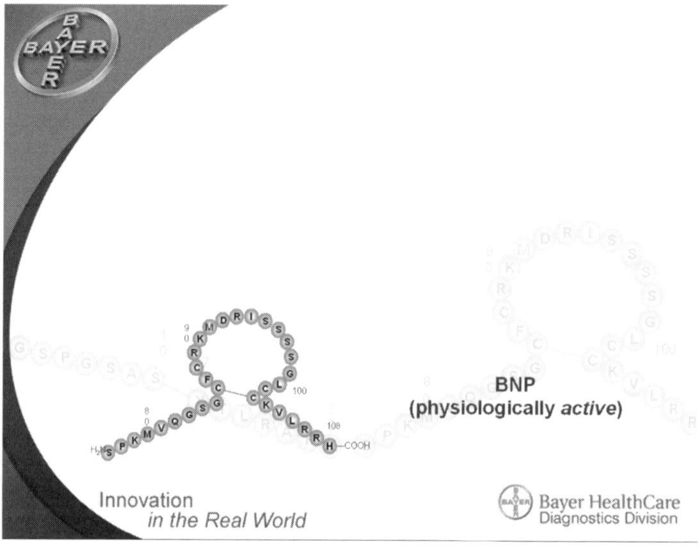

This method of presenting is very powerful. It is engaging. It enters short-term memory and therefore can enter long-term memory. It is also impressive. We believe it is the way we will all present in the future.

The concept of presenting information visually links to a very specific idea, one that is behind the look and working of virtually all the slides we use and recommend. We call this 'four dimensional presenting' (4D). This is probably one of the most powerful concepts in this book and is therefore one of our killer ideas. It is also the most difficult to articulate in this medium as, by definition, this book is a 2D presentation so, while this is shown here as far as is possible, the web link noted at the end of this section will allow you to see the 4D versions of the examples used here more effectively: www.killerpresentations.com/4Dexample.html

Summary

1. Don't use cue-cards, use diagrams and pictures instead.
2. No clip art.
3. Use PowerPoint if it helps to structure your thoughts, but this is the start of the process not the end – don't show this to the audience.
4. Design slides to encourage multi-media not dual media.
5. We have two extra dimensions when we present – use them whenever possible.

Visual devices

Where does the audience look?

For two seconds only turn to the last page of the colour section and look at the logo diagram. How many logos can you remember? More importantly which ones can you remember? Chances are most of you can remember m62's. Why?

The answer lies in where your eye naturally goes to when presented with a new image. In the West we tend to let our eye fix on the top left-hand corner of the screen, move right then diagonally down to the bottom-left and then across to the bottom-right. It is the way we have been taught to read and is therefore almost reflex. The same is true on a large screen. If what you want the audience to see is not in the top left-hand corner then you need to manipulate their focus. We have several techniques at our disposal.

Directed attention

The idea behind 'directed attention' is to create a synergy between the slide animation, the patter and the visual cues given by the presenter. Typically the presenter will set up the build by saying something like 'Moving to a different subject...' – he will then look at the screen, the audience watching him will do the same, and then he CLICK watches the slide build and then makes comments. This idea plays an important part throughout our methods as it requires the slide to be designed correctly and the presenter to present correctly, but the power of the technique is beyond doubt and well worth mastering. While we will mention directed attention in several areas of this book, here we are going to look at several visual devices that enable or *require* this technique...

Basic techniques

Killer Idea Build up

The concept of 'pacing information flow' has led us to use a number of graphical techniques the two most important of these are summarised in our next killer idea 'build up, fade down'.

Build up is the idea that a diagram is often too complex to show all at once. As an example, look at the following diagram.

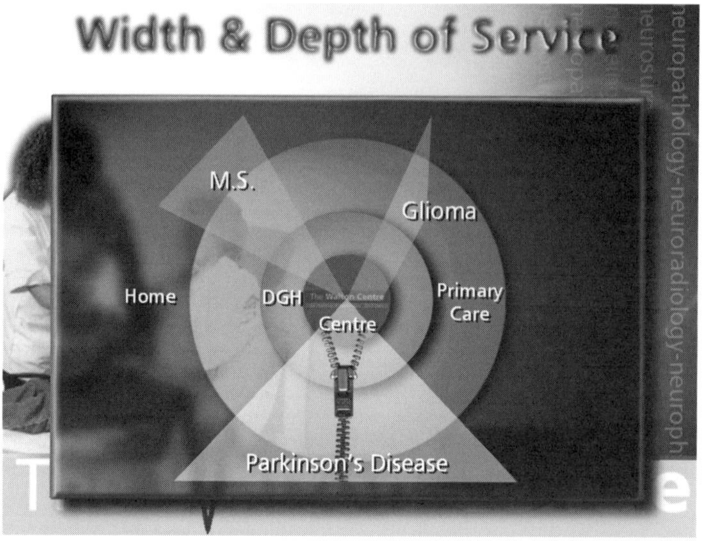

We call this the *Care Map* and it has been used by a client to describe the issues facing his organisation – a specialist centre for neurosurgery. As a complete diagram it is difficult to understand and so is built up in stages from the outside in (helps with the story!) using three CLICKs. At each CLICK the presenter explains what the audience is seeing.

Then the care profiles are laid over the diagram allowing us to show different types of care for different illnesses.

And finally the zip is added, graphically making the point that this needs to be 'zipped' together to form a seamless service to the patients.

This sequence can be seen presented at: www.killerpresentations.com/Walton.html

By building the diagram up we show the audience where to look on the slide, thereby ensuring information transfer. We also control the pace of the information flow.

Killer Idea Fade down

Now suppose we want to talk about the GP's role in the care of patients with Parkinson's disease, then to make this point we would fade down everything except the relevant piece of the diagram.

Actually we often use this to structure a presentation. Here is a sequence in a presentation from Bayer describing the ADVIA WorkCell Automated Diagnostic system. The sequence allows a virtual tour of the WorkCell and positions the information in the audience's mind as it is delivered. (Clearly we have only shown the segue slides; for a definition of segue please see later sections of this book.)

This sequence can be seen presented at: www.killerpresentations.com/fade.html

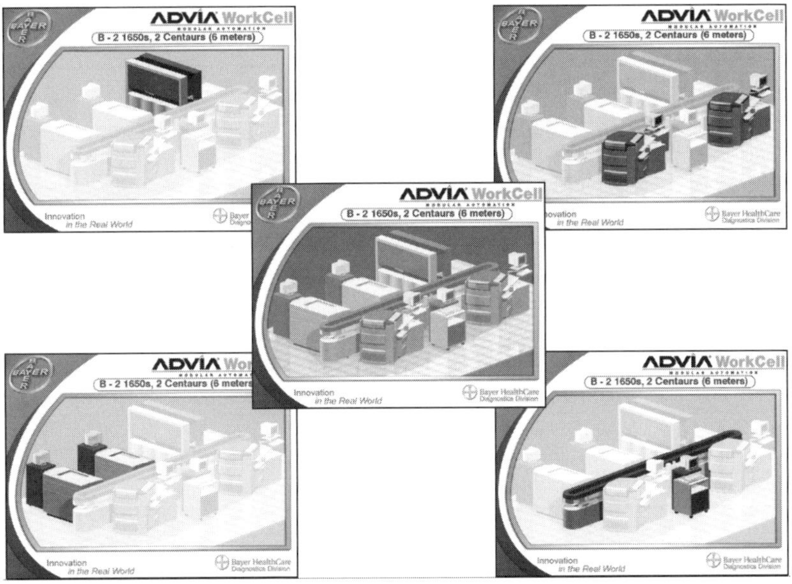

Killer Idea Highlight

Another useful technique and actually easier to recreate in PowerPoint alone is the Highlight. For example, here you can see a map and then an area highlighted in red. Often we will combine the three techniques, first building up a complex diagram and then fading down all but the relevant piece, at the same time highlighting it.

You can view the presentation at: www.killerpresentations.com/highlight.html

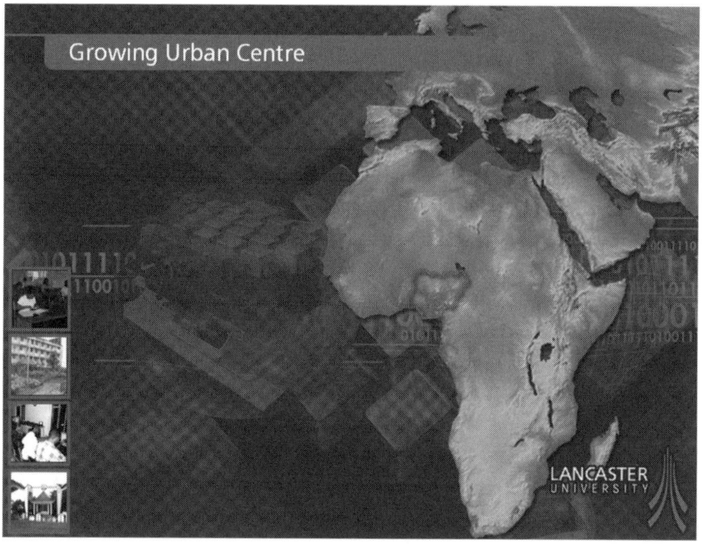

Killer Idea **Zoom-in**

Finally the zoom-in technique, particularly useful for spreadsheets, maps and photographs. The sample opposite shows a spreadsheet for a client of ours, Burns E-commerce. The spreadsheet as a whole is a dashboard, but we need to draw the audience's attention to a specific part of the spreadsheet, and so we show the whole and then zoom into the relevant parts in stages; these can be seen from the sequence.

Once again, these slides can be seen presented at: www.killerpresentation.com/zoom.html

Diagrams

Lozenge

This is probably the most used visual device. The centre of the lozenge represents the main heading and the segments surrounding it the subheadings.

Useful for 'Central Ideas' or, as in the sample here, showing the areas of business that this client operates in. We have also used pictures to key the headings.

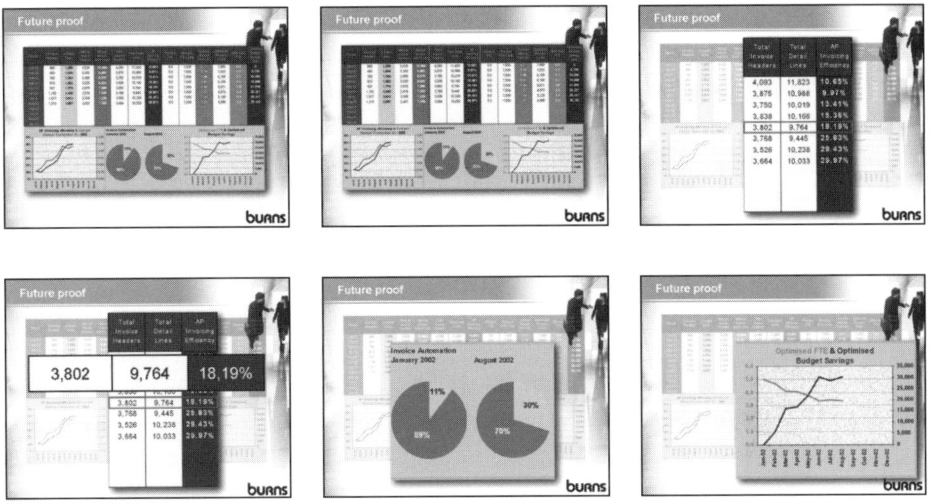

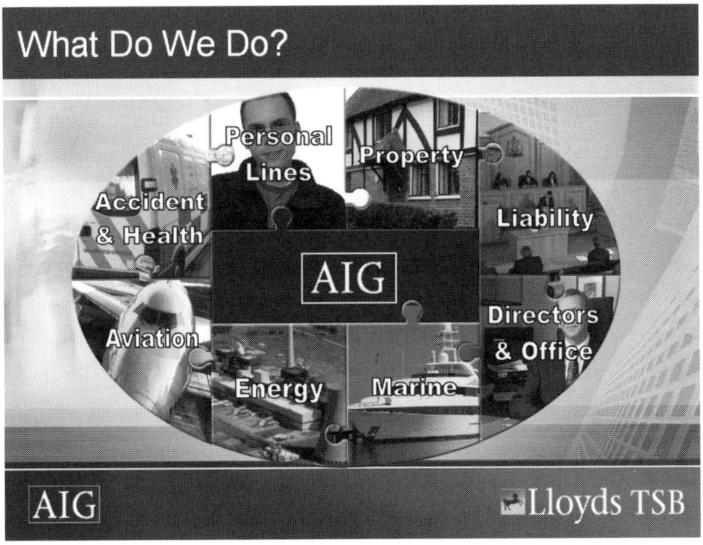

Typically, this will build with the central idea first (although sometimes last – it depends on the patter) and then the other section from the top centre, and clockwise a CLICK at a time; allowing the presenter to add value to each section. It should never be built all at once, there is too much information in it. See: www.killerpresentations.com/lozenge.html

Schematic

The schematic is very common in presentations, especially technical ones. Here we are showing a schematic from StorageTek, it shows how their archiving solution works. The build on these slides is critical, here the slides builds top to bottom on five CLICKs helping to draw the audience into the explanation of the diagram.

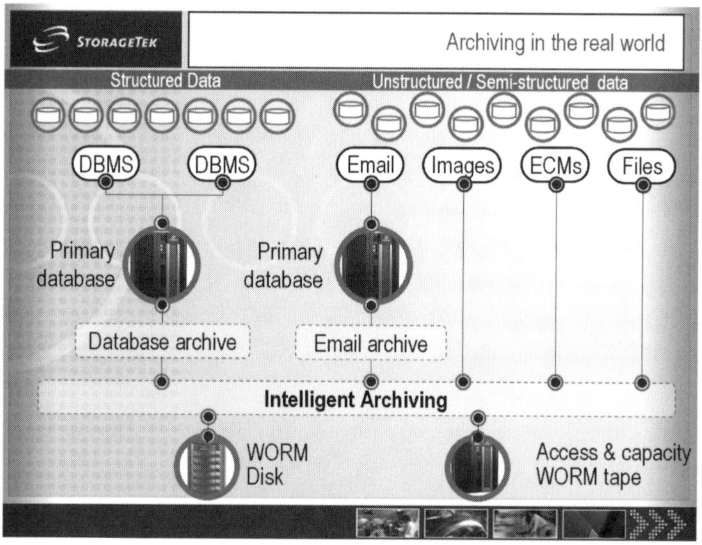

These diagrams need to be built logically following the way the presenter will explain them. Once again, this can be viewed at: www.killerpresentations.com/schematic.html

Pyramid

Both of these examples show a 3D pyramid, clearly a 2D pyramid is a triangle and this is also used to show supporting ideas or a tiered structure where one tier supports another.

It is particularly useful when describing anything to do with market segmentation – most markets can be described as a triangle with the smaller clients (of which there are many) at the foot and the higher value or larger clients (of which there are few) at the top.

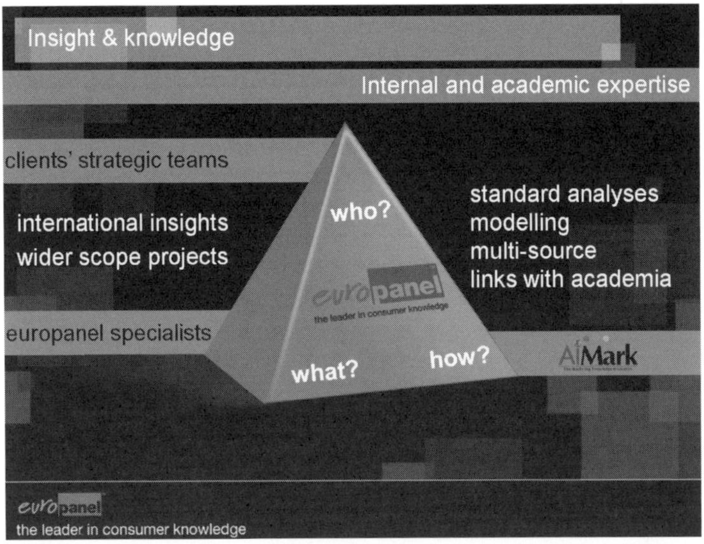

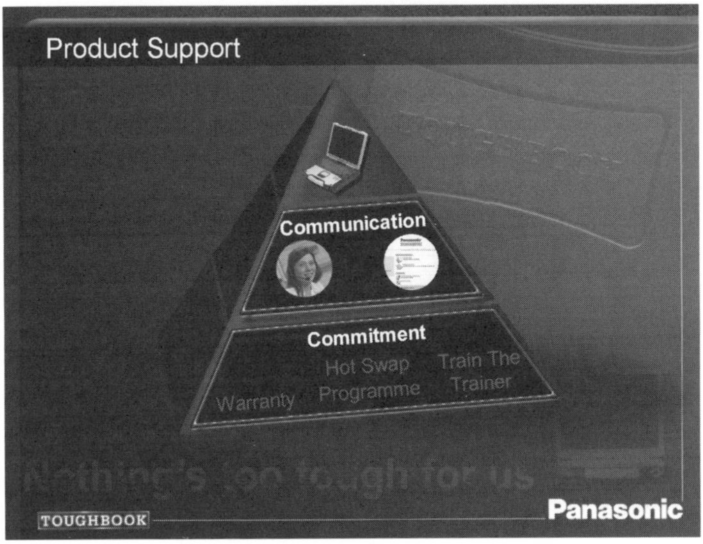

This slide would be build from bottom to top probably on three CLICKs. View this at: www.killerpresentations.com/pyramid.html

Venn

Venn diagrams are very useful. Here we are showing the three areas or initiatives that form part of the client's business area, but they can display expertise, technologies, etc. – anything that implies a collection or an overlap.

Usually this would build on three CLICKs. To see how this builds look at: www.killerpresentations.com/venn.html

Matrix

2 × 2 × 2

Here you can see a 3D matrix. The diagram depicts the changing face of the client's marketplace. In the late 1990s IT was tactical, quantitative and relatively simple, but recently it has become strategic, more qualitative and far more complex. The diagram supports the patter.

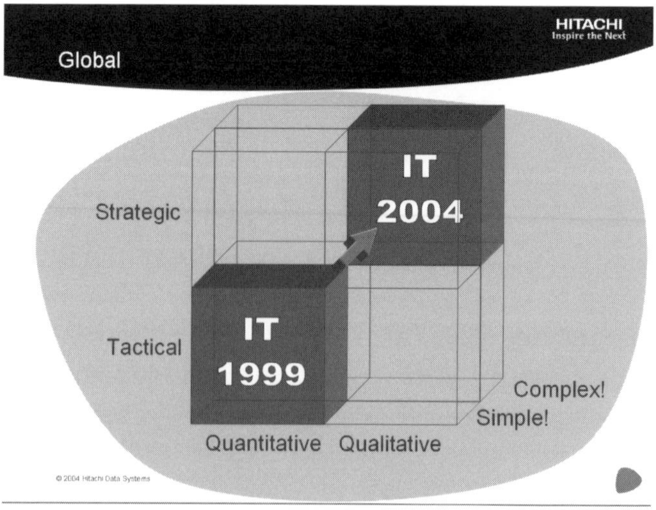

We have many more samples of 2D 2 × 2 matrices, many of you will be aware of Igor Ansoff's famous 2 × 2 matrix, which gets used frequently (and misused as often!).

The build on these matrices is similar to graphs (build axes, then data). To see it presented please use this link: www.killerpresentations.com/2x2x2.html

3 × 3

The most famous one is the GE McKinsey matrix, but again this can be a very useful device.

2D model

2D modelling can be useful to show a cross-section or schematic view of a complex object, especially where attention needs to be directed towards one very specific aspect of its construction and it is important to avoid distraction by unnecessary modelling. See: www.killerpresentations.com/2d.html

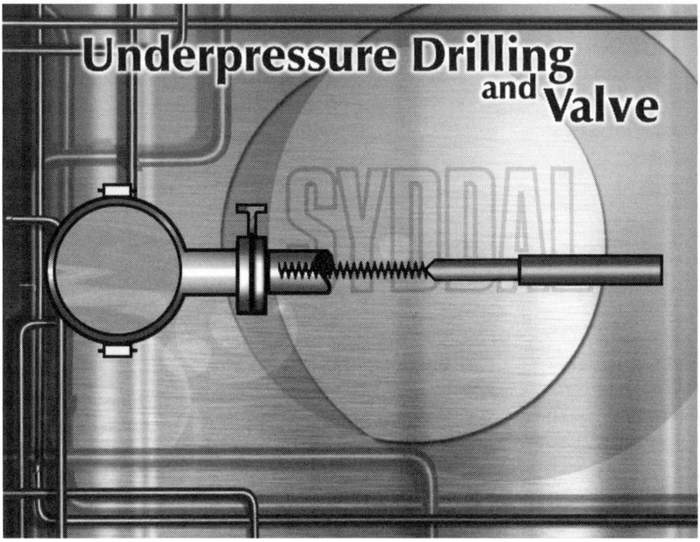

3D model

The use of 3D models can be invaluable to convey understanding, especially for technical subjects. Here we have built a 3D image in Photoshop™ to show a picture of something that has yet to be constructed. See: www.killerpresentations.com/3d.html

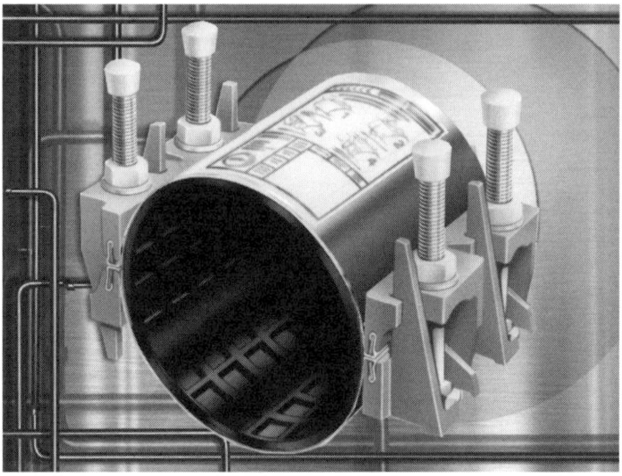

4D model

By a 4D model we mean a 3D model that is built over time; here is the previous example shown in the stages of assembly. View at: www.killerpresentations.com/4dmodel.html

Photographs

There is a danger that photographs can become C.L.I.P.A.R.T (see definition earlier) – they *must* be relevant. Here we are showing a product and then highlighting the two areas of that product we wish to make comment about.

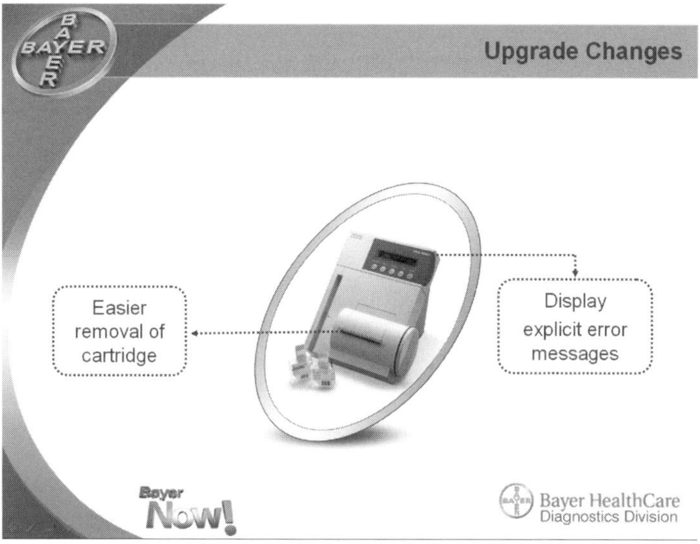

One of the biggest mistakes we see with photographs is poor composition. For example, look at the next three slides:

The first (left hand picture) is a photograph of a mug, except it has been poorly composed. The middle shot is better (actually they are the same photograph but the second one has been cropped using PowerPoint's picture toolbar). The third has been re-shot with better light and the picture then cut-out in Photoshop™ and placed on a virtual table, complete with manufactured shadow and reflection. The point I am trying to illustrate is that photographs display a massive amount of information, sometimes too much. It is often better to eliminate the unnecessary visual information and draw the audience's attention to the bit of the picture that is relevant.

Size

The next biggest mistake when using photographs is to insert high resolution pictures. There is no quicker way to increase your file size than to insert 5Mb pictures. PowerPoint creates slides at 72dpi (equivalent to 960 v 720)* and so inserting pictures at a higher resolution than this is unnecessary and will slow the presentation down. You should either use a package like Photoshop™ or if you are using PowerPoint 2003 there is a button on the toolbar that will compress and delete crops of your picture. As a tip, don't compress all of the images in the document as the feature has a tendency to resize and sometimes move pictures that are used more than once or have the same file name.

Maps

Maps are a great visual device. Here are several examples. Note how we have used colour (you'll need to see the colour section!), as well as the zoom-in technique to use the maps as both information and as a visual key.

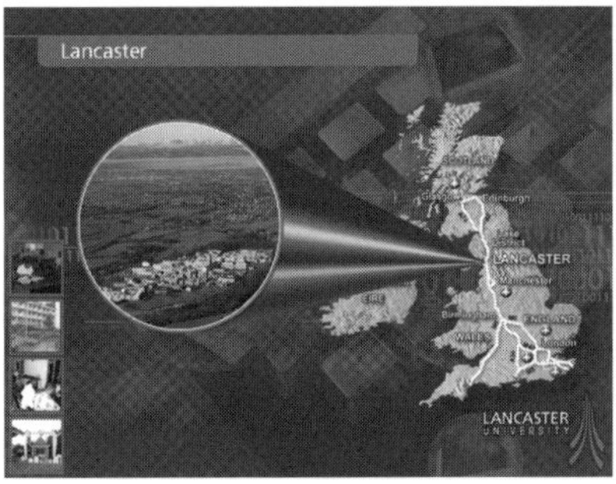

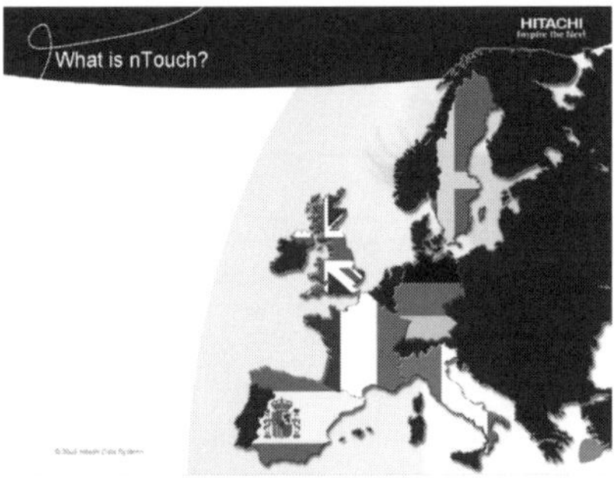

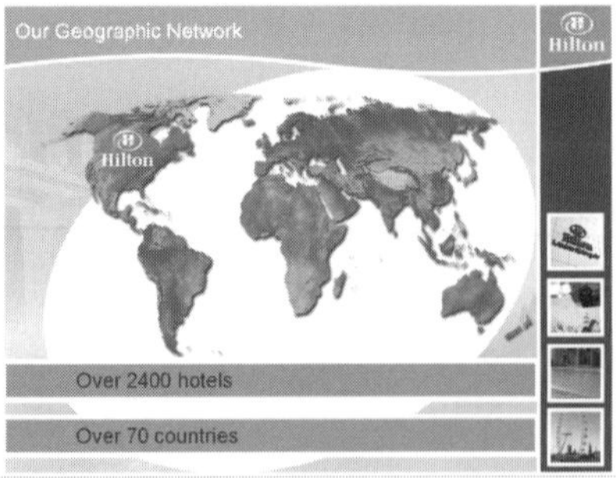

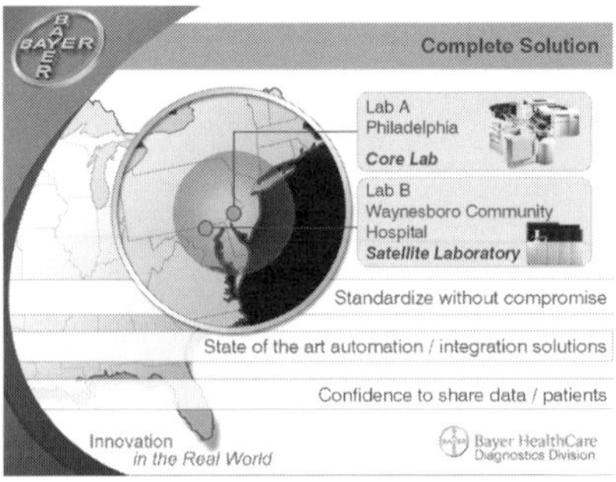

* This is not exact but this is the resolution we import into PowerPoint from Photoshop™ that gives the best results.

Screen grabs

We tend to use screen grabs a lot, particularly in technical presentations; clearly the *Fade*, *Zoom* and *Highlight* techniques are extremely useful here. Below you will see an example of a screen shot from one of our US clients, Yahoo HotJobs. Since the product is a web service they have to show screen grabs. The process is easy: browse to your required screen and press the *Print Screen* key (usually 'Prt Scr') then switch to PowerPoint and select Paste (or 'CTRL+V').

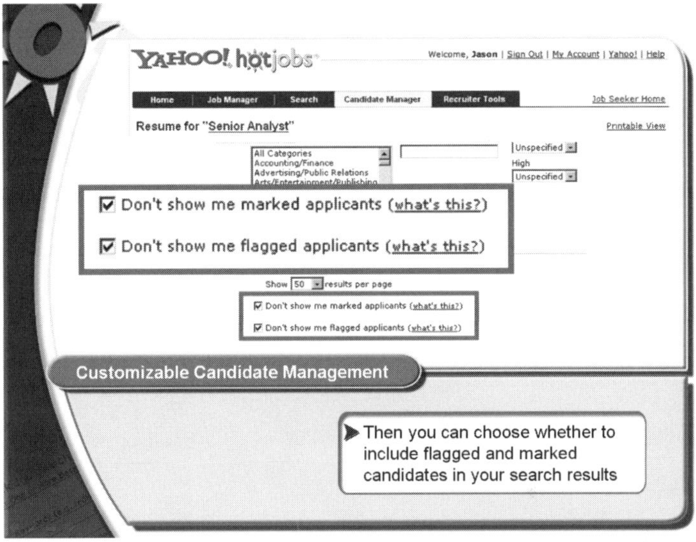

However, there are some issues with this, especially if you intend to zoom in. *Print Screen* (or any other method of screen capture) will only capture at whatever screen resolution you are running. The first trick is to increase your screen resolution on the PC before doing the capture, but this is rarely enough. Generally we have to capture the image (at as high a resolution as possible) then print it (again at as high a resolution as possible), then scan it in as if it were a high-resolution photograph. The result is fairly impressive. You can see these slides animate with the following link: www.killerpresentations.com/screengrab.html

Killer Idea Visual segue

To *segue* means to effect a smooth and unhesitating transition from one stage or area to another. In the context of presentations, this concept is very useful. Segue slides are those which develop and enhance their message by gradually removing and adding graphical elements to an unchanging background. This helps the audience to concentrate because it avoids the 'break' that occurs when moving between static slides. It creates an impression of dynamic flow that encourages the audience to keep up, and matches what the patter is – or should be – doing.

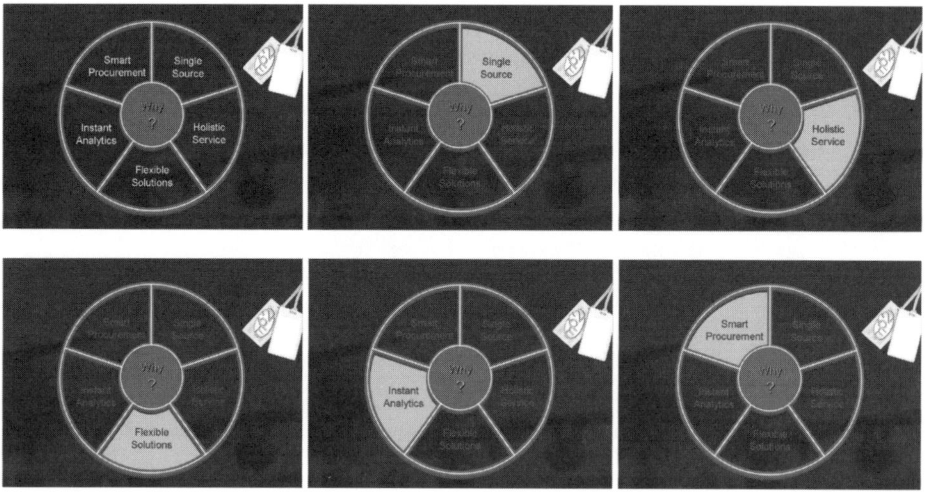

www.killerpresentations.com/wheel.html

Structure is important to the audience as it helps short-term memory; they feel comfortable and know where they are in the presentation. This is best done with non-verbal communication. Hence the visual segue. The example here is of how we use a 'value proposition' from a sales presentation to structure the presentation into five sections, each proving the presenter's ability to deliver.

We use visual segue to segue the presentation but we also use it to segue the slides. Titles in an m62 presentation have to be visually different from the body text, usually a complete contrast. This involves using a graphic we call a Title Bar under the titles to allow the text to be contrasted. We then use this title bar to alert the audience that the slide title has changed by having it disappear with the last slide, animate in followed by the heading. This animation drags the eye to the title bar, making sure that the audience notices that the slide title has changed and reads the new one. This theory can be seen reflected in our objective quality rules.

Title bars

Although linked to its template by design, the title bar is eye catching and contrasting; its job is to draw attention to a new topic. It does this by animating in prior to the heading changing. It does not animate on every slide, only on the slides where headings have changed. This subconsciously alerts the audience to the change of heading and compels them to read the heading. Please view this animation at: www.killerpresentations.com/titles.html

Graphs

Unfortunately, graphs are sometimes added not to support an argument or make a point, but to spice up an otherwise boring presentation. Presenters using bullet points often insert graphs simply to break the monotony.

Graphs should be used either to aid understanding and comprehension or to offer proof of a point, sometimes adding credibility. Edward Tufte's (see earlier reference) biggest complaint about PowerPoint (or 'slide ware' as he refers to it) is that computers often cannot show the resolution to depict accurately the true data. In this assertion he is correct, but to my mind he misses the point of a presentation: we are not trying to show the entirety of the data, just explain our conclusions from it.

Often we will see graphs that simply have far too much data in them to be effectively presented. Remember the comments earlier about the pace of information flow. On paper in 2D we can show lots of data and let the reader interpret it themselves, in a presentation we cannot. In fact, we *should* not. The purpose of a presentation is almost always to *share our* conclusions, not to allow others to draw their own; there is little time in a presentation to form opinions based on data. The data is mostly used to add weight to the presenter's argument.

To this end we invariably want to remove data from a graph in order to allow the points we need to make to be clearly seen.

There seem to me to be several different things that graphs can successfully illustrate. They can be used to show:

- increase or decrease
- two data sets merging or diverging
- change in trend.

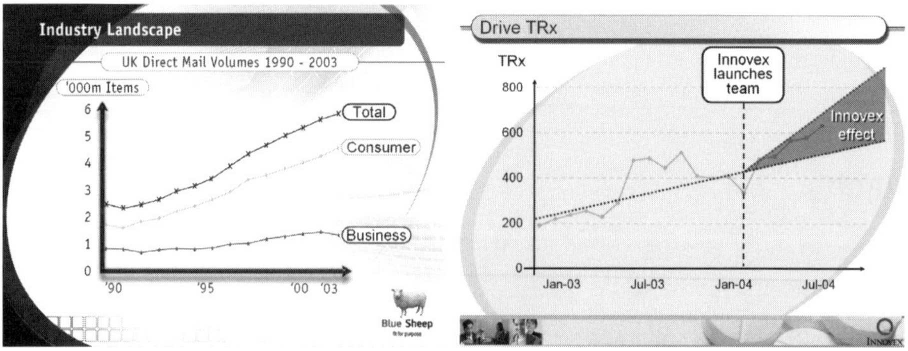

www.killerpresentations.com/linegraph.html

These comparisons, alongside the concept of 'pace the information flow', have led us to adopt the following sequence for animating graphs that show comparators:

1. Animate axes, then explain them.

2. Add the first data set, describe it.

3. Add the second data set, describe it.

4. Add the comparator, make your conclusion.

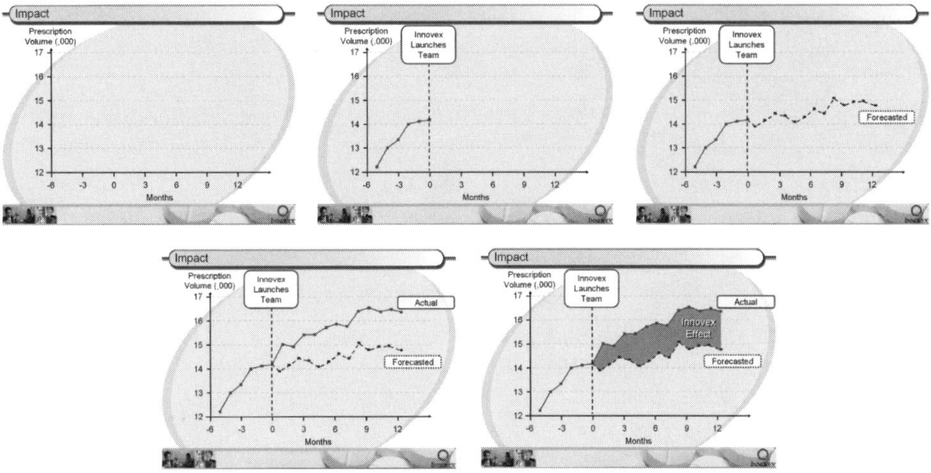

Here is a sequence that makes the point well: www.killerpresentations.com/graph2.html

The right graph for the right purpose

A great variety of graphs and charts can be produced at the click of a mouse. Each must be well-chosen. By all means ring the changes a little, but only if each can be justified in its own right as being well-chosen for its purpose.

Pie charts

These show the relationship of a part to the whole, i.e. a percentage. This is ideal for showing, for example, the breakdown of a company's turnover by sector but irrelevant if we are to show revenue growth year on year.

This example shows the breakdown of labour required to run a laboratory. The second slide shows how, after automating, 70% of these manual tasks disappear. The graph supports the argument and the transition from one slide to the other makes a dramatic statement. Clearly this is best actually seen animated and can be viewed at: www.killerpresentations.com/pie.html

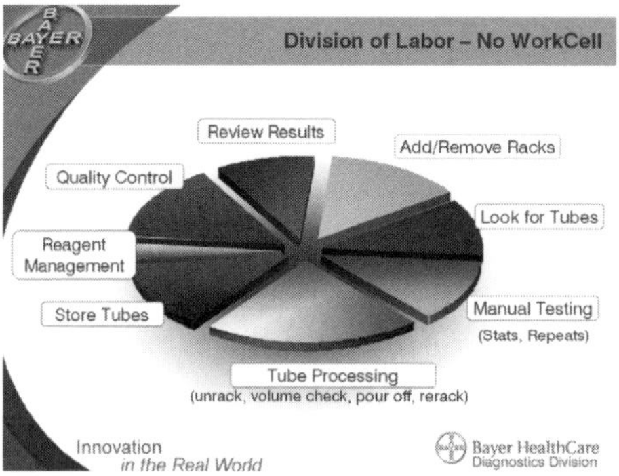

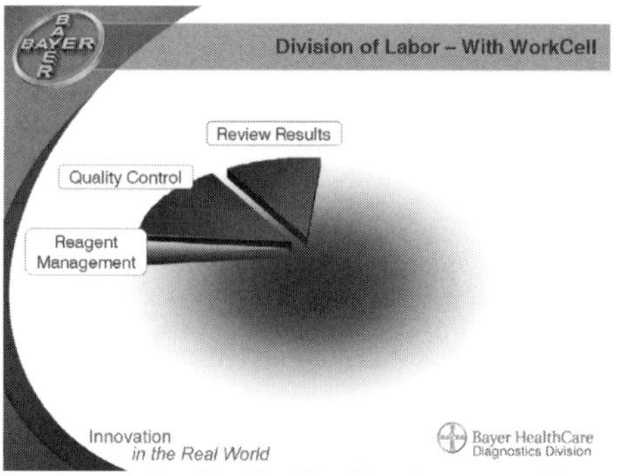

Line diagrams

These are best used to show a trend.

3D bar charts and line charts

These are not the easiest graphs to read and therefore should not be a first choice method.

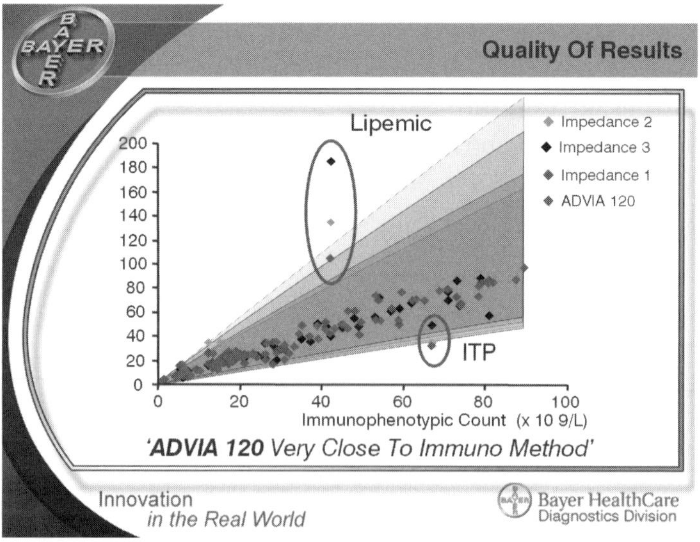

Scatter plots

This type of graph is great for showing statistical analysis, but difficult to use well in a presentation. Here is a good example of data used to show that Bayer's haematology systems are more accurate than their competitors'. This has a complicated build and really needs the patter to make it clear and can be seen at: www.killerpresentations.com/scatter.html

Bubble charts

The danger with these is that they typically have too much information contained in them. The rule of thumb is to remove the unnecessary data so that the point can be made visually. They do, however, work very well in 4D (e.g. show where you are now and where you want to be by having the bubble actually move over the graph).

Bar charts

Bar charts are best used if we are to compare two sets of data. They also work well if mixed with a line diagram as this example shows. We show the discreet data as a bar chart and then fade this leaving the trends to emphasise, in this case, the impact of a project on prescribing behaviour in a GP practice. Clearly the reprint here is only of the final picture – to see the whole slide build follow: www.killerpresentations.com/bar.html

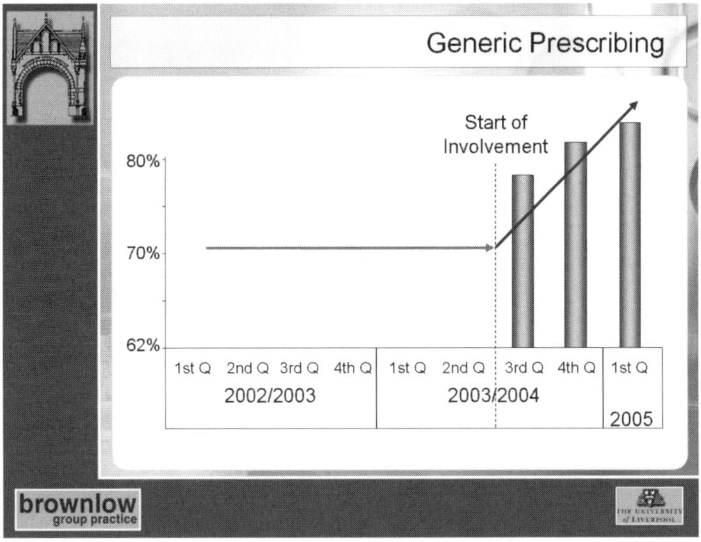

Importing Excel™ graphs

Clearly this is possible and provided the Excel™ file is with the presentation, any changes in the data can be updated to the presentation. However, we do not use it that often. We typically want to animate the graph according to our objective quality standards and this is tricky on linked graphs. We normally paste the graph in and then ungroup them (converting to a PowerPoint object). The graph can then be manipulated a lot easier, although you have lost the actual data and so updates have to be done manually.

Ordered lists: flow chart

There are two types of flowchart, linear and iterative. Generally if a list has an order to it (i.e. you can number it or it runs chronologically) then it will look better as a flow chart. Linear flows have a start and beginning, iterative end where they start. Clearly linear flows should ideally be laid out left to right (in the West) or top to botto0is more space left to right because of the aspect ratio of the screen). Iterative should work clockwise (most audience members will be right-handed and find anti-clockwise counter intuitive. Please see: www.killerpresentations.com/flowchart.html

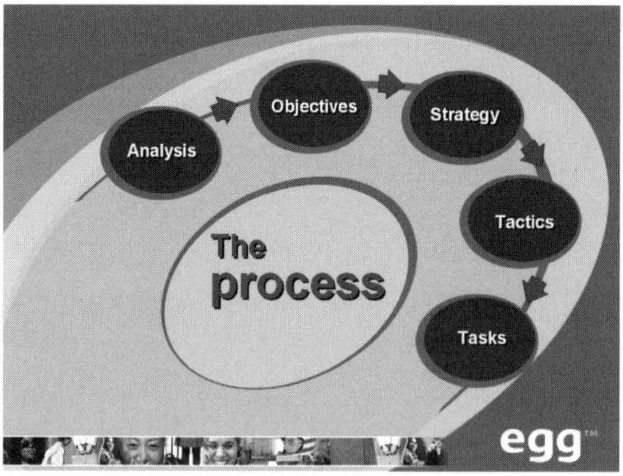

The use of media

Multi-media

About a year after I started m62 we were approached by a famous camping stove manufacturer who wanted a presentation. The MD was hugely passionate about his products and after we had taken the brief for the presentation he showed me some video he wanted to include. The video footage was a 60 minute documentary about a team of mountaineers climbing one of the world's tallest mountains. During the black and white film there was a great shot of the company's equipment being used to boil water, no mean feat so far above sea level and a great piece of video to include in the presentation. However, where I wanted to include 30 seconds of the video, the MD wanted all 60 minutes. I refused and we lost the contract which has taught me a valuable lesson about customers always being right. The point of this is that 30 seconds of good well-shot video that makes an important point is worth the effort, but be warned – including footage that *you* enjoy or find interesting is not a good idea; only use enough to support the argument. It is highly unlikely that the audience shares the same passion for the subject as you.

Sound

If you are using animation – either PowerPoint animation (building a slide, etc.) or embedding some external animation (movie or flash file) – then ten seconds of silence is acceptable: more than this will become uncomfortable for the audience. You can extend this by adding sound – usually music – to around 90 seconds. Longer periods of self-running animation need either narrative or interaction, both of which start to step out of the realms of presentations and into the realm of video production.

We rarely use sound during a presentation, perhaps the occasional customer quote, but this works better as video. Sound really needs to be accompanied by something happening on screen: either an animation or a build. As soon as music starts the audience will look at the screen, and if there is nothing there they may disengage.

Summary

1. No lists of bullet points, definitely no lists of lists.

2. Appropriate visual device.

3. Pace the information.

4. Control the audience's focus.

5. Avoid too much too quickly.

Section Four
Design

It is only shallow people who do not judge by appearances.

Oscar Wilde

Before I start this chapter a word of caution, I am not a designer. What you are about to read needs to be put into context. The design of the PowerPoint slide is important, but not as important as the *purpose* of the slide or the content. At the risk of boring you and repeating myself, look at this slide again.

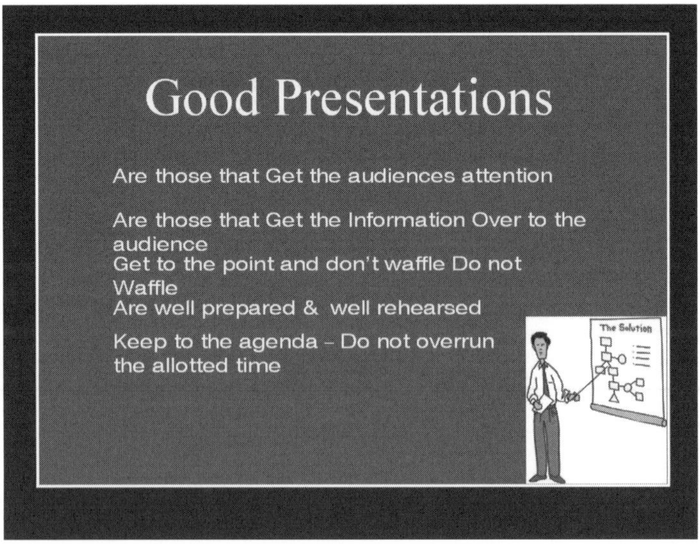

When I present this to a new audience I always point to the graphic in the right hand corner and ask 'What is this?' The correct answer is 'rubbish', however I usually get 'clip art' as a response.

Then I ask them to do something: next time you see a piece of clip art in a presentation, find the person who put it there originally (because chances are it was not the current user!), and ask them this question, 'Why did you do it?'

The interesting thing about this question is that it doesn't matter where in the world they are, or in what language they speak, the answer is broadly the same: 'Well, it's a dull boring slide, so I though I would give it some visual interest!'

Half points. This *is* a dull boring slide, however why do people insist on adding graphics to make up for it? Here is a version designed by my Creative Director, Alison Sleightholm, (probably the finest PowerPoint designer on the planet). Is it any better?

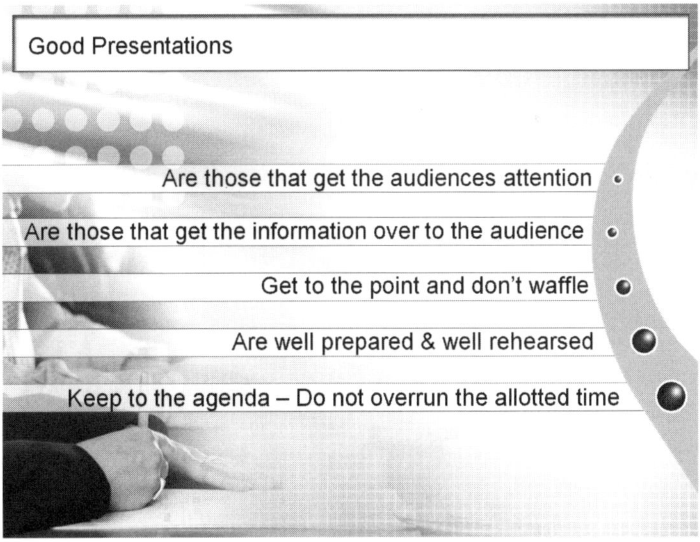

A lot of people would think so. Indeed as a piece of design it is better, nicer to look at, easier to read and the imagery 'keys' the content (see later). But ask yourself this important question, 'Does this new slide improve the information transmission?' Answer: NO.

So why do we do it? The answer, I believe, lies in the fact that as presenters we have been audience members and we know what a heading and five (or six in this case) bullet points feels like. At m62 we call it 'audience abuse'. We all know that, regardless of the quality of the graphics, this dull and boring slide is going to need a presenter of rare gift if it isn't going to send us to sleep. So we add a little Clip Art to do nothing else but appease our conscience a little for what we are about to do: *abuse the audience*. Spending time worrying about background images when we could spend time worrying about content is a crime – don't bother.

The purpose of design

It may sound as though I don't value design. I do. I think it can make a massive impact on audiences on an emotional level and a smaller impact on a rational level. Slides need to look good, primarily because they are a showcase for your organisation.

Another thing that has always puzzled me is the lack of design in corporate presentations. Can there be a major organisation on the face of the planet that does not put a massive amount of time, effort and often money into getting the corporate communications right? Brochures, web sites, stationery all designed by a designer, carefully co-ordinated so as to maximise Consistent Integrated Marketing Communications. Then the salesperson gets up with a presentation he knocked together on the flight!

What I find bizarre about many of these organisations is that they will spend fortunes on the literature which is designed to initiate dialogue with a prospect but then refuse to spend money on the piece of communication that could make that prospect a client. When was the last time you heard a client say 'I gave you the order because your brochure was exceptional!'? I have lost count of the number of times clients of mine have heard their clients say the decision was based on the presentation.

So I begin this section on PowerPoint design by saying this: don't do it yourself, hire an expert. It's too important to leave to amateur designers such as myself or your PA.

The rest of this section is therefore really aimed at professional designers who have to create presentations for other people to present, although some of the ideas are pretty essential for the actual presenter to understand.

The communication problem: perception

One man's ceiling is another man's floor.

Paul Simon

Look at this picture, 'My wife and my mother-in-law', published in 1915 by W.E. Hill. I am sure you have seen this before; it is very famous. What do you see? Old hag or beautiful woman? Perhaps both or nothing? The really interesting question is what did the person next to you see and how do you know it was the same?

This is the problem with communication: people's perception is subjective. What one person sees as an advantage others see as a problem. The trick with really good presentations is to minimise the opportunity for misinterpretation and that takes considerable effort.

We are once again touching on De Burgh and Steward's concept of *Actual vs Intended Messages*. I have seen many slides that inadvertently convey a different meaning from the intended, not always serendipitous; here is an example:

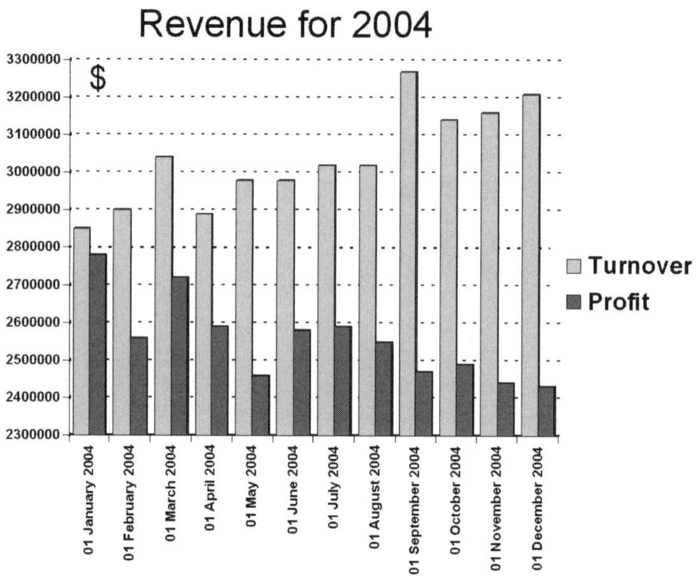

This, one of the few slides created solely for this book, is actual data from a presentation given to us on behalf of a client but it was not designed and not used; here is why.

The presenter wants to prove credibility by showing that his company's revenue is growing (a common misconception that size in business matters!). However, *I* look at this graph and see a company that is trading profit for sales and will shortly run out of cash: not so credible! But I am a sceptic. Again this is a reference to Tim Steward and Hugo De Burgh's concept of Intended and Actual messages. The question we have to ask is 'Can this data be interpreted in a different way?' And if so how do we prevent it? The answer here was to remove the profit line – now it just shows a growing company!

The single most common presentation error

In my experience the most common mistake made by presenters is to present too much information too quickly. It is a mistake I have made and will, I am sure, make again. Once we have defined the objectives we need to ensure we only present information that is strictly relevant to achieving the objectives and not cloud the issues by adding partially or wholly irrelevant information.

Graph axes

Graphs on paper are primarily used to help people interpret data, so they are often printed with a lot of detail to enable study. In a presentation the audience has neither the time nor, often, the inclination to study the data. It is a mistake to present something too complicated. For example look at this slide:

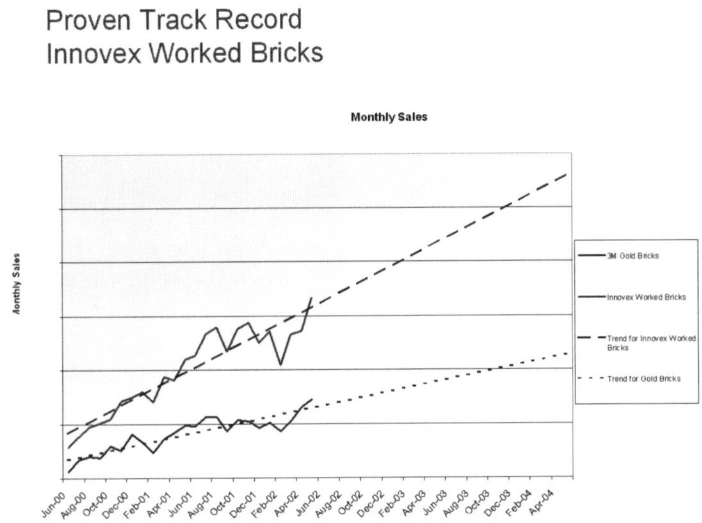

This is a before slide for a presentation for a UK client of ours, Innovex.* Innovex provide contract sales forces for pharmaceutical companies. This slide displays a very good reason for their client to leave the current contract with Innovex in place. As a piece of data it is essential to the pitch; however as a slide it does little to advance the argument. There are a number of issues.

- You cannot read the text on the left hand axis as you cannot turn the screen through 90%
- The text on the *y* axis (bottom) is too small to be seen by the audience.
- The legend, even if you could read it, is difficult to use as you may have to move your head to move your focus from it to the actual data.
- There is too much information here to take in at a glance. Where do you start?

* Clearly we have removed the *x* labels, the client name and logo in order to protect confidentiality.

Here is the sequence we used:

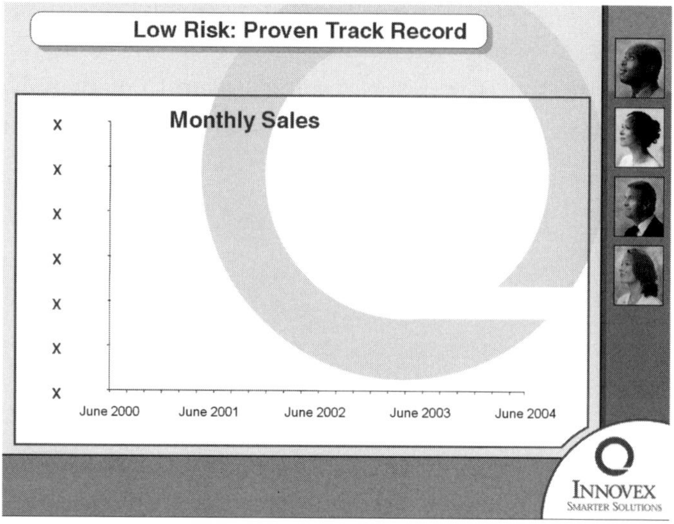

1. Build one shows the axes. We are plotting the same data over the same period but we are only using five data labels, so that it can be clearly seen that we are showing four years' data (in his patter the presenter explains this, saying '*we are going to show two years' actual data and two years' projected data…*')

   CLICK

2. We show the Innovex Sales data and let them see the positive trend, then

CLICK

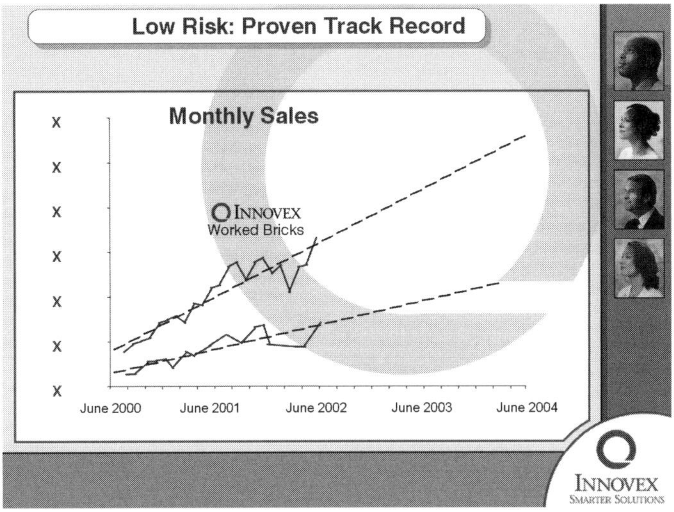

to show them the control data (in this case their own sales team's sales figures). The comparison is now obvious: Innovex's sales team is consistently outselling the in-house team.

CLICK

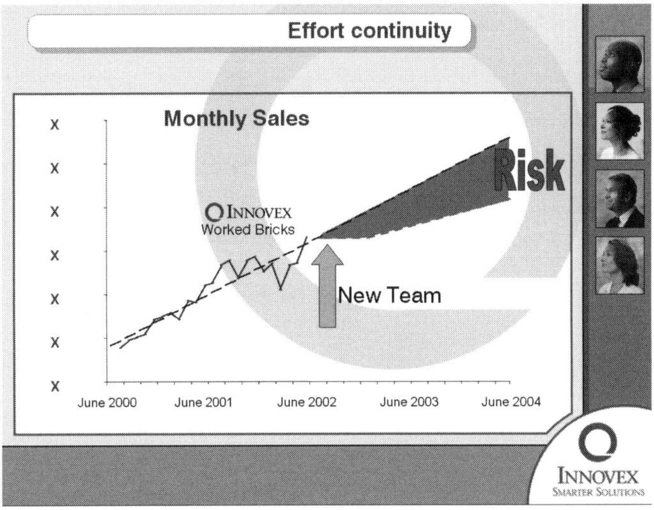

We highlight the fact that if the client was to pass the contract to another supplier the forecasted trend could not stay in place, representing a massive risk on their behalf.

This sequence can be seen presented on:
www.killerpresentations.com/innovex.html

Innovex secured their client's repeat business.

Explain graphs clearly

Legends, which often appear in a box alongside a graph, should be avoided. On paper this description works well as the eye can flick conveniently between the legend and data point. On a big screen at a presentation this is too difficult for the audience. The best idea is to label the data point directly with notes as close to the data set as possible. Beware too of taking graphs from elsewhere, for instance within a report, and reproducing them unaltered as slides, often they contain too much information – more than you want to present – and end up confusing rather than clarifying.

Keep the amount of information on graphs manageable

Do not use more than eight (12 max.) horizontal labels or six vertical labels on a graph, although more data points may be used unlabelled.

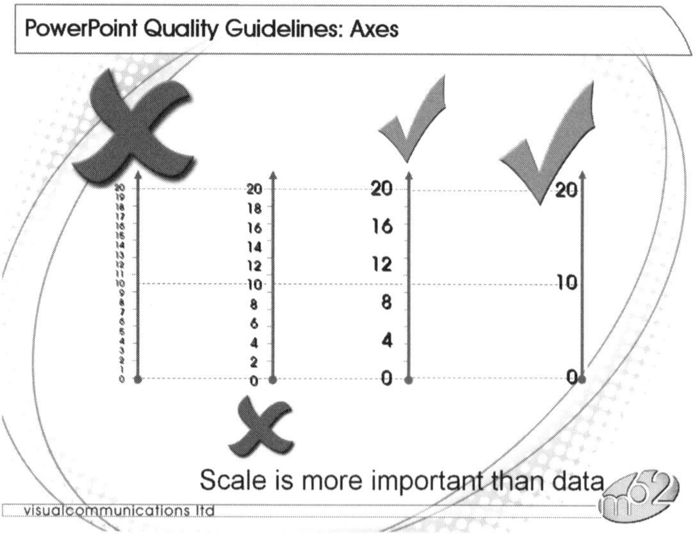

Check marks should signify the presence of additional data, for example, for a 24-month revenue chart use 24 data points, 24 marks on the axis but only eight labels (one every three months is perhaps best).

For example look at the slide opposite. Here we have shown four *x* axes all of which show the same scale. Which is easiest to understand?

Effective communication not just impressive presentation

Visual keys

Successful presentations should not only be consistent in content (messaging), but also in style. Slides should be designed so that the imagery directly reflects and links to the message being communicated. This way the audience finds it easy to see how points are interlinked with the general message. For example, using a map of Europe on a slide when you are discussing your company's performance in the European market will reinforce the point and add clarity. We call this 'keying' the slide; the graphic helps the audience place the information in context.

When we started in 1997 we worked with some people from BBC Wales, one of whom was a former editor of *Newsnight*. The BBC use 'visual keys' to help key current affairs information during telecasts. Watch the news tonight and look for the key, it is usually in the top right-hand corner above the newsreader's head. The purpose of this graphic, picture or heading is to help the audience place the information they are hearing into context. It works because it allows the right side of the brain to help the left side of the brain interpret the information it is receiving.

Visually keying information is important in presentations for the same reason; we would typically *key* the background with relevant photography (pictures of cranes for a crane hire company, PCs for an IT company, etc.). After the initial viewing this visual information pales from the audience's conscious attention and only becomes noticed again if it is changed.

It is for this reason that we don't often change the background on slides. We always have a good argument for changing the images: either it adds value to the presentation *or* the client is ignoring sound advice and prepared to pay for the extra work!

Integrated marketing communications and branding

This is not the place for a lengthy discussion about the necessity of having a consistent look and feel for your presentations, or for your entire marketing communications as there are much better texts around than I am capable of producing.* However I want to point out that the presentation is a highly visible piece of communication that for some reason tends to get left out of the branding guidelines. It is probably seen by more people for longer than any other piece of marketing collateral and so ought to be at the top of the list when considering branding.

At m62, we put considerable effort into promoting consistency with our clients and will often modify the design of a presentation to make it fit with a consistent approach to communication even if they do not have a policy. To this end we almost always produce a corporate ID presentation that helps promote this consistency both in my team and in the client's presenters. I highly recommend that you produce one for your own organisation.

Look and feel

I learnt very early on in m62's development that design is a personal thing. Having produced over 3,000 PowerPoint presentations and therefore seen well over 6,000 backgrounds all with different layouts, colours, images, etc. I can say with some clarity that it doesn't really matter. Some people will love it, others will not. The important thing is that it is unique to you and it has been designed by a designer and not put together on the plane.

Good backgrounds have some things in common: contrast, good usable space, attractive visual keys and visible but not over-facing branding. Whilst most of these are self-explanatory let me touch on the first one and explain it.

---

* *Integrated Marketing Communications* by Schultz, Tannenbaum and Lauterbaum (Contemporary Books).

Contrast

The human eye cannot see brightness. For example, if you were to look at a torch at night and a different torch in the day, could you determine which was the brighter? Probably not. What the human eye can do is compare brightness levels: this is of course called contrast.

Take the two torches and put them side by side in a dark room and you can tell which is brighter. The same goes for computer projection devices; side by side you can see a difference but isolated and in different ambient light conditions you can't. There is a myth about projectors that says brighter is better, but as you actually need a 100 × increase in light output to see any perceived increase in brightness levels, I am not convinced of its worth. If your image is washed out, it may be considerably cheaper and quicker to control the ambient light than to change the projector for a more expensive, brighter version. I am not advocating that we all sit in the dark to watch presentations (although this can help you sleep if the presenter is using bullet points!) but turning off the fluorescent lights in favour of bright down lighters can have a dramatic effect on contrast levels.

The human eye is a contrast meter, hence find a dark wall to project on to, do not use south facing rooms (north in the southern hemisphere) and avoid bright lights sending rays onto the screen.

As far as the look and feel goes, the bigger the contrast between the background and the foreground colours, the easier it is to see. So dark blue backgrounds and bright yellow text can be seen clearly because of the relevant contrast differences. Not that we are advocating using blue and yellow, it's just that you don't put yellow text over a yellow background and then wonder why people can't see the text.

Corporate ID presentation

What is an ID?

m62 have designed nearly 3,000 PowerPoint presentations over 7 years, and our conclusions are that the template facility in PowerPoint is somewhat limited when you need to speed up the process of slide production, improve quality and consistency and therefore reduce the amount of time and effort required to produce a professional-looking presentation. The purpose of the ID is to extend the usefulness of the PowerPoint template and to allow users access to additional pieces of design that help them produce visual slides instead of a presentation that is essentially a 'list of lists' using headings and bullet points.

Every m62 presentation begins with the production of, or enhancement of, a client ID.ppt.

Why do our clients use them?

While m62 believe that we offer a good slide production service in terms of value for money and service quality, we recognise that some presentations need to be put together immediately. Slides may be added to an m62 presentation and it is important that the additional slide does not stand out from the rest by being of poor quality or inconsistent with the rest. To this end our clients find the ID an invaluable tool. It ensures:

- quality
- consistency
- design
- corporate regulation adherence

and reduces the:

- time
- effort
- cost

involved in in-house slide production.

What is a PowerPoint template?

PowerPoint templates provide all presentation material with a consistent look and feel. A considerable amount of effort goes into the design of these templates and once complete there are no restrictions on their use within the client organisation.

> Microsoft PowerPoint provides design templates (design template: A file that contains the styles in a presentation, including the type and size of the bullets and fonts; placeholder sizes and positions; background and design and fill; color schemes; and a slide master and optional title master) that you can apply to a presentation to give it a fully designed, professional look.
>
> © Microsoft Corporation

This is a PowerPoint tool that carries some, but not all, of the information to brand a presentation each .pot should be programmed with the following information:

- main background
- title screen background
- default font
- default colour scheme
- default animation scheme.

What is contained in an ID?

A sample ID presentation can be found by following this link at: www.m62.net/ID.zip, but broadly the file contains the following items.

PowerPoint template (.pot)

A fully designed and configured template file for use with all versions of PowerPoint, although some features of the template for PowerPoint 2003™ will not work in older versions of the software.

Main background

This is a 960 × 720 .jpg file inserted into the presentation to be used should a user need to patch an image or use the design outside of PowerPoint. This image is the background used for the majority of the slides in a presentation with the exception of the title slides.

Title background

As well as giving a presentation structure, this helps the audience organise the information and encourages 're-tuning' after they start to 'sample', thus improving the amount of information received and therefore retained from your presentation. It is important that the title slides have a different background from the rest of the slides. The design ought to be similar to the main background, often using the same images in the same position to allow for an attractive but not distracting transition between backgrounds. This is also placed in the ID as a 960 × 720 .jpg.

Heading banner

m62 believe that slide titles ought to be visually different from the main body of a slide and, as such, most presentations require the addition of a heading banner to lie beneath the title on certain slides. As PowerPoint .pot files do not allow for this facility, we add this to the ID including the correct animation for the banner and title text. Although in actual presentations m62's objective quality standards require this animation setting to be removed on slides where the title has not changed from the previous slide (the idea is that the animated banner draws the audience's attention to the fact that the heading has changed without distracting them each time a new slide is used). For this reason most banners contrast with the background and allow for contrasting text colour.

Font information

Included in the ID is a slide that has a 'picture' of the correct font alongside a PowerPoint box of the font. The purpose of this is to help the user identify whether or not they have the correct font installed on their PC.

WordArt and font style information

Configuring WordArt to look professional takes time and effort – it has the potential to look considerably amateurish. This slide contains sample designs that can be cut and pasted into future presentations ensuring both quality and consistency.

Subjective *vs* objective quality

One man's Picasso is another man's art!

NBO

We found quite early on in the business that there are two definitions of quality, which we now call 'objective' and 'subjective'. Subjective quality is a bit like art; whether you like it or not depends largely on the individual. Look through some of the examples in this book of slides we have designed: some of them you will like and some of them you will not. I personally have a thing about pink! I hate it, and I generally prefer dark backgrounds – but we have clients who really like the opposite.

If a presentation we have produced fails a subjective quality test we don't worry too much, we just redo it for the client. We try to ensure that these matters of taste are decided early on, but generally we will not be hard on the designers if somebody doesn't like the design.

Objective quality is another issue. On these things they are either right or wrong – it is *not* down to taste. Spelling, conformity to the brief, the way things animate and the way things are lined up all form part of our objective quality standards, and it is against this list that our quality audit process runs.

The list of objective quality standards below may help you with your presentations; they certainly help in producing ours.

Text rules

- Text must be readable from the back of the room (20pt minimum and only on graph labels otherwise 24pt minimum). No point in having text that most of the audience cannot read.
- No scripted fonts – they are difficult to read.
- Avoid serifed fonts – also difficult to read.
- Maximise contrasting colours to background.

- Avoid curved text.
- Use consistent capitalisation.
- Avoid using vertical text.

In the West it is a safe bet that your audience is comfortable reading from left to right. So by the time they have figured out what the vertical label on a graph reads, they may have missed the whole point of the graph itself. It is best not to place unnecessary strains on your audience's attention. It is a hangover from the printed world where it is possible to turn the image through 90° to read the text. However attempting this in a presentation can cause serious irritation for other audience members, assuming you can actually lift the projector.

Spell out acronyms

TLAs are of course Three Letter Acronyms. Examples of this phenomenon are ENT, CAB, CIS, TCF, RRS, NUT. How many did you recognise? TLAs may be punchy, but they are not meaningful. At worst, your audience may be so intrigued that they begin to idly guess at their meanings or even, if they are really bored, to invent their own TLAs to describe you! Avoid this, and avoid even longer ones too, while perhaps keeping one four letter one in mind: KISS (keep it simple, stupid).

Use non-serif type

Serifs are the tails and tassels that adorn type fonts such as Times New Roman and Garamond. Serifs are used to provide a kind of 'visual hand-rail' that guides the eye smoothly along the printed line; sometimes they are simply picked to give a more elaborate effect. For presentation slides it is advisable to avoid using fonts of this sort because their appearance when combined with graphics and when projected can be quite distracting. It is better to use 'sans-serif' fonts such as Arial or Verdana, and if possible to use 'TrueType' (.ttf) fonts, which guarantee the same appearance on paper or in graphics as on the computer screen.

Layout rules

- Evenly space objects.
- Centre objects around the middle of the useable presentation space.

- Don't align by eye, use the tools in the draw menu. What looks straight on a 17in monitor can be 20cm out on screen.

Graph rules

- Build the axes and then pause to explain what the audience are seeing.
- Then build the data by series. Pause to allow the audience to digest information.
- Fade, highlight or zoom to show the relevant data or comparisons.
- Possibly fade graph and overlay inference.
- Use two or three data labels per axis – you never need one for each data point.
- The title of the slide is usually the *x* axis.
- Slide titles ought to be visually different from the main body text, usually in a box of a contrasting colour, and above all else consistent.
- Use labels not legends.

Keep your own checklist

While all the above are rules that we feel strongly about, regard as tried and tested and follow ourselves at m62, it is doubtless possible to both adapt these and to add others. If you do so then it makes sense to create an 'operating manual', setting out guidelines that can usefully be followed consistently around an organisation to create a sound – and impressive – corporate style.

Having a clear idea of the way you want things to look and basing that, in turn, on the reality of how presentations work (particularly the reality of what audiences expect, enjoy and respond to) is the key to producing slides and presentations that will work effectively.

Tips and tricks

Create you own toolbar with your favourite tools

All of our designers create their own toolbars. Overleaf is a picture of the one I use. To create your own, simply go to 'Tools/customize/toolbars'. Click 'new' and name your tool bar.

Next flip into commands and drag and drop your favourites onto the new toolbar. The best tool to add in here is in 'format/pick up object style' and 'apply object style'. This will copy all effects and styles applied to text, word, shapes, etc. – very useful.

The 'Shift' key

Holding the 'Shift' key while using the mouse will affect the action, for example:

1. Depressing the 'Shift' key while dragging to create your line will create a line that is perfectly horizontal or vertical.
2. Select the first object, then while depressing the 'Shift' key, click the other objects to select more that one object at a time.
3. Selecting the top animation in the animation window, then selecting the bottom one while holding down the 'Shift' key will select all animations in a sequence.
4. Depressing the 'Shift' key while dragging to create your rectangle or oval will draw a perfect square/circle.
5. Clicking on the *Slide View* icon (at the bottom-left of the screen), while depressing the 'Shift' key will quickly access the 'Slide Master'.

'Alt' key

Using the 'Alt' key in conjunction with the mouse or the keyboard will allow you to move, size or crop in smaller increments.

Shift select

The biggest productivity tip we can give you is SHIFT Select and it's impact on Custom animation. When you need to animate multiple objects on a slide in a certain sequence hold the SHIFT key down while selecting the objects, if you do this in the order you wish them to animate then when you apply the custom animation settings to this group PowerPoint will pick up the order in which you selected them. If you are using 2003 you will need to change the timing to After Previous but you will see the objects appear on the animation window in the correct sequence. This tip will save you hours of time.

The 'Ctrl' key

Using the 'Ctrl' key in conjunction with the mouse or the keyboard will alter the point of anchor of an object (e.g. when creating a square, circle or line, usually the first place you click anchors a corner, but with the 'Ctrl' key pressed it anchors the centre of the object).

Select all animations in a sequence

Select the first animation in the animation window then select subsequent animations holding down the 'Ctrl' key.

'Ctrl' drag

You can duplicate an object by holding down the 'Ctrl' key and then selecting and dragging the object. This works in slide sorter view as well, although it doesn't work in the slides window of the normal layout. (This also works in other office applications: for example, double click a word and then press 'Ctrl', now drag the word and it will duplicate.)

Combinations

Most of these will work together, for example holding down Alt, Ctrl and Shift will allow an object to be created in small increments, anchored in the centre with regular dimensions.

Fine-tune curves, lines and shapes

Select the 'edit point' tool in the draw menu or right click the edge of the shape or line. (Note: this can only be done with drawn objects, not with 'Autoshapes'.)

Select object

Press the 'Esc' key first to de-select any object that may be correctly selected. Then repeatedly press the 'Tab' key to cycle round all the objects on the current page.

Autoshapes

1. Double-click on an AutoShape to format it.
2. Select *Change Autoshape* from the *Draw* menu to change the type of shape.

Right clicking

Right click on an object to bring up a menu with a series of shortcuts, grouping, order (front-to-back), cut and paste, etc.

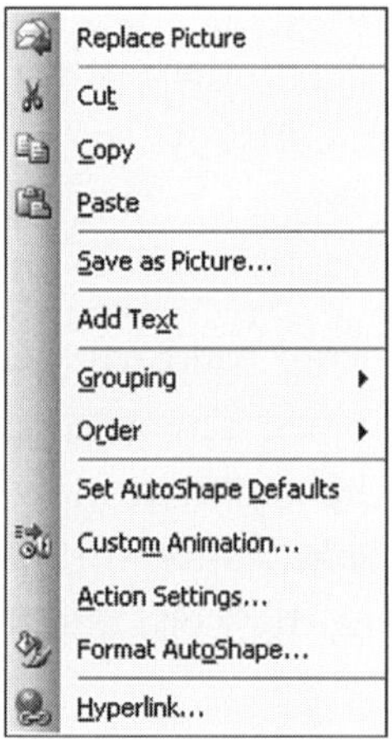

Typing shortcuts (any office programme)

- Copyright © symbol: enter (c).
- Trademark ™ symbol: enter (tm).
- Registered ® symbol: enter (r).

Changing from caps to lower case (or vice versa)

Shift+F3 will toggle the text case between ALL CAPS, lower case, and Initial Capital. You'll be surprised how often you use this once you get the hang of it!

Text resizing

Select the text and to make it larger repeatedly press 'Ctrl+]', or to make it smaller press 'Ctrl+['.

Guides

First turn guides on by using the *Guides* command on the *View* menu (PowerPoint will allow up to 8 guides in each direction). To get more guides, hold down the 'Ctrl' key while dragging on a guide. To remove a guide, drag it off the page.

Summary

1. Effective communication not just impressive presentation.
2. Avoid clip art.
3. Be consistent.
4. Use design to help the audience understand the message.
5. Text no smaller then 24pts (20 for graph labels).
6. Build data along with the argument.
7. Avoid too much information too quickly.

The art of animation

The ability to simplify means to eliminate the unnecessary so that the necessary may speak.

Hans Hofmann

Purpose of animating slides

The purpose of animating a slide is to control what the audience are seeing and when. Good animation directs the audience's attention to *where* it is required *when* it is required. Bad animation is distracting. Done well, animation can add considerable non-verbal information to the overall communication. Done badly, it can ruin a good slide and therefore a good presentation.

The problem with this section of the book is that it is difficult to know where to talk about animation. It is integral to the visualisation, the design, the delivery and almost all of the other sections in this book; it is a core skill.

Build types

There are two basic types of animation (build) effects: those that leave the object where it is in relation to the slide (*static builds*), and those that move the object in relation to the slide (*motion builds*). Generally it is the latter that grab more attention, usually too much, and therefore they are frequently distracting. Static builds, on the other hand, are much more useful: the most frequently used static build is the *Random Bars Vertical*, but I have listed the effects that fall into each category below.

Flying objects really look amateurish. Whether it is text flying in from the left or a picture crawling from the right, this effect tends to look unsophisticated primarily because it is not subtle. Subtlety is the watchword for animations.

Below I have listed all of the various build types available in PowerPoint 2003, I have categorised them into static and motion builds. As a rule try to use the static builds as much as possible as they will make your presentation look more polished.

Static Builds

Basic
Appear
Blinds
Box
Checkerboard
Circle
Diamond
Dissolve In
Flash Once
Plus
Random Bars
Split
Stripes
Wedge
Wheel
Wipe

Subtle
Expand
Fade
Faded Swivel

Moderate
Color
Typewriter
Unfold
Zoom

Motion Builds

Basic
Crawl In

Moderate
Ascend
Centre
Revolve
Compress
Grow & Turn
Descend
Ease In
Peek In
Fly In
Rise Up
Spinner
Stretch

Exciting
Boomerang
Bounce
Credits

Subtle
Curve Up
Flip
Float
Fold
Glide
Lightspeed
Magnify
Pinwheel
Faded Zoom

Sling
Spiral In
Swish
Swivel
Thread
Whip

Build times

The principal aim of animating is to draw the audience's attention to the correct place on the screen at the right time. It is not to impress them with how well we know PowerPoint, and using the same animation types over and over again is only ever boring to the presenter. Perhaps the reason that presenters use various animation types is that they know their content is so bad they hope some variation in the build types will add something! Good animation should be unnoticed by the audience who should be engaged by the message, not the medium. To this end consistency is a prerequisite for quality animation.

Build Time is the time it takes between a CLICK and the moment the animation ceases. We tend not to have continuous animation (except on a title slide where we want to draw attention to the slide and will not be presenting over it) as this can be too compelling, and audiences have difficulty paying attention to the presenter if things are moving. Because of this, we recommend that build times do not exceed three seconds. As we also recommend that presenters say nothing over slide builds, to allow the audience to concentrate on assimilating the information just displayed, three seconds is a comfortable amount of silence. Silences much longer than that require a great deal of self-control from the presenter, which is difficult with raised adrenalin levels.

Animating

Most of our rules (or suggestions) are common sense, ignore them if you wish (unless you work for m62 in which case ignore them at your peril).

Arrows

Flying arrows don't work. Generally, arrows should be 'wiped' in the direction of their indication, as this naturally draws the eye towards what they are pointing to.

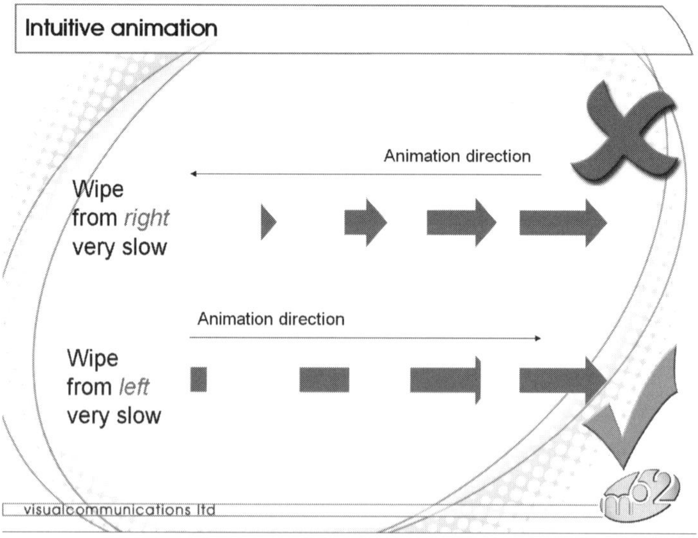

Clearly this is difficult to do in 2D – you can see a more detailed demonstration of how to do this by following this link:
www.killerpresentations.com/intiativeanimation.html

Wheels

If you read the section on persuasive presentations then you will know that we use a wheel graphic to display the value proposition. This slide, known as the killer slide, articulates the reasons for dealing with the presenter but it then forms segue slides to give the presentation structure. The first time the slide appears the graphic animates in 'static' followed by the first benefit. The presenter would then explain this benefit to the audience and then CLICK for the next. Each of these needs to appear with a static animation.

To see our killer slide animated please follow this link:
www.killerpresentations.com/killerslide.html

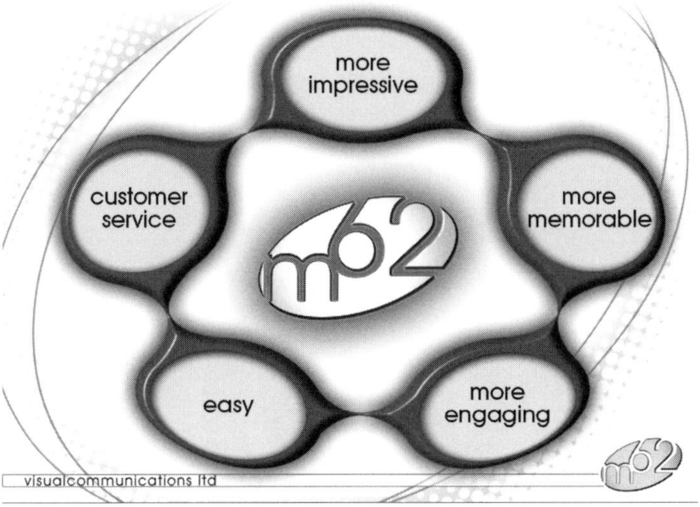

Flow charts

There are two types of flow charts, linear and iterative (see the visualisation section for explanation). They need to animate from the start of the process to the end. For example here is one of our own slides.

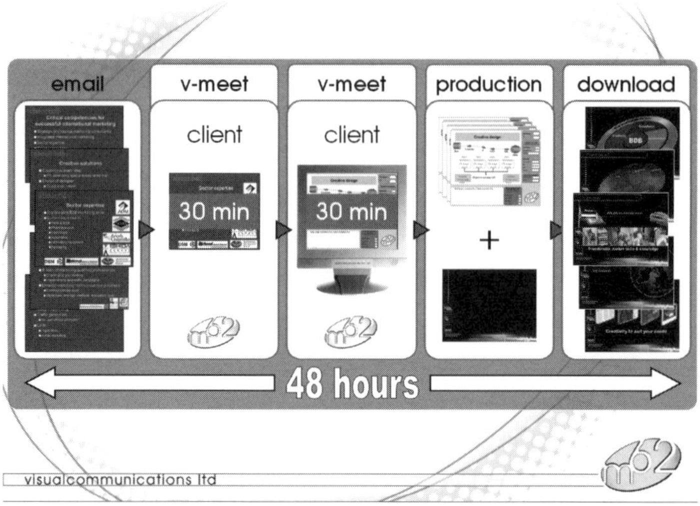

Here the flow chart needs to be built from left to right using four CLICKs (ending with 'download'). The final click adds the box behind the stages and the 48hrs, showing that the whole process of producing a presentation can take less than two working days. To see this presented use this link: www.killerpresentations.com/flowchart.html

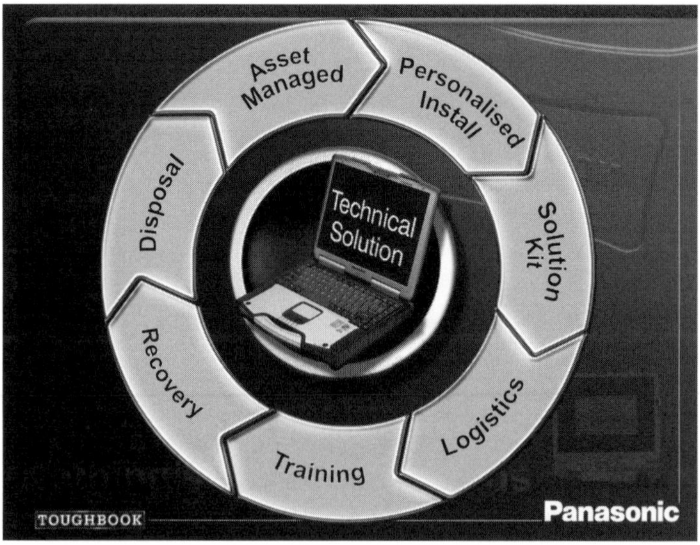

The iterative chart example at bottom left shows a sequence of stages that is ongoing – the process does not end with the final stage, it continues back to the first stage to give a continuous process. In this example, the slide builds from the first step (1 o'clock) clockwise to the last, and the stages are arranged to show the cyclic process.

Graphs

Axes are usually built using any static build, but data is usually *wiped* again in the intuitive direction. So bar graphs are *wiped from bottom*, line graphs *wiped from left*, etc. Comparators are usually *random bars horizontal* – again these are more easily demonstrated online: www.killerpresentations.com/graphs.html

Repeated slides

The first time a slide appears in a presentation it should build, but if it appears again the repeated build will just irritate the audience. We therefore recommend that the whole slide just builds at once (unless the title changes, in which case I prefer to build the title bar, then the title and then build the rest of the slide).

Again this is demonstrated online:
www.killerpresentations.com/repeats.html

Repeated objects

In the same vein, objects that are repeated on adjacent slides and do not move (see later) should not disappear only to reappear immediately after in the same place.

Examples of this can be seen online:
www.killerpresentations.com/repeatedobjects.html

Slide transitions

The observations about custom animation above largely apply to slide transitions as well. Motion transitions (*Push Left*, etc.) are seldom used in a presentation, although www.killerpresentations.com/hds.html shows how

my design team have used this type of slide transition to create a very nice, subtle effect throughout the presentation. The most frequently used motion transition is *Push Left* which is often used to show Microsoft Project™ files. The link below also demonstrates how *Push Down* can be used to show a spreadsheet that is too large for one slide.
www.killerpresentations.com/slidetransitions.html

Objective quality rules

Animation can be the difference between a highly-polished professional presentation and an obviously amateur effort. It is so critical that most of these suggestions form part of m62's objective quality standards (and therefore our disciplinary procedure). The list below captures most of them.

Animation rules

- The second time a slide is used, i.e. repeated, we do not build it as it will annoy the audience.
- If an object appears on one slide it should not disappear and reappear on an adjacent slide; it should stay during the transition.
- No motion animations, only use static transitions (unless you are trying to draw attention).
- Don't distract the audience with the builds.
- Build slides in a logical manner.
- Never present a complete diagram first; build it and then fade and highlight sections (build up, fade down).

Summary

1. The purpose of animation is to help the *audience look at the right thing at the right time.*
2. Animation is about focus and pace.
3. Build logically.
4. Three seconds maximum.
5. Don't distract.
6. Don't re-animate.

Section Five
Delivery

Vision without action is a daydream.
Action without vision is a nightmare.

Japanese proverb

By now we have set the objectives, from this decided on a structure, produced the content and designed and animated the slides. Now for the crucial bit, the piece that brings it all together into a presentation: the presenter.

Killer Idea Role of the presenter

In most presentations the presenter is the centre of attention. They used to be centre stage, the main flow of communication being 80% from presenter and 20% from the visual aids. Along with the shift from '*presentations with visual aids to visual presentations*' comes a shift in the balance of where the audience receives its information: from 80:20 to more like 20:80 (well, this is the aim, in reality it is probably less!).

The reasons that this is desirable have been covered at length elsewhere in the book but the psychology of it is this: we are *visual* beings – sight is our primary sense and we process visual information much faster than language.

Let me give you an example. When my son Matthew was a year old I would ask him if he wanted a banana and get no response. When he was five (if I could get his attention away from 'Bob the Builder' for ten seconds) he would pause, think about it and give me an answer.

The process is slow by comparison to my holding up a banana and asking whether he wants it. Instant response, usually affirmative both now and when he was one year old. Why the difference in response times?

At one year old he had yet to learn that the sound 'banana' was associated with the sweet yellow fruit. When he was five he knew what it meant (he could even read it) but he still had to decode the sound, remember that the word means sweet yellow fruit and then make a decision. He had to process the sound, which psychologists tell us takes longer than the visual processing that goes into seeing the fruit. We have to learn language, and that takes longer than learning what bananas taste like and whether we like them or not!

It is the same now if we are presenting to an audience in a language other than their mother tongue: say 'banana' and maybe get no response. Show a picture, everybody understands.

So if this is what we are going to do, 'show rather than tell', then the role of the presenter has to change from primary source of information (verbal) to providing supporting narrative to the visuals. This is the power of visual presenting, but it requires a complete change of behaviour for the presenter.

Bad habits, like reading the text, are difficult to stop, but ultimately presenting this kind of presentation is significantly easier than trying to make boring dull slides seem interesting and engaging. Most presenters take to it quickly and it becomes addictive.

Language – precision and clarity

Use of language is a broad topic, but some aspects of this are worth a mention here.

- **Jargon:** this is perhaps best described as professional slang, a useful device between people who know each other around an organisation, a company, etc. Yet if words are used out of context it creates problems. There may not only be a lack of understanding, but people are reluctant to ask and check. They will let the word go by and hope to pick up the gist of what is said as the presentation continues; if they do not do so, sense is inevitably diluted to some extent. What is more, it becomes more embarrassing to ask the more time goes by, and thus often less likely to happen.

- **Abbreviation:** much jargon takes the form of abbreviation, and this aspect of it is worth a mention in its own right. So much these days is reduced to initials – acronyms. Of course this is useful, indeed well known ones are said as a word (for example, NATO and CBI), others make a word – as does Language Abbreviation and Initialisation Disorder: LAID, a mnemonic to boot!

In both cases, what is being said must be checked and spelt out, at least to begin with. In business, language often links to the special nature of industries, products, organisations, processes and technology (if there is a more jargon-rife area than information technology, I cannot think of it). In every setting language must be matched to the audience. Do they, all of them, understand the kind of jargon you will instinctively use, or must you modify your language somewhat? The tone adopted must always suit the individual group to which you are speaking.

A final point about language: description is a powerful thing, or rather it can be. It is worth some thought to be sure that what you say does contain the right turn of phrase. Certainly you should avoid any bland language where something more powerful is going to have more impact: it is unlikely that anything you present in a business context should talk about something being *quite good*, or *very practical.* If there is a positive point to make, make it. Conversely, people appreciate it when things they expect to be complicated, are explained easily and quickly. It shows a confidence and expertise that assist credibility. A powerful, perhaps unusual, description is more likely to stick in the memory than something more routine. For instance, no one hearing something smooth described as: *as slick as a freshly buttered ice rink* is going be see it as anything but very, very shiny, or my favourite '*The spaceship hung in the air exactly the way a brick doesn't*'.*

* From *The Hitchhiker's Guide to the Galaxy* by Douglas Adams (Pan).

Audience focus

At any particular moment of a presentation, how do you know where your audience's attention is focused? How can you be sure that everyone is looking at the right diagram, or shifting their focus to the right areas, and at the right moment? Keeping your audience correctly focused is achieved by careful design of visual cues, building slide transitions, and ensuring the visuals do not stay on the screen for longer than necessary. If you get this right, you can hold them in the palm of your hand for as long as is necessary.

Directing audience focus

To the screen

The easiest way to direct attention to the screen is to gesticulate (point to) and at the same time make something happen on the screen – an animation or build. If you also turn and look at the screen yourself (potentially breaking a traditional rule of not talking to the audience with your back to them!) you will compel them to look at the screen.

To the presenter

This is often harder to do. First ensure that there is nothing to distract them on screen. If necessary press 'B' or 'W' to blank the screen (they almost immediately look at you!). Secondly use silence to compel their attention, nothing works better than saying nothing to make the audience stop what they are doing or thinking and look at the presenter expectantly.

Levels of presenting

First, in preparing and delivering, the overriding consideration is the audience. Everything that is done must be audience focused. A presentation cannot consist of your saying it as you see it; rather the presenter's job is to work with an audience to help them understand the message and put things in a way designed – specifically designed in every way – to ensure that the objectives (persuasive or otherwise) are achieved.

To get it right, it helps to bear in mind that there are, in this context, three levels of presenting:

1. **Level One** presenters run in this sequence: CLICK (to bring up the next slide), read (go through what is on it – often verbatim), and explain (add to what is on it – too often leaving the slide there to distract after the relevance of what it presents has passed). Remember that people read *seven times faster than you can read out loud.*

2. **Level Two** presenters are more familiar with their presentation and will begin to explain, CLICK and show a slide, this is much better and from the audience's point of view looks slick.

3. **Level Three** is the integrated approach: using the visualisation and the patter in a cohesive whole. The effect is best described as seamless, and if asked which contributes most – what they see or what they hear – an audience should be hard-pressed to disentangle the different elements. The best example of this is good, well-produced television; my personal favourite example is the BBC's *Newsnight* daily current affairs programme.

If anything needs to be read, rather than reading verbatim it may be better to paraphrase or to reverse the words: as in *aim to get attention or getting attention should be your aim.* Sometimes there are things that must, by their nature, be put over verbatim. One example of this is testimonials in a sales pitch, others might be a definition, quotation or anything where the exact wording matters.

This may not initially be easy to execute (remember the story of the New York visitor asking directions? *How do I get to Carnegie Hall? – Practise!*), but the effort is well worthwhile because this style of presenting does the most powerful job for you and marks you as a real professional. As was said in the first few pages, professionalism in presenting rubs off; because of it, people assume that you must also be expert, experienced, capable and so on.

Don't read the text

Reading text that appears on the screen is counter productive and can distract the audience. The role of the presenter is to add value to visuals, not to clash with them. One technique we find useful is to use different words to say the same thing, for example if on screen the slides reads 'Customer

Service' we would encourage the presenter to say '*We consider the most important aspect of our business to be you, the client, and servicing your needs is a critical skill for us*'. Alternatively you can produce a half-way effect by reversing the order of the words. In the example above we could just say '*Servicing our customers is extremely important to us*'.

Of course the best plan is to have no words on the screen, thus eliminating the temptation to read them in the first place. Be warned this is easy to say but difficult to do; you have to spend a considerable amount of time practising the art of reading!

How to present quotes

Nowhere is it more important to not read the text than when presenting a quote. We recommend that you follow these steps to presenting quotes effectively:

1. Slide builds with heading and client logo.
2. Explain the relevance of the quote.
3. CLICK, turn to the screen and read the quote to yourself silently. (This compels the audience to do the same plus it allows you to estimate the time needed for them to read it. They will be slower than you as this is the first time they have seen the quote.)
4. Turn to the audience and when they make eye-contact (thus signalling that they have completed reading the quote) then build the reference's credibility.

You will find this a powerful way of presenting quotes.

It has often been remarked to me that surely it is OK to occasionally read text in a presentation in order to emphasise a point. Again, I feel that whilst this is right, it is the exception to the rule. I would prefer to present a quote like this:

Here you can see that we have picked out four words in red, the audience will be tempted to read just those four: 'didn't read bullets, brilliant!' and get the essence of the quote. I would nevertheless still present this quote as we outlined above, talking about who Celia is and what she does for a living (makes sure PowerPoint works in every language). If you want to see and hear me do this visit: www.killerpresentations.com/quote.html

Tips for presenting

Finally in this section some general tips for your presentations:

- If you are using media, cue it, i.e. make sure it is rewound. We tend to put video and animations into PowerPoint as .wmv files, if we are running a large piece of video we will put the file onto DVD format and use a player.
- Round figures off in patter, e.g. 76.4% is '*about three quarters*'.
- If you forget what you were going to say, CLICK and move on – they won't notice.
- If the slide makes perfect sense without explanation it won't engage the audience so build it, change it or delete it.
- Know what is going to happen when you CLICK.
- Pause for effect.

- Don't apologise.
- Never criticise your own presentation or the slides.
- In patter use a different frame of reference e.g. £1.2m per annum says '£100k each and every month'.
- Never contradict a figure.

Summary

1. Add value, don't read text.
2. Don't clash with animation.
3. Allow time to read the text – silence is OK.
4. Know your slides and the animations.
5. Explain what the audience are seeing.
6. Practise.
7. Practise.
8. Practise.

Final details

Success is the sum of details.

Harvey S Firestone (1868–1938)

The purpose of a business presentation is to convey information to a group of people in order to educate or persuade. Everything we have talked about, (getting the message right, visualising it, designing it, rehearsing it) means nothing if we don't actually get to deliver it. Over the last 15 years as a professional presenter I have experienced every possible hiccup. I have turned up at the wrong venue, at the wrong time; I have had equipment fail or not show up, laptops crash in the middle of a presentation, projectors die half way through; you name it, it has happened to me. Most of these were not my fault. None of them prevented the presentation from going ahead (except the lack of an audience, which did throw me off my stride a little). Why? Because you learn very quickly as a presenter, or presentation organiser, to have a backup plan.

Most of our presentations get used face-to-face, either one-to-one with a laptop or one-to-many with a projector. However, we are producing more and more presentations for delivery over the web. Let us treat these separately for the moment.

Presenting face-to-face

By now you know your message and have a coherent presentation with the patter worked out and practised. Now comes the bit that makes a difference: bringing it together for a performance. Ultimately, that is what this is, a performance, equivalent to being on stage front and centre. That's why it is anxiety-provoking (anybody who tells you otherwise is either lying or dead). Everybody gets nervous before a presentation; the trick is to turn those nerves into enthusiasm to fuel the performance.

One-on-one

When presenting to small groups or individuals you can usually get away with using a single laptop screen. With audiences of over four it is difficult to work on a small screen and some kind of additional large screen is needed (projector, plasma, etc.) Here are some hard-earned tips for these situations.

1. Connect the laptop first, turn on the monitor and then boot up the PC, this way the PC will see the external monitor and enable it. If this doesn't work you may need to 'toggle' the screen with one of the function keys (my laptop is function F5, but they are all different).
2. Make sure that the resolution you are driving from the PC is compatible with the projection device. It is best to feed the projector its highest native resolution, which is not the highest resolution it will detect and display; but the highest resolution that it will not resize. This gives a much clearer image.
3. Have a backup. We use PowerPoint *Package for CD* to put a backup (including the PowerPoint 2003 Viewer™) on to a USB memory stick. The attraction of this as a backup is that all we need is a PC – it does not need to have the right version of PowerPoint – and a fast USB 2.0 port will allow us to run most presentations direct from the storage device.

Large meetings

1. Have a backup PC. While it is acceptable to ask one person to wait for three minutes while a PC reboots, 100 people look like a mob.
2. Test the equipment prior to the presentation (especially if you have an AV technician available).
3. Use a remote mouse if possible.
4. Make sure that people at the back can hear you (sound check) and see the screen (the bottom is usually the hardest if there are people in front of them).
5. Be strictly under time, especially at conferences. Nothing irritates people more than a presenter exceeding his or her allotted time. If they are behind and you get them back on time, they will be grateful.

6. If you have to give your presentation to a technician to run on a PC that is not your own, make sure they have the correct version of PowerPoint and that it has the latest patches and security updates, otherwise it may not look or behave as you expect.
7. Breathe.

Handouts

On the whole, we don't recommend the use of handouts; controversial, I know. It has become a collective habit to print the slides three or six to a page and give it to the audience, sometimes ahead of time. I have several objections:

1. I want their attention on me or the screen and I want to be able to manipulate that attention as best I can. This is difficult if they are reading something else.
2. I want to control the pace and flow of information – again this is difficult if they can read ahead.
3. In a sales presentation the message is the most important information I have. If I print it I lose control of it, and that strikes me as counter-productive (if the CEO wants to see the presentation *I* want to deliver it, not let somebody who works for him/her present it). It is also a safe bet that as soon as you put it on paper it ends up with the competition.
4. The definition of a good PowerPoint slide is that it should not make sense to the audience until it is explained by the presenter. The printed slides probably do not make sense, so why hand them out and leave them open to interpretation?
5. We use four dimensions to present, by giving them 2D you lose information as well as impact.

Evaluation

When we help clients make pitch presentations we are successful more than 85% of the time. The downside of this is that winning doesn't help us improve as we generally always win. Sales people who are always fixated on closing the order (at least the successful ones are) tend to relax when they have the order, believing everything went OK because they won.

I think it is important to attempt to find out what we could have done better and so we always ask for a debrief after a presentation and ask what they thought went well and what could have been done better. It is the only way to improve.

Summary

1. Have a backup plan.
2. No handouts.
3. Have a debrief.

Memorable presentations

I'm always fascinated by the way memory diffuses fact.

Diane Sawyer

How good is your memory?

Most people think that their memory is pretty good but that's primarily because they struggle to remember the things they have forgotten, they therefore have little or no idea how much they have forgotten. Depressingly most of us can not even remember how much we remember. Clearly we forget more than we remember and clearly, as a presenter, it is safe to assume that the audience will do likewise.

As we have discussed earlier people forget much of what they are presented with. Since you can not forget what you don't know, the first trick with presenting is to gain, and hold, the audience's attention. This is where *Visual Cognitive Dissonance*™ comes.

The purpose of a presentation is surely to get the audience to remember the content. Presentations are about delivering information, usually to modify behaviour either to persuade the audience to our point of view (i.e. sell them something) or to educate them (which is less about persuasion and more about imparting knowledge). Either way we need audiences to remember the content. Presenters should care about memory in particularly how do we get the audience to pay attention to our content? and then how do we encourage them to remember the key messages? To do this we need to understand how 'Working Memory' which is essentially the bit of your brain that governs what you are paying attention to, works and how it interacts with 'Long Term Memory'.

The research

Let me start this chapter by saying I am not an academic and have absolutely no wish to pretend otherwise, my interest is in the practical application of memory research in a presentation. So while I have included some references to the research that I am aware of, clearly it needs to be read within this context: I am a presenter looking for ways of enhancing communication and not a psychology student looking to pass a mid-term assessment.

That said, memory research began with a German Psychologist called EBBINGHAUS over a hundred years ago. What is clear now is that memory is a complex thing and we do not have a simple model for it. Ebbinghaus invented a series of non-sense symbols and used it to test his recall ability, he was the first to show that memory (or to be precise the ability to recall memories) decays over time. In the late 19th century a man called JAMES (1890) was the first to suggest that there are different types of memory, one for immediate things like the last sentence you just read, and one for older memories, such as what you had for breakfast 3 years ago today or maybe just the best meal you have ever had!

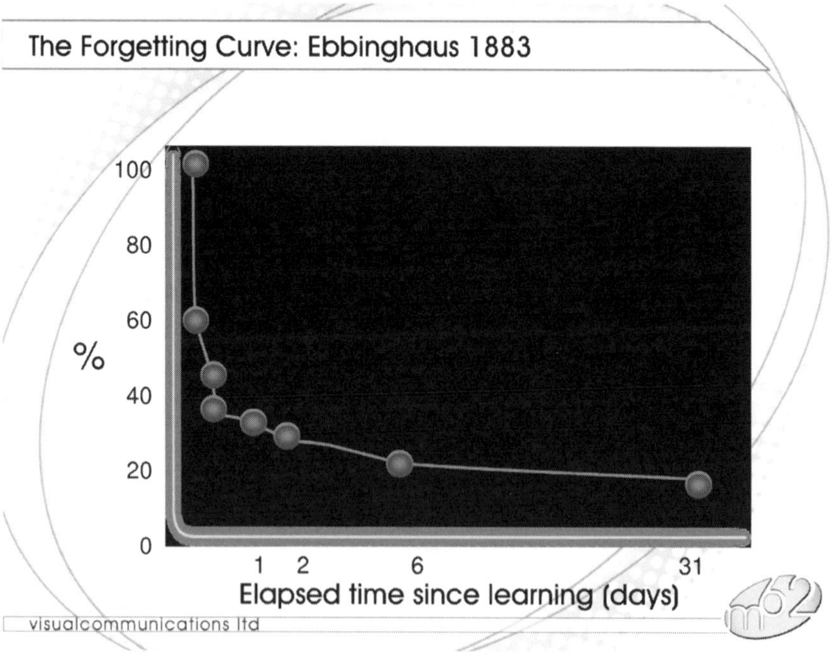

Killer Presentations Implication: Audiences will remember more today than tomorrow, more tomorrow than next week, etc. as presenters we need to be aware of this, don't assume that just because you presented information before, it will be instantly familiar to the audience.

JAMES called these '***Short Term Memory***' and '***Long Term Memory***' and suggested that they had different categoristics. More recent theories propose a multitude of different types of memory, '***Working Memory***' and '***Long Term Memory***' being the categories but each dividing further (Badderly 1986). I will discuss Working Memory later since it impacts presentations more directly but Long Term Memory divides in to Sensory Memory, Procedural Memory and Declarative Memory; which in turn can be divided into Episodic and Semantic.

We know from research done by MILLER (1956) that Working Memory is finite and probably a relatively small 7, plus or minus 2 items (see the section below on "chunking"). However, Long Term Memory appears to be infinite or at least very large and it is into this store that we as presenters need to transfer information since it is here that it will affect behaviour. It seems probable that your Working Memory is the principal gate keeper to your Long Term Memory and so an understanding about how this may work will help us comprehend how we should present information if we indeed want it to be remembered or recalled by the audience at some point in the future. Before we leave Long Term Memory its worth noting that it has been shown that Long Term Memory is less than exact and then people have a tendency to remember things in a way that makes sense to them but doesn't actually reflect what happened, a point worth remembering!

If Miller was correct and Working Memory is 7 +/– 2 the moment you present a slide with more than seven facts on it you loose control over which of these the audience will recall. By limiting the information to no more than 5 facts on a slide you increase the chance of recall. The same goes for the complete presentation, more than 5 arguments or ideas in the presentation and you are increasing the amount they will forget and decreasing your effectiveness.

Killer Presentations Implication: Five (or less) pieces of information on a slide, five chunks of information in a presentation (or less). The more information you present, the less in percentage terms they will recall.

Working Memory

There are four distinct functions in the Working Memory: Articulatory Loop, Primary Acoustic Store, Visio-spatial Scratch pad and the one that pulls them together, the Central Executive (BADDELEY 1981) As you can tell from the names, even without the descriptions, half of these are to do with processing sounds; which is part of the reason bullet points are so ineffective in presentations.

Articulatory Loop

The *Inner Voice*, your ability to talk to yourself and rehearse what you will say.

Primary Acoustic Store

The *Inner Ear*, listen to sounds or acoustic information.

Visio-spatial Scratch pad

The *Inner Eye*, the ability to mentally picture an image, a cube for example.

Central Executive

The *Attention System*, the bit that accesses the Long Term Memory and decides what to pay attention to.

Why isn't text effective in a presentation?

When presented with text on screen the audience is compelled to read it, this usually involves saying the words with their Inner Voice (Articulatory Loop) which makes it difficult to listen to if the presenter is talking

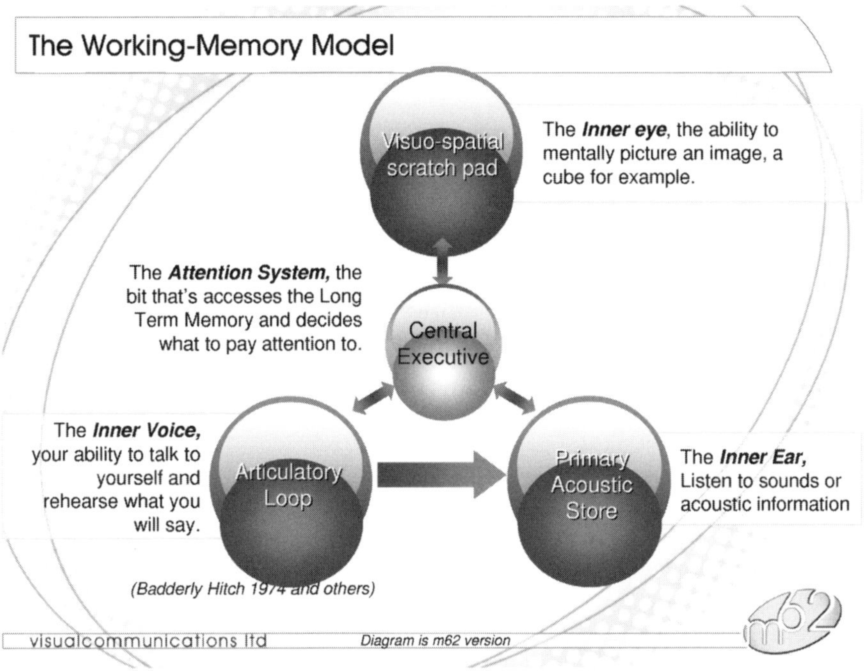

(Primary Acoustic Store). Therefore, the brain (Central Executive) chooses to ignore the presenter until it has deciphered the text, then provided the information hasn't distracted it onto a line of thought (Articulatory Loop) it may pay attention to the presenter. The bottom line is that if there is no or little text, the brain finds it a lot easier to listen to the presenter.

Killer Presentations Implication: The less text you have on the screen the better, since the Visual Assimilation rate is faster allowing cognitive load to be diverted to paying attention to the presenter.

How does *Visual Cognitive Dissonance*™ impact Working Memory?

If the audience sees an incomplete image, this image is held in the Visio-spatial scratch pad (inner eye) the Central Executive then attempts to make sense of it by accessing Long Term Memory to see if it has seen something similar. If it can't find this it has to switch attention to the Primary Acoustic Store and see if there is an explanation from the presenter, thus compelling engagement.

There is a well known system call the RAS that activates when we see or hear something incomplete; it is the bit in our Working Memory that wants to complete patterns. I suspect the reason Sudoku is having such a revival at the moment, is because we love filling in missing numbers and making things complete. If we can not complete things the drive to do so is fairly strong ***Visual Cognitive Dissonance***™ uses this to encourage the audience to pay attention to the presentation.

Killer Presentations Implication: Images that do not make sense encourage active audience engagement.

Mnemonic processes

Active Processes

Suppose I ask you to remember the following number 4476262458404, what would you do to remember it? Both of my boys can recite my mobile phone number, my daughter (18 months) can remember the first 6 digits. They can do this because I set out to teach them the numbers in case of emergencies. I used several well established techniques, Chunking, Rehearsal, Visualisation, Narrative Association and Acoustic Association to get the children to remember it. Almost certainly you know all of these tricks, you use them every day, you were probably taught them by your parents and you will teach them to your children, possibly without even being aware of what you are doing.

As an experiment write out your mobile telephone number on a piece of paper for me and then look at what you have written, 90% of you will have just demonstrated Chunking without realising it. Look carefully at the number, did it look like this: 4476262458404 or did you do what most people do, which is this:

4476 2624 584 04?

Note the gaps. When you are on the phone ask somebody to give you their number, they will split it up for you with each section less than 5 numbers. We do it instinctively, some people will say that it is so the other person can write it down but if that was the issue we would put a space (or pause) between each number. It is actually a reflection of how we remember the number, if you like, how we encoded it into our Long Term Memory. Miller called this Chunking and believed that a normal person could hold 5-7 chunks of information in their Working Memory.

This process is an example of what we call an Active Mnemonic Process, active because it is employed once an individual decides to remember something. If we mimic these processes in our presentations, for example breaking the presentation up into 5 logical chunks, we refer to this as a Passive Mnemonic Process™.

Here is a brief description of some of the more prominent Passive Processes that we embed into presentations and how we can use them to improve the amount of information audiences recall.

Passive Mnemonic Processes™

Chunking

As I described above, this is the process of structuring the information into meaningful logical chunks and then presenting it in sections, we segue these sections with a Graphic that acts as a visual clue to where in the presentation they are. We have shown countless times that by splitting the presentation up into sections, we both increase the amount of information recall and significantly we can impact which information is recalled.

Killer Presentations Implication: Break your argument down into understandable bite sizes, if this ends up being more than five then look for ones that could collapse for example: 'Lower costs' and 'More revenue' could be collapsed into "Increased Profit"

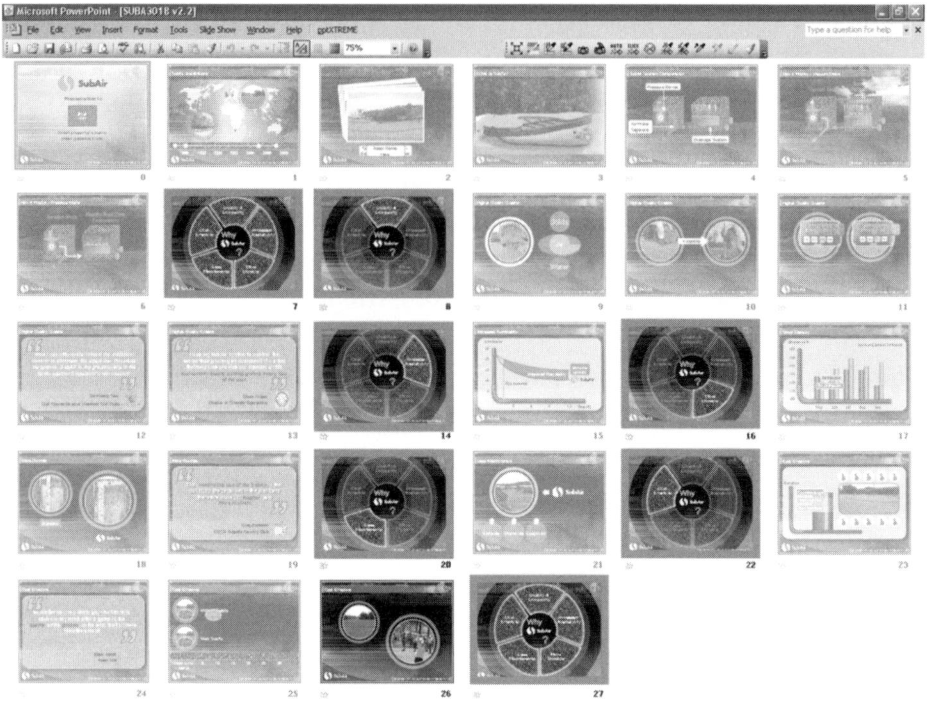

Rehearsal

Rehearsal or repetition is a primary mnemonic process but it can be used in two ways; simple rehearsal is where we take the key messages and repeat them throughout the presentation (for example a value proposition wheel is shown at least 7 times in one of our sales presentations). However, CRAIK & WATKINS (1973) demonstrated that simple rehearsal or "Rote" is less effective than "Elaborative rehearsal" which is what we encourage presenters to do when presenting the value proposition wheel, connect the 5 issues with a story or a Narrative (sometimes called Narrative Story Method Bower & Clark 1969).

When I am teaching I use a simple exercise to illustrate how repetition can impact recall. I read out 5 numbers and then give the audience 5 seconds during which time I ask them to repeat the numbers in their head (using their Inner Voice) and then write them down, predictably there is an average of 80% recall. We then repeat the exercise but this time we disrupt the mnemonic processing by not allowing the repetition and forcing them to count out loud from 10 down to 0 and then write down as much as they can recall, this time we get 20% recall. This exercise is called the BROWN-PETERSON technique and was researched in 1959.

Killer Presentations Implication: For presenters the useful observations from this is that if you do not allow pauses (5–6 seconds) for the audience to think about the information you have presented, they do not have time to mnemonically process the information and therefore will have low recall. However, if we do pause and allow, indeed even encourage the audience to actively process the information, then we can achieve extremely high levels of recall.

Elaborate rehearsal

This is essentially the key to 4 Dimensional Presenting, taking the visual information and creating an elaborate semantic repetition of it in the patter. That's not simply repeating the text on the slide but adding to it. We encourage paraphrasing as well as elaboration and so for example if the slide has the words "***More Memorable***" on it, we would actually say

> *"You need your presentations to be remembered by the audience after the presentation"*

Thus elaborating without using the same words.

Killer Presentations Implication: Don't read the text on the screen use different words to describe the same thing, this will increase the audiences recall as well as preventing the disengagement caused when somebody starts to read something that is written in front of them.

Relevance

This is important for two reasons, firstly it encourages engagement, since people will pay attention to information they know or think will be of direct use to them and secondly, people tend to remember facts more easily if they are related to something that they already know (association to Prior knowledge). Clearly this is part of getting the message right but it is also about demonstrating how the information is useful and reminding the audience of why it will be useful (since they are likely to forget unless you re-expose them to this fact).

While this impacts the decision to include information in the content of the presentation it also impacts the narrative, since the presenter needs to help the audiences build connections to things they already know. The best example of this is during a sales presentation, where we encourage sales people to use the value proposition as a questioning aid before the presentation is delivered to find facts about the prospect that can be worked into the patter of the presentation to help prove relevance.

In the example above "*More Memorable*" patter would become:

> *"You need your presentations to be remembered by the audience after the presentation, because as you agreed, earlier audiences do not make a purchasing decision during the presentation but afterwards. Meaning they are basing their decisions on what they remember of your presentation and not what was actually in it!"*

Killer Presentations Implication: Strive for relevant content but also explain to the audience specifically how and why this information is relevant to them.

For example, if I know I am going to talk about improving the prospects of customer service with a product, before I pitch I would ask how their current levels of service were perceived, if during the response they make reference to an annual survey, then during the actual presentation I might work this into the patter like this: "*As you where saying earlier, if we provided this product it would impact the perception of your customer service and alter the results in next years survey*" thus referring to something they already know. Incidentally this is making use of another mnemonic technique called priming.

Visualisation

If you have delved into the rest of the book it will be apparent that this is the corner stone of our business, taking ideas and turning them into visual interpretations by combining these with the narrative, we produce a very powerful mnemonic.

A psychologist call BOWER showed over 30 years ago (1972) that by asking audiences to formulate mental images along with lists of words, recall could nearly be doubled showing 80% recall vs. 45% without these instructions. Clearly by showing the linked images you turn an active technique into a passive one, we believe you can easily show 70% recall on visualised slides vs. 15% on bullet points.

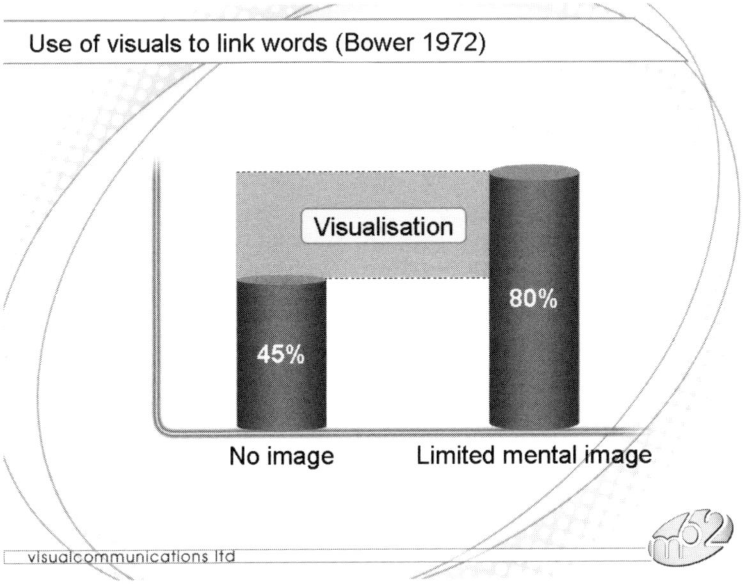

Part of the impact of this technique may be because we are encouraging something. Mayer (2002) calls dual encoding, that is to say the brain processes visual and auditory information in different ways, by encoding information simultaneously visually and aurally, Mayer has shown the material can be better recalled.

Killer Presentations Implication: Visual messages work better than oral ones, visual messages with oral explanation works better than either. However, a visual message is not just a photograph pasted into your slide, the image has to convey a specific message otherwise it is just Clip Art.

Primacy – Recency

MURDOCK (1962), using a similar technique to the number recalling exercise I explained before, managed to show that audiences are more likely to recall the first and last items in a list, this is probably because the audience have an opportunity to rehearse the first, as it is the first and the last is followed by silence which allows rehearsal of this item, the others do not have the time to be rehearsed because the various sections of the Working Memory are busy.

Killer Presentations Implication: We use this to select the order of our value propositions putting the most powerful first and the second most powerful last. That is unless there is a better story (Narrative Association) if the presentation order is different, in which case we assume that the story will override the effects of Recency.

Narrative Association

Properly called Narrative Story Method and researched in 1969 by BOWER & CLARK their original experiments involved telling a story to link words together, this showed a clear increase in recall. We use this to link ideas, such as arguments to buy, into a story that help the audience recall the benefits. For example, if the benefits of our system were, Productivity, Rapid Turnaround Time, Quality results, Constancy and Patient Care we might suggest that the salesperson uses patter like this:

> *"Our clients have told us that the use of our medical diagnostics equipment impacts their facility in five key areas, they are all struggling with staff*

shortages (Productivity) and at the same time need to provide their Doctors with test results quicker and quicker (Rapid TAT). These results need to be accurate (Quality results) to prevent retesting and miss-diagnosis and follow-up tests need to be consistent (Consistency) if they are to have an impact on Clinical outcomes (Patient Care)"

But if they have the soft skills to cope then this will work better:

"Imagine it from the patients point of view, once the Doctor has drawn the blood for the tests the patient doesn't want to be told he has to wait because the laboratory is short staffed (Productivity), he wants the results as quickly as possible to remove the anxiety of uncertainty (Rapid TAT) while he is still in the ER. The last thing he wants to hear is a miss-diagnosis because of poor quality (Quality) and if this is his second visit he will want to know that the test is the same and not different because it's a different technician running it (Consistency) and finally he wants the best clinical outcomes possible (Patient Care) wouldn't you?"

The story of a patient turning up to the Emergency Room having to wait for test results that turn out to be inaccurate and not comparable to those on his record; leading to the wrong diagnosis and treatment, will help the audience recall the five benefits. If you don't believe me try it, put the book down and relive the story writing benefits as you go, you will find you can easily recall 5 out of 5. Getting salespeople to do this is another story!

Acoustic Association

Honestly I can't recall using this in a presentation, but this is how my 18 month old daughter is learning my mobile phone number, we are singing it to her as a nursery rhyme! On the whole it's probably better left for remembering social things rather than business facts but it is a fundamental trick in marketing slogans, Cantor, Rhyme and Rhythm will help slogans or strap lines become memorable, here is one of ours:

Effective Communication not just *Impressive Presentation*!

The rhyming couplet works even if you read it (your inner voice again!)

Structured information

TULVING (1968) showed that in the absence of structure to information (he called it organisation) the audience creates their own. He called one structure *Subjective Organisation* and the other *Experimenter Organisation* (to represent the fact that the experiment designer imposed organisation on the data). BOWER, BLACK & TURNER (1969) showed that by providing structure to the information, recall could be trebled. This is presumably because if the Audience does not have to create Subjective Organisation they free up Cognitive Load to mnemonically process the information.

Killer Presentations Implication: Give your presentations a **Visual Structure** by making the structure of the information visual we make it apparent to the audience, even if we do not make this explicit in the patter we help the audience make sense of the information, thus increasing the amount it can be recalled.

The importance of structure can not be understated, but there are many ways of structuring information and a linear sequence is not always the most appropriate, despite the fact that the information must be presented in a linear fashion (Chronologically) we can still represent the information non-linearly visually.

This has a massive impact on the presentation, during the messaging phase of a presentation development we are looking to structure the arguments and therefore the information but also during the visualisation stage we are looking to make this structure apparent to the audience.

Types of information (presentation) structure

Linear

This is the most common presentation structure, simply because unless you have a very small group, or you are an extraordinary presenter, presentations are by nature a linear flow of information. This is why the output from our consulting service is a word document we call a *Linear*

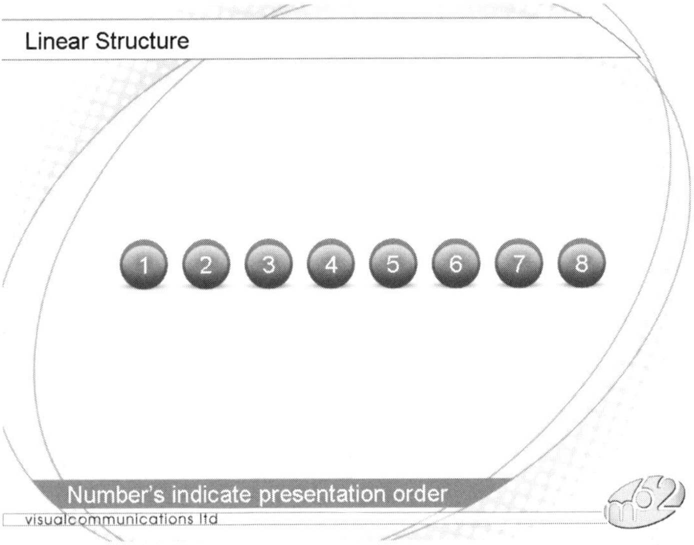

Information Flow, it is essentially an ordered list of information we feel needs to be presented and the sequence it should cover. However, as we have demonstrated earlier a list has little or no mnemonic properties and is not a good basis for visual structure.

Visualising this and using it as Visual Structure helps the audience know where they are in the presentation, we occasionally show a diagram such as this full screen, highlight the section we are about to talk about and then have the graphic shrink and move to one of the corners of the screen to act as a visual key for the information.

Hierarchy

COLLINS & QUILLAN (1969) demonstrated that presenting information in the form of a hierarchy can improve recall. The critical issue is actually making the audience aware of this order. The diagram (overleaf) shows the visual interpretation of the structure and the ideal presentation order.

Matrix

A matrix structure can be extremely useful, again as with the hierarchy the issue is making this structure apparent to the audience and then walking through the material in a logical sequence.

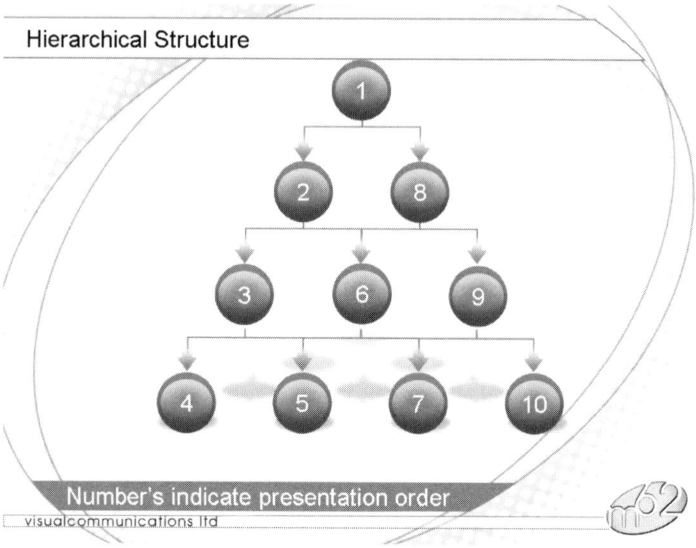

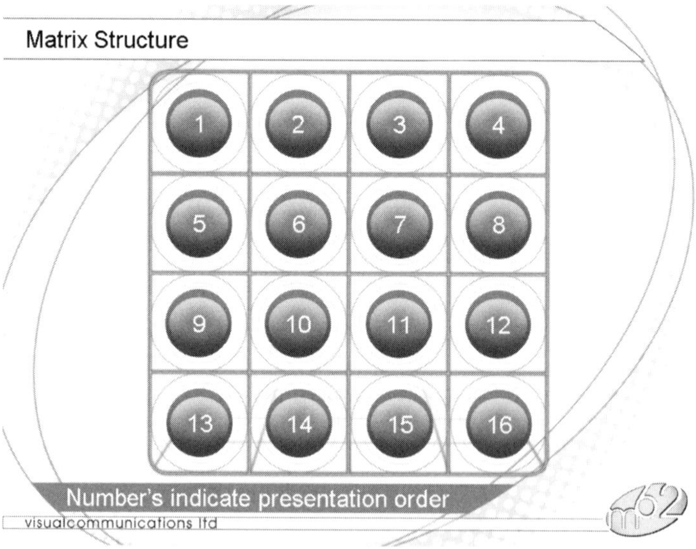

Spreading-activation models

COLLINS & LOFTUS (1975) which to most of us would be called a mind map. The interconnection of ideas is important but so to is the relative position of the information. The real mnemonic benefit to using this layout comes if the audience see the building of the diagram.

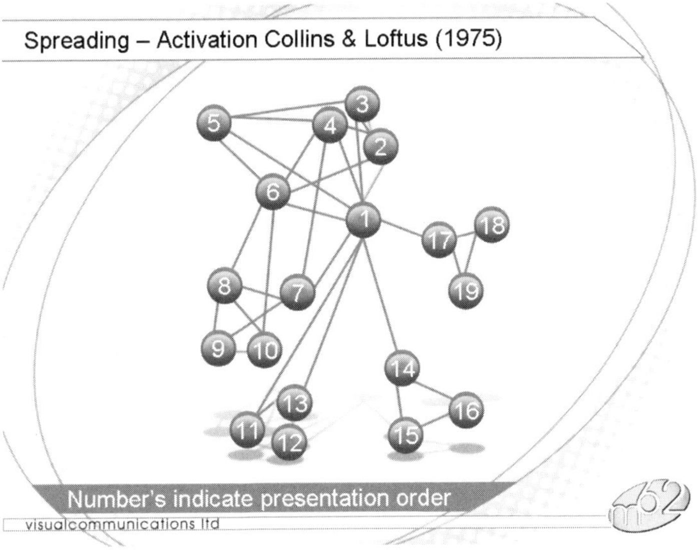

Radial

This is the one we use most (see the Value Proposition section earlier), five spokes giving five sections.

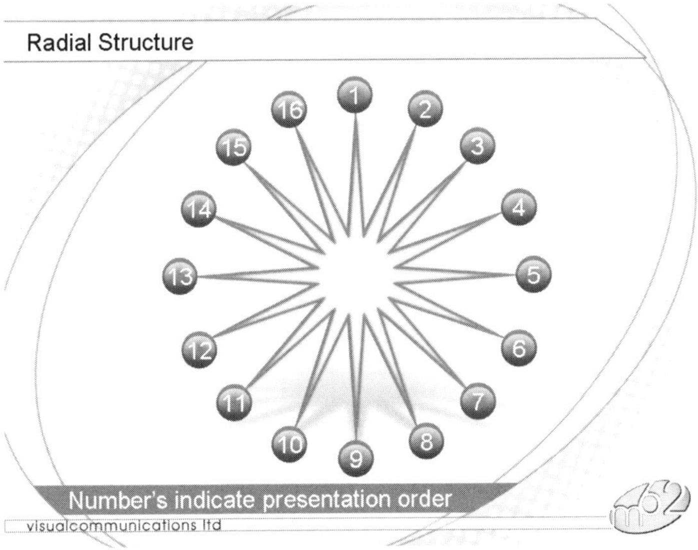

Summary

Just to be clear, I am not suggesting that these are slide layout's but presentation structures, all of them structure the information and this demonstrably helps audiences recall. Our innovation is to make the structure apparent and visual; we call this Visual Structure. The beauty of this is it helps re-enforce the message.

Value Proposition Mnemonics

The most basic Passive Mnemonic Technique we use is the repetition of the value proposition. Our Value Propositions all have 5 elements to them (Mnemonic 1) our own is More impressive, more memorable, more engaging, easy and takes 48 hours. We build the slide the first time building a narrative association to the five points (Mnemonic 2). They are displayed as a graphic producing a visualisation of the Value Proposition (Mnemonic 3) and then repeated up to 7 times as it is used to segue the presentation (Mnemonic 4). During each section we are striving to show relevance (Mnemonic 5).

All in all we work very hard to increase the chances of the audience (prospect) recalling the five reasons for buying from us rather than the competitor and it works.

Summary: Effective Mnemonics

1. Make sure the content is relevant.
2. Limit the content to a manageable amount (i.e. not 125 facts delivered in 12.5 mins).
3. Chunk the content into five sections (More than 3, less than 7).
4. Select an appropriate structure for the information.
5. Make this structure apparent to the audience, ideally visual.
6. Use a visual or graphic slide as a presentation segue.
7. Visualisation the information to use Visual Cognitive Dissonance™ to encourage Attention.

8. Visualise slides for 4D presentations, i.e. they only make sense when presented.
9. Limit the information shown at anyone time to 5 facts.
10. Develop narrative to explain the relevance to the audience of the information included.
11. The more elaborate the Rehearsal, the more likely they are to recall.
12. The presenter's role should be to explain the visuals to the audience.
13. Pause for 5–6 seconds to allow the audience time to mnemonically process the information.
14. Avoid excessive eye contact as well as too little. Make it appropriate.
15. Where possible use rhetorical questions, since this helps force Mnemonic processing.

Of course this is a list and lists are difficult to remember so here is a chunked version:

Content
- Relevant
- Manageable
- Chunked

Structure
- Appropriate
- Apparent
- Visual

Visualisation
- Visual Cognitive Dissonance
- 4D presentations
- 5 facts per slide max

Narrative
- Explain relevance
- Elaborate Rehearsal
- Explain visuals

Passive Mnemonic Processes
- Pause to allow processing
- Appropriate eye contact
- Rhetorical Questions

And if I really want you to remember them I would give you a visual:

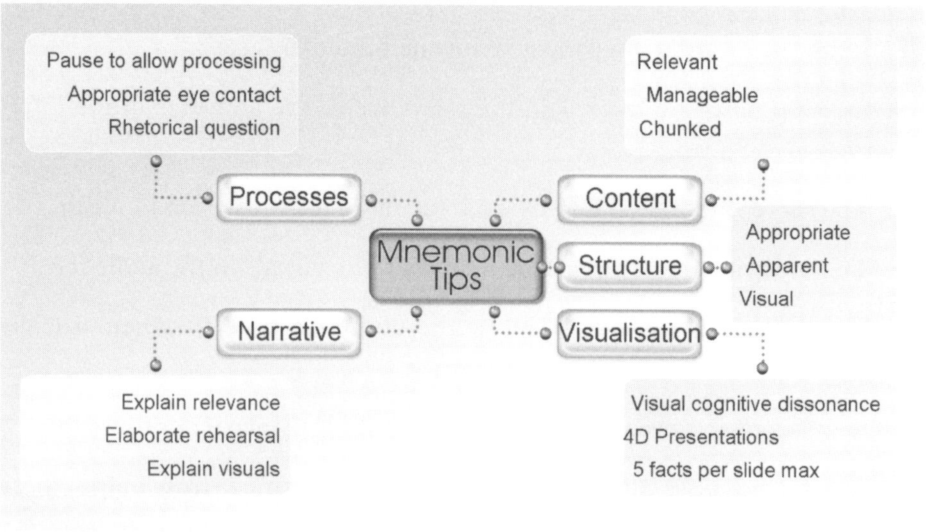

Or better may be:

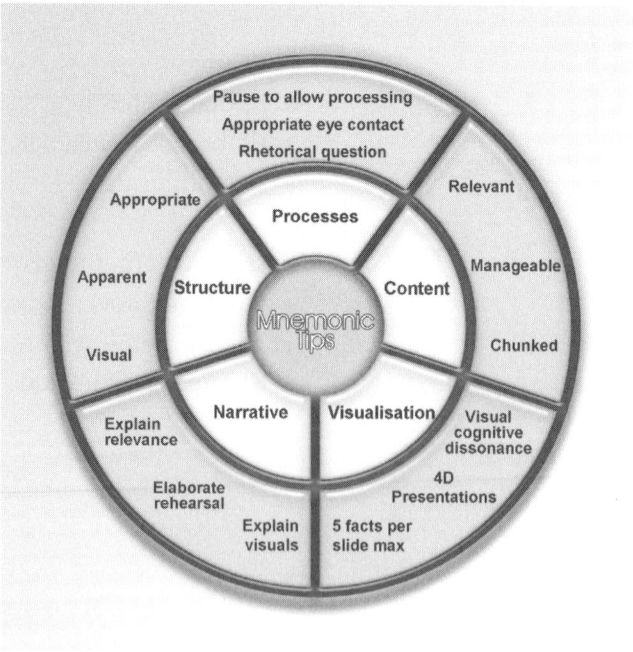

Now try and recall the 15 points!

Memorable Presentations: Conclusions

Memory is important for presenters to understand as it impacts the whole process from message development through visualisation, design and ultimately delivery. Everything we do at m62 is built on the assumption that the purpose of the presentation is better achieved if the audience are paying attention and can remember more than 10% of the content. Which on the whole seems like a fair assumption.

References

Baddeley, AD. (1981) *The concept of working memory.* Cognition, 10, 17–23.

Baddeley, AD. (1986) *Working memory.* Oxford University Press.

Bower, G.H., Clark, M.C (1969) *Narrative stories as mediators for serial learning.* Psychonomic Science, 14, 181–182.

Bower, G.H., Black, J.B & Turner (1979) *Scripts in memory for text.* Cognitive Psychology, 11, 177–220

Collins, A.M & Loftus, E.F (1975) *A spreading-activation theory of semantic processing.* Psychological Review, 82, 407–428.

Collins, A.M & Quillian, M.R (1969) *Retrieval time for semantic memory.* Journal of Verbal Learning and Verbal Behaviour, 8 240–247.

Craik, F.I.M & Watkins, M.J. (1973) The role of rehearsal in short-term memory. Journal of Verbal Learning and Verbal Behaviour, 12, 599–607.

Ebbinghaus, H (1885) *On memory.* Leizig: Duncker.

James, W (1890) *The Principles of Psychology.* New York: Henry Holt & Company.

Murdock, B.B (1962) *The serial position effect in free recall.* Journal of Experimental Psychology, 64, 482–488.

Tulving, E (1968) *Theoretical issues in free recall.* In T.R. Dixon & D.L. Horton (Eds) Verbal Behaviour and General Behaviour Theory. Englewood Cliffs, NJ: Prentice-Hall.

Conclusions – why rules?

Presentations are complex. Many things are happening at once and the details act cumulatively. You may get away with one thing being done inappropriately, but any more than one and the totality of the presentation will suffer. Conversely, get details right and each one adds strength to what you do. As was said earlier, presentation is, in part, an art: the soft skills matter and a speaker with flair can add something to a presentation at any level.

But presenting is also a science.

There are elements about it, or more particularly about how people find information easiest to take on board, that are well-proven. Use these factors and your presentation will be more powerful than if you do not. The rules we use are designed to make sure that we maximise the power of all these factual areas. They may be apparently simple things like never using a smaller typeface than will be visible. Or they may be more complex, influencing the whole way a message is put over. Having these as a mandatory routine and checklist prevents us forgetting the factors that make a difference – they act to instil good habits and make us see PowerPoint for what it is, not a simple list-maker, but rather an overall communications tool.

The rules define our approach and make us put our presentational messages and ideas into pictures; then we explain the pictures and, by so doing, add appropriate patter.

At m62 we produce many presentations for ourselves and for our clients every week. Doing it this way now comes naturally, because we have taken the time to learn it. So can you.

Summary

Killer Idea **Effective communication not just impressive presentations**

If what an audience is talking about after the presentation is the graphics you have lost, it is the presentation you have lost; if they talk about the content and discuss the argument rather than the medium, then you are on the way to a positive decision.

The definition of a good presentation is one that gets the message across: nothing else matters.

So whilst it may be desirable to impress the audience, communication is the purpose of the task so 'effective communication not just impressive presentations' is rightly one of our killer ideas.

FAQs

1. **If my slides don't make sense, what do I leave my customer with?**

   Response: I would rather leave nothing behind; certainly not my carefully-prepared value proposition, but I won't repeat the arguments for this. If you must then Click on *File > Send to> Word*, this will automatically send each slide of your presentation into a document along with the speaker notes – at least this will then make sense to a reader.

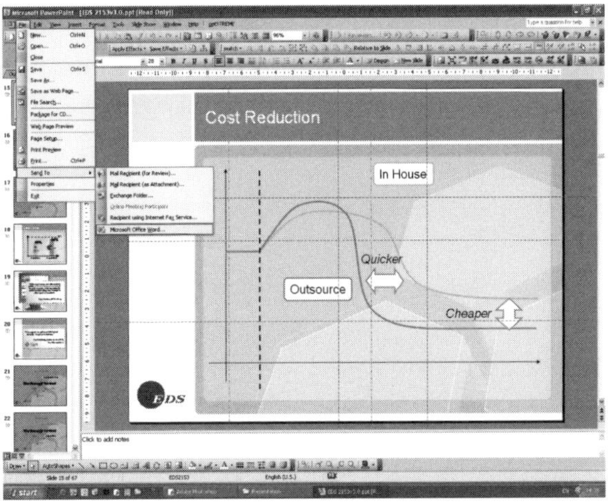

2. **Sometimes we cannot use a screen and we need to print the presentation and present using the slides on paper.**

   Response: again, I would reschedule for a time when we could use an audio/visual presentation. Remember that the audience will remember three to four times more information if you present using our techniques – worth the wait I think. However if you must use paper then you will have to eliminate all of the 4D information in the presentation.

3. **I want to send the presentation in advance.**

   Response: don't if possible, try using the explanation that the slides follow m62 guidelines and don't make sense until they are explained. We have never known anybody to insist after this.

4. **My audience does not have great English; they want the slides to be self-explanatory as it helps them follow the presentation.**

   Response: my experience is that the less text there is the better as there is less to translate. Pictures are universal. This is perhaps the only time I would use handouts but I would get them translated into the local language. Frequently we will run dual screens and have two identical looking slides, one in one language and one in another. While this is time-consuming (and therefore expensive) it is the best solution.

5. **How many slides do I need for a 20 minute presentation?**

   Response: this is old-style thinking. I can show you a single-slide presentation that lasts 20 minutes and a 45-slide presentation that also lasts 20 minutes. The important thing is that they last 20 minutes and not 55!

Afterword

If in the last few years you haven't discarded a major opinion or acquired a new one, check your pulse. You may be dead.

Gelett Burgess

The view expressed above confirms the point made here that any presentation must focus on the customer and meet their objectives, and that to do so with sufficient power in today's dynamic and competitive markets, may need a shift of approach. No amount of bluster will persuade, however much it may be dressed up. The approach advocated here is certainly 'dressed up' compared with a routine bullet-point-led style of presentation, but that is not the point. It looks different, better, yes; but it only works if it is well-directed and well-focused and if the question, *Why is this presentation being made?* can be answered clearly in terms of a specific customer-focused objective.

It will be clear at this point that objectives are key. On any presentations that m62 make, practising what we preach is only sensible; in fact we regard having a clear objective with almost religious fervour. It is just the same when we are advising clients: but what about the message here? What objectives have we had in mind for this book?

At its simplest this can be stated as follows: this book aims to change your view of presentations and of PowerPoint presentations in particular.

This is actually too general. First, our objectives go beyond this – we want to change practice and thus improve results. You might have quite liked the way you have used PowerPoint to date, but have now changed your view regarding it, seeing what you normally do as failing to make best use of all the possibilities. Unless you are exceptional (and we are not so arrogant as to suggest that we alone use PowerPoint in a truly effective way), that is certainly the first step – we aimed to change your view in this way.

Additionally, however, we hope you see the message spelt out here as a starting point and that in future you will be prompted to use more of the possibilities. So, a suggestion: do not just put this book to one side now, even if you do so with some good, albeit vague, intentions to change.

Rather, do two things:

1. Get out a recent presentation and critique the material. Look at it objectively, and ask questions: was the objective clear, or was it simply a presentation 'about' something? How well did it put over its message and how likely was it to prompt both attention and retention? You may pick something where there were results to check back on too, and you can bear your own prevailing strike rate in mind if you selected one of the sales presentations you give yourself. Overall, the key thing to ask yourself is: could it have been better, more likely to achieve what you wanted and even do so with some real degree of certainty?
2. Assuming you do discover some shortfall, resolve to take a more conscious approach to the next presentation you prepare. The way the approach has been presented here can act as a guide and template. If a revised approach makes your next one go better, then you will want to repeat that success. You can make the next one better still, and so on.

Once you move away from the routine of preparing a presentation, in part at least, on automatic pilot, simply re-using ideas and methods from the past, then you are creating a new way forward. It is a way that will be appreciated by your audiences, and a way that will be more likely to produce the results that you want.

No magic is involved: utilising elements of what is set out here is, at root, only common sense. This approach is tried and tested. It works for people in many organisations around the world, and it can work for you.

It is worth some time and effort to get it right. Remember the phrase quoted '*A presentation is the business equivalent of an open goal*'. It is just that – and the aim must be to score again and again. Making an effective presentation is not a matter either of successfully 'winging it' or of good luck. So, we do not end by wishing you good luck, you have the basis here to create killer presentations of your own; we wish you well with them.

Glossary

Animation	Effects that cause elements of a slide to appear, disappear, and move around the screen in various ways. The most useful feature of a computer based presentation.	
Animation build sequences	Sequences which build up the sections of the slides to convey the message in a dynamic way.	81
Application hunting	Positive audience response – looking for ways in which your message is relevant to them.	40
Attention Span	The length of time an audience can fully concentrate on a presentation.	20, 28, 35, 53, 61, 62
Audience Abuse	A presentation consisting mostly of bullet-points that are read out to the audience by the presenter. Blue background, yellow text and an irrelevant piece of Clip Art (see definition) added in the bottom right hand corner. The most common type of PowerPoint presentation.	114
Autoshape	A drawing option in PowerPoint allowing you to easily create or change basic shapes.	131
Backup	Copy of a file in a different location from the original.	150
Bar charts	Charts featuring vertical or horizontal bars that show quantity.	109
Boot	Restarting a PC, or footwear, or euphemism for redefining somebody's career.	150
Breeze	See Macromedia Breeze.	
Bubble charts	Charts which demonstrate distribution across several axes.	109
Build Time	Time it takes between a CLICK and the moment the animation ceases, should not be confused with time it takes a builder to complete a job, which approximates infinity.	134
Build Up/Fade Down	An m62 concept that describes building up a slide in sequence and then fading out everything except the most relevant section to draw attention to it.	140

Builds	Animations which cause a slide to be constructed in sections, building up a complete picture.	
Bullet points	Most common definition of this would be: Lines of text summarising points the presenter wishes to make. However at m62 we prefer 'Spawn of the Devil' as a more accurate description. Bullet points add no value and almost certainly distract from good presentation, but you must have read about this already!	
Carrying a Bag	US slang for sales activity.	20
CLICK	To click the mouse during a presentation.	
ClipArt	Crass Little Inserted Pictures, Always Rubbish & Trite.	72
Composition	Term used to describe the way a photograph has been framed and shot. This used to be important for good photography but less so now we all have Photoshop.	101
Compress	A picture editing function in PowerPoint2003 that can reduce the resolution and size of pictures to reduce file size.	
Computer Projection Devices	Devices that plug into a PC to project the screen image like a slide projector.	123
Consultative Selling	A sales process developed by Mack Hanan.	55
Contrast	The definition of one colour shade against another.	123
Corporate ID	A PowerPoint file created by m62 containing background designs and graphic elements, fully-programmed with fonts and colour palettes.	122
Cue	To prompt (usually an actor).	68
Cue Card	List of bullet points (see definition) serving to 'Cue' a presenter, best printed onto card and kept with the presenter. On no account should they be shown to the audience.	68
Curved Text	Text produced in WordArt or Photoshop that is purposely warped or bent.	128
Cut	Shortcut CTRL+X – removes a selected item and places it on the clipboard.	
Cyclic process	A process that passes through a number of stages and returns to the start to reiterate (see iterative process).	139

Delivery	How the presentation is shown and explained to the audience.	14
Design	Visual technique and devices used in presentations.	14
Directed Attention	Use of animation/build to ensure that the audience's attention is focused on the correct part of the slide.	91
Download	Process of recording a copy of a file placed on the Internet.	
Drag and drop	Clicking on an object and moving the object by holding down the mouse button, then positioning it by releasing the button.	130
Dual Media presentation	An m62 concept that describes the usual use of PowerPoint: visual information displayed via PowerPoint and a separate verbal presentation delivered by a presenter – occasionally linked, usually at the beginning of a slide!	82
Education	Type of presentation – would include training, teaching or most technical presentations.	45
Entertainment	Type of presentation (best left out of the business world).	45
Esc	The Escape key.	
Event support	Management of the presentation venue and technical support.	11
Excel™	A Microsoft application for calculating and creating spreadsheets.	
Firewall	An application which protects your computer from Internet privacy threats.	
Flash	A Macromedia animation program, widely used in Internet applications.	
Flow chart (Iterative)	A sequence of events which ends where it starts.	110
Flow chart (Linear)	A sequence of events displayed as a flow chart.	110
Flying Objects	PowerPoint build. A motion build, best not used.	134
Font	Text design, e.g. Arial, Verdana, Times New Roman.	
GB	GigaByte (1000MB).	
Guides	Construction lines used when creating a slide to facilitate drawing.	
Hard Breaks	Definite break allowing the audience to think about other things, change of location or format.	38
Hard skills	An m62 concept used to describe a set of skills based on science and theory which can be learnt and reproduced. Could also be termed Explicit Skills.	1

Heading Banner	A strip at the top of the slide on which to type the title, this should animate in when a title changes in order to draw attention to the change. Clearly it should not animate on every slide.	126
High Resolution Picture	A picture or photograph of high definition, suitable for print, usually 300 dpi as apposed to 72dpi (see definition) needed for PowerPoint.	102
Highest Native Resolution	LCD projectors work by passing light through a transparent glass on which the image is formed. This glass has a fixed resolution (usually 1024 × 768) this resolution is called Native and if your PC uses this resolution to display graphics the image will look its best. Other resolutions need software algorithms in order to be displayed on the screen, these will always reduce quality.	150
Hole hunting	Negative audience response – looking for faults and flaws in your argument.	40
I.T.	Information technology.	
Importing	Inserting a non-native object (e.g. a photograph or movie file) into PowerPoint.	110
Information Transfer	Purpose of a presentation.	92
Initial Purchase Decision (IPD)	The point at which the audience makes a decision whether to go into application-hunting or hole-hunting mode. This is usually reached within the first five minutes of a presentation, although you can often see the results in the audience's body language as early as five seconds. The best example of this is a presentation using bullet points (see definition) which typically results in a sleep within 5 seconds.	40
Integrated Marketing Communications	The concept of having consistency of image and message in all customer (prospect) facing communications – the bedrock of a good marketing plan.	114, 122
Jargon	Professional slang.	142
Keying the slide	Using visual imagery to complement the message.	121
Killer Presentation	Our concept of an audience-focused, impressive and engaging presentation with the right message and the right delivery.	33, 46, 71 158

Killer Slide	The slide which communicates the main point of your presentation, for example in a sales presentation this would be your Value Proposition (see definition).	20, 61, 62 72, 137
Killerpresentations.com	The website accompanying this book, access to which requires the following code: 1512596262PPT.	
KISS	Keep It Simple, Stupid.	128
Laptop	If you need a definition of this you are reading the wrong book.	
Latest Patches	Software fixes for bugs in either the application or the operating system, actually some people believe this is just a marketing ploy to force you to upgrade.	151
Legends	Explanatory labels added below a graph.	120
Line Diagram	Graph that uses lines to show data progression.	108
Linear	Progressing in a straight line one step at a time.	
Logo	Company's identifying symbol.	
Lozenge	Bar-shaped graphic.	94
m62	The road that connects Liverpool (the centre of the presentation universe) and Hull (the back end of beyond). Also the name of a small presentation company based conveniently in Liverpool, near the start of the m62 (which interestingly starts at Junction 3, presumably Junctions 1 and 2 were stolen!).	
Macromedia Breeze	Software allowing screen-sharing over the web, web conferencing and remote presenting. Although there are many applications of this type, this is our preferred solution as it works the best with PowerPoint 2003.	151
MAT	Moving Annual Totals.	86
Matrix	A rectangular array of numbers (or objects). Also used to describe the situation where the sequel in a series disappoints the promise of the first (usually used in a film context).	98
Matrix Selling	An m62 concept for radically improving the effectiveness of a sales force.	
MB	MegaByte (1000 KB).	
Medium	A means of conveying information (singular of media).	134
Messaging	The purpose of the presentation and how the content should be structured.	

Microsoft Project™ files	Project plans created in Microsoft Project.	140
Mind Map™	A method of displaying information which highlights the relationship between ideas as much as the ideas themselves.	25
Motion Build	Build where the object does not appear in its final resting place relative to the slide e.g. Fly In (from Left).	134
Motion Transitions	Opposite of a Static Transition, i.e. a slide transition that moves the background as it animates. Generally creates amateurish looking presentations.	139
Motivation	Type of presentation.	45
Movie	A piece of animation or video.	
Multi-media	Using more than one form of communication to convey the same point, e.g. pictures and music, as apposed to Dual Media Presentations (see definition).	82
Muppet	Cloth puppet with no brain, used to refer to people who do things without thinking them through. The best example of this is a person who thinks that a good presentation consists of a series of bullet points read out to the audience and believes that it can be enhanced by printing speaker notes and handing them out before the recital.	
Negative Correlation	Two values are said to correlate if changing one affects the other. A negative correlation means that increasing one decreases the other, also referred to as inverse correlation (although to be entirely accurate inverse correlation and negative correlation are different mathematical terms – one to do with multiplication and the other addition).	37
Non-Cognitive Decision	An unconscious decision, one where the maker is not aware that they are coming to a decision or opinion. A good example is the IPD (see definition) or, more commonly, the decision of a woman to buy a new pair of shoes.	40
Objective Quality Rules	m62's design standards; conditions that should apply to every presentation we produce.	127
Office Applications	Microsoft programs in the Office Suite, including Word, PowerPoint and Excel.	131

OHP acetate	Overhead Projector Acetate. An old technology for displaying Visual Aids, now only ever used to identify presenters over the age of 80!	
Online	Connected to, or accessible through, the Internet.	
Operating Manual	Manual setting out guidelines that can usefully be followed consistently around an organisation to create a sound corporate style. Most devices have them but the male of the species will never read them!	129
Paste	Shortcut CTRL+V – inserts whatever is on the Clipboard into the open application.	
Patter	Term used to describe the words said during a presentation.	
Persuasion	Type of presentation.	45
Photoshop ™	Adobe's professional graphic design software.	30, 100
Pie-chart	A chart shaped like a pie and used to show proportion of parts to the whole.	108
Pitch	A presentation designed to win business or further a sales process.	
Placeware	Online presentation software similar to WebEx, see Breeze.	151
Plasma	A large visual display device.	150
Platform	Area of a train station used to keep passengers waiting in the vain hope of boarding a train. Can also be used to describe the operating system on your laptop, which is a piece of software designed to keep you waiting in the vain hope of using an application!	151
Positive Correlation	See Negative Correlation.	37
PowerPoint™	The most prolific, certainly the most misused, probably the most important piece of software to be developed by Microsoft.	
PowerPoint™ Package for CD	A feature in PowerPoint 2003 allowing you to easily create self-starting CDs of your presentation that will run on any PC.	150
PowerPoint ™ Template	A design template file (.pot) containing the presentation background design and colour and font palettes.	124
PowerPoint ™ Toolbar	User-created toolbar for manipulating objects on slides.	101

Presenter support	Services to aid the presenter, e.g.presentation training.	11
Push Down	A slide transition pushing the current slide downwards to be replaced by the next.	140
Push Left	A slide transition pushing the current slide to the left to be replaced by the next.	140
Random Bars	A static animation build.	
Random Bars Vertical	A variation on Random Bars.	134
Remote Mouse	A device that plugs into the PC running the presentation allowing the presenter to click through the slides without a mouse.	150
Sans-serif	Font without 'tassels', e.g. Arial or Verdana.	128
Scatter Plots	A graph displaying data, very difficult to use well in a presentation.	109
Schematic	A technical map-type diagram showing interrelations between parts.	96
Screen Grab	A picture of graphics on a computer screen.	
Scripted Fonts	Fonts designed to mimic handwriting.	127
Security Updates	Downloads provided by Microsoft to improve the protection of your PC against threats.	151
Segue	A smooth transition from one stage, section or message to another.	93, 104
Serifed Fonts	Fonts adorned with 'tails' and 'tassels', e.g. Times New Roman and Garamond.	127
Show mode	PowerPoint mode that displays the slides full-screen as a presentation.	20
Slide Show	A presentation.	
Slide Sorter	PowerPoint mode that displays the complete slide deck in mini-view.	
Slide Ware	Disparaging US slang for PowerPoint slides.	105
SMART	Acronym for: Specific, Measurable, Action-orientated, Realistic, Timed.	43
Soft Breaks	Change of pace/new topic.	38
Soft Skills	An m62 concept used to describe a set of skills based on personality and interpersonal skills that can be practiced and honed but are difficult to teach. Could also be termed Tacit Skills.	
Solution Selling	Offering an integrated solution to a set of requirements, rather than focusing on individual products and offerings, Also a sales process developed by M Bosworth.	55

Specific Sales Presentation	A presentation designed specifically to close an order or win new business.	23
Spin	Giving subtle different meanings to.	
SPIN™	Patented approach to selling.	55
Static Build	Build where the object animated in appears in its final resting place relative to the slide, e.g. Random Bars.	
Storyboard	A PowerPoint sketch of the presentation content.	81
Strategic Selling	A sales process developed by Miller Hieman.	55
Subjective Quality	Judgement of presentation style based on the individual's own tastes and preferences.	127
Testimonials	Positive feedback statements from clients.	
Title Bar	See Heading Banner.	
Toggle	Most laptops disable the external monitor socket in order to save power. The happy consequence of this is that if a laptop is not connected to the projector prior to turning it on it will not display the image when it is connected. Many people believe this feature is less about saving power and more about amusing the engineers who design laptops who generally don't get invited to presentations. The solution is to Toggle the screen which involves pressing a series of keys on your laptop in order to enable the external monitor port. To make this game more entertaining every laptop is different, mine is Function f3, yours will probably not be, it's worth finding out, just don't ask an engineer, they won't tell you.	150
Typeface	See Font.	
USB 2.0 port	Universal Serial Bus – a high speed input/output slot on your PC.	150
USB memory stick	A keying-sized drive fitting into the USB slot, ranging in capacity from 32MB to 1GB.	
Value Proposition	The key reasons why an audience should buy from/work with your company.	20, 23, 40 67, 58–66
Venn Diagram	Implies a collection or an overlap.	97
Visual Aid	A term used to describe 'old' style presentations where a Visual was used to Aid comprehension. Irrelevant in today's world where audiences have been trained (via television) to assimilate information in a visual medium, see dual media presentations.	

Visual Cognitive Dissonance	An m62 concept that refers to the effect achieved by an intentional inconsistency between the visuals and the patter, the result is increased attention.	26
Visual Keys	Using visual imagery to complement the message. The term originates from the world of TV production, specifically from the BBC current affairs broadcasting where an image is used above and to the right of the presenter's head in order to lock or 'key' the information contained in the bulletin.	121
Visual Segue	An m62 concept of using visuals to segue (see definition) the presentation, i.e. we design the slides so as to allow the audience to follow a change of subject or topic by an obvious change in visual, different background imagery or colours.	104
Visualisation	The process of turning text into pictures and diagrams.	80
WebEx	Software allowing screen-sharing and remote presenting online, see Breeze.	151
Webinars	Online presentations or demonstrations.	81
Wheels	Graphic objects that display text or pictures. Commonly used in m62 presentations to display Value Propositions.	137
Wipe	A static build animation effect.	136
WordArt	Means of displaying text as a stylised graphic.	126
.jpg file	A compressed file format for pictures, this is the best format to use with PowerPoint as this is the format that PowerPoint itself uses to store picture information.	125, 126
.pot files	PowerPoint Templates. Files that determine the default design of your presentation – a very useful and underused function of PowerPoint.	126
.ttf	TrueType fonts. This type of font has been designed to appear the same in print and on screen with no loss of definition. We recommend always using TrueType fonts, such as Arial.	128
.wmv file	Windows Media file. This is a movie/sound file that is optimized for playing within Windows applications such as Media Player and PowerPoint. Whilst it is possible to use other formats and codecs we recommend this one for	147

	best results with PowerPoint 2003 and Windows Media Player 10.	
20pt/24pt	Text size. m62 recommend never using body text that is below 24pt, as people with average eyesight in a normal presentation environment will struggle to read it.	127
2D Presenting	Traditional presentation style – static text slides that are read to the audience by the presenter.	16
4D Presenting	The m62 presentation method – as well as slides building over time, patter (see definition) is added at the correct stages to explain the progression.	16, 90, 109
72dpi	72 dots per inch – the standard resolution of PowerPoint slide graphics.	102

References

Abraham Lincoln's Gettysburg (PowerPoint) *Address*, P Norvig, (http://www.norvig.com/Gettysburg/)

Attention Span and It's Implications for Trainers, N Oulton, (Critical Thinker, 1993)

The Cognitive Style of Powerpoint, E R Tufte, Yale, (Graphics Press, 1 July 2003)

Emotional Branding: How Successful Brands Gain the Irrational Edge [Chapter 6 'Right brain, Left brain, no brain at all'], Daryl Travis, (Prima Tech, 1 September 2000)

Hitchhikers Guide to the Galaxy, D Adams, (Pan Macmillan, October 12, 1979)

Integrated Marketing Communication, Schultz, Tannenbaum & Lauterbaum, (NTC Business Books, 1993)

The Management Speakers Handbook, P Forsyth, (How To Books, 2002)

My Wife and my Mother-in-law, W E Hill, (Puck, 1915)

Power Corrupts PowerPoint Obfuscates, J Naughton, (Guardian)

That Presentation Sensation: Be Good, Be Passionate, Be Memorable, M Conradi & R Hall, (Financial Times Prentice Hall, 29 August 2001)

Video Applications in Business, H de Burgh & T Steward, (Random House Business Books, 19 November 1987)